ENGLISH SYNTAX

CSLI LECTURE NOTES NUMBER 185

ENGLISH SYNTAX

An Introduction

JONG-BOK KIM & PETER SELLS

CSLI
PUBLICATIONS
Center for the Study of
Language and Information
Stanford, California

Copyright © 2008
CSLI Publications
Center for the Study of Language and Information
Leland Stanford Junior University
Printed in the United States
12 11 10 09 08   1 2 3 4 5

Library of Congress Cataloging-in-Publication Data

Kim, Jong-Bok, 1966–

English syntax : an introduction / by Jong-Bok Kim and Peter Sells.

p. cm. – (CSLI lecture notes ; no. 185.)

Includes bibliographical references and index.
ISBN-13: 978-1-57586-567-6   (alk. paper)
ISBN-10:   1-57586-567-X   (alk. paper)
ISBN-13: 978-1-57586-568-3 (pbk. : alk. paper)
ISBN-10:   1-57586-568-8 (pbk. : alk. paper)
1. English language—Syntax. 2. English language–Grammar.
I. Sells, Peter, 1957– II. CSLI Publications (Firm) III. Title.

PE1361.K56 2008
425–dc22   2008004362
CIP

CSLI was founded in 1983 by researchers from Stanford University, SRI International,
and Xerox PARC to further the research and development of integrated theories
of language, information, and computation. CSLI headquarters and
CSLI Publications are located on the campus of Stanford University.

CSLI Publications reports new developments in the study of language,
information, and computation. Please visit our web site at
http://cslipublications.stanford.edu/
for comments on this and other titles, as well as for changes
and corrections by the authors and publisher.

Contents

Preface

One important aspect of teaching English syntax (to native and nonnative undergraduate students alike) involves the balance in the overall approach between facts and theory. We understand that one important goal of teaching English syntax to undergraduate students is to help students enhance their understanding of the structure of English in a systematic and scientific way. Basic knowledge of this kind is essential for students to move on the next stages, in which they will be able to perform linguistic analyses for simple as well as complex English phenomena. This new introductory textbook has been developed with this goal in mind. The book focuses primarily on the descriptive facts of English syntax, presented in a way that encourages students to develop keen insights into the English data. It then proceeds with the basic, theoretical concepts of generative grammar from which students can develop abilities to think, reason, and analyze English sentences from linguistic points of view.

We owe a great deal of intellectual debt to the previous textbooks and literature on English syntax. In particular, much of the content, as well as our exercises, has been inspired by and adopted from renowned textbooks such as Aarts (1997, 2001), Baker (1997), Borsley (1991, 1996), Radford (1988, 1997, 2004), Sag et al. (2003), to list just a few. We acknowledge our debt to these works, which have set the course for teaching syntax over the years.

Within this book, Chapters 1 to 5 cover the fundamental notions of English grammar. We start with the basic properties of English words, and then rules for combining these words to form well-formed phrases and, ultimately, clauses. These chapters guide students through the basic concepts of syntactic analysis such as lexical categories, phrasal types, heads, complements, and modifiers. In Chapter 4, as a way of formalizing the observed generalizations, the textbook introduces the feature structure system of Head-Driven Phrase Structure Grammar (HPSG, Pollard and Sag (1994), Sag et al. (2003)) which places strong emphasis on the role of lexical properties and the interactions among grammatical components.

From Chapter 6 on, the book discusses major constructions of English within a holistic view of grammar allowing interactions of various grammatical properties including syntactic forms, their grammatical functions, their semantic roles, and overall aspects of clausal meaning. In Chapter 6, we introduce English subject verb agreement, and concentrate on interrelationships among different grammatical components which play crucial interacting roles in English agreement phenomena. In particular, this chapter shows that once we allow morphological information to interface with the system of syntax, semantics, or even pragmatics, we can provide good solutions for some puzzling English agreement phenomena, within a principled theory. Chapter 7 covers raising and control phenomena, and provides insights into the properties of the two different constructions, which are famously rather similar in terms of syntactic structures, but different in terms of semantics. Chapter 8 deals with the English auxiliary system, itself remarkable in that a relatively small number of elements interact with each other in complicated and intriguing ways. This chapter assigns the precise lexical information to auxiliary verbs and constructional constraints sensitive to the presence of an auxiliary verb. This allows us to express generalizations among auxiliary-sensitive phenomena such as negation, inversion, contraction, and ellipsis, which we would otherwise have missed.

From Chapter 9 through Chapter 12, the textbook discusses how to capture systematic relations between related constructions. Chapter 9 deals with the relationships between active and passive voice clauses. Studying this chapter, students will be able to fully understand why, how, and when to choose between canonical and passive constructions. Chapters 10 and 11 deal with *wh*-questions and relative clause constructions, often called non-local or long-distance dependency constructions, in the sense that a gap and its filler are in a potentially long-distance relationship. These two chapters present the basic properties of these constructions and show how the mechanism of feature percolation is a crucial part of a systematic account for them. The final chapter of the book covers the so-called 'tough' constructions, extraposition, and cleft constructions. These constructions are also based on long-distance dependencies, but different from the constructions in Chapters 10 and 11. The goal of all these chapters is to present a groundwork of facts, which students will then have in hand, in order to consider theoretical accounts which apply in precise ways.

We have tried to make each chapter maximally accessible. We provide clear, simple tree diagrams which will help students understand the structures of English and develop analytic skills for English syntax. The theoretical notions are kept as simple yet precise as possible so that students can apply and use them in analyzing English sentences. Each chapter also contains exercises ranging from simple to challenging, aiming to promote a deeper understanding of the factual and theoretical contents of each chapter.

Jong-Bok Kim and Peter Sells

February 2008

Acknowledgements

Numerous people have helped us in writing this textbook, in various ways. We especially thank Aaron Broadwell, Suk-Jin Chang, Rui Chaves, Chan Chung, See-Youn Cho, Gwang-Yoon Goh, Shin Sook Kim, Ivan Sag, and Kap-Hee Lee for reading the manuscripts and giving us valuable comments. We also thank the following people for their comments in various places, help, and interest in our textbook: Sung-Ho Ahn, Arto Anttila, Emily Bender, Francis Bond, Bob Borsley, Joan Bresnan, Hee-Rhak Chae, Myong-hi Chai, Hye won Choi, Incheol Choi, Jae-Woong Choi, Stan Dubinsky, Dan Flickinger, Kazuhiko Fukushima, Danièle Godard, Chung-Hye Han, Young-Jun Jang, Wooson Kang, Sun-woong Kim, Tibor Kiss, Beth Levin, Bob Levine, Chung-min Lee, Kiyong Lee, Nam-geun Lee, Kyung-Sup Lim, Seung Chul Moon, Michiko Nakano, Byung-Soo Park, Myongkwan Park, Carl Pollard, Yooha Song, Eunjung Yoo, James Yoon, Tom Wasow, Stephen Weschler, among others. We also thank teachers and colleagues in Kyung Hee University and Stanford University for their constant encouragement over the years. Our gratitude also goes to undergraduate and graduate students at Kyung Hee University who used the draft of this as the textbook and raised so many questions that help us reshape its structure as well as contents. We also owe our thanks to Dikran Karagueuzian, Director of CSLI Publications, for his patience and support, as well as Lauri Kanerva for his help in matters of production. We also thank Kaunghi Un for helping us with LaTeX problems.

Lastly, but not the least, we also truly thank our close friends and family members who gave us unconditional love and support in every possible regard.

1

Some Basic Properties of English Syntax

1.1 Some Remarks on the Essence of Human Language

One of the crucial functions of any human language, such as English or Korean, is to convey various kinds of information from the everyday to the highly academic. Language provides a means for us to describe how to cook, how to remove cherry stains, how to understand English grammar, or how to provide a convincing argument. We commonly consider certain properties of language to be key essential features from which the basic study of linguistics starts.

The first well-known property (as emphasized by Saussure (1916)) is that there is **no motivated relationship between sounds and meanings**. This is simply observed in the fact that the same meaning is usually expressed by a different sounding-word in a different language (think of *house, maison, casa*). For words such as *hotdog, desk, dog, bike, hamburger, cranberry, sweetbread*, their meanings have nothing to do with their shapes. For example, the word *hotdog* has no relationship with a dog which is or feels hot. There is just an arbitrary relationship between the word's sound and its meaning: this relationship is decided by the convention of the community the speakers belong to.

The second important feature of language, and one more central to syntax, is that **language makes infinite use of a finite set of rules or principles**, the observation of which led the development of **generative linguistics** in the 20th century (cf. Chomsky (1965)). A language is a system for combining its parts in infinitely many ways. One piece of evidence of the system can be observed in word-order restrictions. If a sentence is an arrangement of words and we have 5 words such as *man, ball, a, the*, and *kicked*, how many possible combinations can we have from these five words? Mathematically, the number of possible combinations of 5 words is 5! (factorial), equalling 120 instances. But among these 120 possible combinations, only 6 form grammatical English sentences:[1]

(1)   a.   The man kicked a ball.

        b.   A man kicked the ball.

---

[1]Examples like (1e) and (1f) are called 'topicalization' sentences in which the topic expression (*the ball* and *the man*), already mentioned and understood in the given context, is placed in the sentence initial position. See Lambrecht (1994) and references therein.

1

     c. The ball kicked a man.

     d. A ball kicked the man.

     e. The ball, a man kicked.

     f. The man, a ball kicked.

All the other 114 combinations, a few of which are given in (2), are unacceptable to native speakers of English. We use the notation * to indicate that a hypothesized example is ungrammatical.

(2)   a. *Kicked the man the ball.

      b. *Man the ball kicked the.

      c. *The man a ball kicked.

It is clear that there are certain rules in English for combining words. These rules constrain which words can be combined together or how they may be ordered, sometimes in groups, with respect to each other.

Such combinatory rules also play important roles in our understanding of the syntax of an example like (3a).[2] Whatever these rules are, they should give a different status to (3b), an example which is judged ungrammatical by native speakers even though the intended meaning of the speaker is relatively clear and understandable.

(3)   a. Kim lives in the house Lee sold to her.

      b. *Kim lives in the house Lee sold it to her.

The requirement of such combinatory knowledge also provides an argument for the assumption that we use just a **finite** set of resources in producing grammatical sentences, and that we do not just rely on the meanings of the words involved. Consider the examples in (4):

(4)   a. *Kim fond of Lee.

      b. Kim is fond of Lee.

Even though it is not difficult to understand the meaning of (4a), English has a structural requirement for the verb *is* as given in (4b).

More natural evidence of the 'finite set of rules and principles' idea can be found in cognitive, **creative** abilities. Speakers are unconscious of the rules which they use all the time, and have no difficulties in producing or understanding sentences which they have never heard, seen, or talked about before. For example, even though we may well not have seen the following sentence before, we can understand its meaning if we have a linguistic competence in English:

(5)   In January 2002, a dull star in an obscure constellation suddenly became 600,000 times more luminous than our Sun, temporarily making it the brightest star in our galaxy.

A related part of this competence is that a language speaker can produce an infinite number of grammatical sentences. For example, given the simple sentence (6a), we can make a more complex one like (6b) by adding the adjective *tall*. To this sentence, we can again add another

---

[2]Starting in Chapter 2, we will see these combinatory rules.

adjective *handsome* as in (6c). We could continue adding adjectives, theoretically enabling us to generate an infinitive number of sentences:

(6) a. The man kicked the ball.

   b. The tall man kicked the ball.

   c. The handsome, tall man kicked the ball.

   d. The handsome, tall, nice man kicked the ball.

   e. ...

One might argue that since the number of English adjectives could be limited, there would be a dead-end to this process. However, no one would find themselves lost for another way to keep the process going (cf. Sag et al. (2003)):

(7) a. Some sentences can go on.

   b. Some sentences can go on and on.

   c. Some sentences can go on and on and on.

   d. Some sentences can go on and on and on and on.

   e. ...

To (7a), we add the string *and on*, producing a longer one (7b). To this resulting sentence, we once again add *and on* and generate (7c). We could in principle go on adding without stopping: this is enough to prove that we could make an infinite number of well-formed English sentences.[3]

   Given these observations, how then can we explain the fact that we can produce or understand an infinite number of grammatical sentences that we have never heard or seen before? It seems implausible to consider that we somehow memorize every example, and in fact we do not (Pullum and Scholz (2002)). We know that this could not be true, in particular when we consider that native speakers can in principle generate an infinite number of infinitely long sentence. In addition, there is a limit to the amount of information our brain can keep track of, and it would be implausible to think that we store an infinite number of sentences and retrieve whenever we need to do so.

   These considerations imply that a more appropriate hypothesis would be something like (8):[4]

(8) All native speakers have a **grammatical competence** which enables them to generate an infinite set of grammatical sentences from a finite set of resources.

This hypothesis has been generally accepted by most linguists, and has been taken as the subject matter of syntactic theory. In terms of grammar, this grammatical competence is hypothesized to characterize a **generative grammar**, which we then can define as follows (for English, in this instance):

---

[3] Think of a simple analogy: what is the longest number? Yet, how many numbers do you know? The second question only makes sense if the answer is 0–9 (ten digits).

[4] The notion of 'competence' is often compared with that of 'performance' (Chomsky (1965)). Competence refers to speakers' internalized knowledge of their language, whereas performance refers to actual use of this abstract knowledge of language.

(9)   Generative Grammar:

An English generative grammar is one which can generate an infinite set of well-formed English sentences from a finite set of rules or principles.

The job of syntax is thus to discover and formulate these rules or principles.[5] These rules tell us how words are put together to form grammatical phrases and sentences. Generative grammar, or generative syntax, thus aims to define these rules which will characterize all of the sentences which native speakers will accept as well-formed and grammatical.

1.2   How We Discover Rules

How can we then find out what the generative rules of English syntax are? These rules are present in the speakers' minds, but are not consciously accessible; speakers cannot articulate their content, if asked to do so. Hence we discover the rules indirectly, and of the several methods for inferring these hidden rules, hypotheses based on the observed data of the given language are perhaps the most reliable. These data can come from speakers' judgments – known as intuitions – or from collected data sets – often called corpora. Linguistics is in one sense an empirical science as it places a strong emphasis on investigating the data underlying a phenomenon of study.

The canonical steps for doing empirical research can be summarized as follows:

- Step I: Data collection and observation.
- Step II: Make a hypothesis to cover the first set of data.
- Step III: Check the hypothesis with more data.
- Step IV: Revise the hypothesis, if necessary.

Let us see how these steps work for discovering one of the grammar rules in English, in particular, the rule for distinguishing count and non-count nouns:[6]

[Step I: Observing Data] To discover a grammar rule, the first thing we need to do is to check out grammatical and ungrammatical variants of the expression in question. For example, let us look at the usage of the word *evidence*:

(10)   Data Set 1: *evidence*

a. *The professor found some strong evidences of water on Mars.

b. *The professor was hoping for a strong evidence.

---

[5]In generative syntax, 'rules' refers not to 'prescriptive rules' but to 'descriptive rules'. Prescriptive rules are those which disfavor or even discredit certain usages; these prescribe forms which are generally in use, as in (i). Meanwhile, descriptive rules are meant to characterize whatever forms speakers actually use, with any social, moral, or intellectual judgement.

(i)   a.   Do not end a sentence with a preposition.

b.   Avoid double negatives.

c.   Avoid split infinitives.

The spoken performance of most English speakers will often contain examples which violate such prescriptive rules.

[6]Much of the discussion and data in this section are adopted from Baker, C.L. (1995).

c. *The evidence that John found was more helpful than the one that Smith found.

What can you tell from these examples? We can make the following observations:

(11)　　　Observation 1:

    a.　*evidence* cannot be used in the plural.

    b.　*evidence* cannot be used with the indefinite article *a(n)*.

    c.　*evidence* cannot be referred to by the pronoun *one*.

In any scientific research one example is not enough to draw any conclusion. However, we can easily find more words that behave like *evidence*:

(12)　　　Data Set 2: *equipment*

    a.　*We had hoped to get three new equipments every month, but we only had enough money to get an equipment every two weeks.

    b.　*The equipment we bought last year was more expensive than the one we bought this year.

We thus extend Observation 1 a little bit further:

(13)　　　Observation 2:

    a.　*evidence/equipment* cannot be used in the plural.

    b.　*evidence/equipment* cannot be used with the indefinite article *a(n)*.

    c.　*evidence/equipment* cannot be referred to by the pronoun *one*.

It is usually necessary to find contrastive examples to understand the range of a given observation. For instance, words like *clue* and *tool* act differently:

(14)　　　Data Set 3: *clue*

    a.　The professor gave John some good clues for the question.

    b.　The student was hoping for a good clue.

    c.　The clue that John got was more helpful than the one that Smith got.

(15)　　　Data Set 4: *tool*

    a.　The teacher gave John some good tools for the purpose.

    b.　The student was hoping for a tool.

    c.　The tool that Jones got was more helpful than the one that Smith got.

Unlike *equipment* and *evidence*, the nouns *clue* and *tool* can be used in the test linguistic contexts we set up. We thus can add Observation 3, different from Observation 2:

(16)　　　Observation 3:

    a.　*clue/tool* can be used in the plural.

    b.　*clue/tool* can be used with the indefinite article *a(n)*.

    c.　*clue/tool* can be referred to by the pronoun *one*.

[Step II: Forming a Hypothesis] From the data and observations we have made so far, can we make any hypothesis about the English grammar rule in question? One hypothesis that we can make is something like the following:

(17)   First Hypothesis:
         English has at least two groups of nouns, Group I (count nouns) and Group II (non-count nouns), diagnosed by tests of plurality, the indefinite article, and the pronoun *one*.

[Step III: Checking the Hypothesis] Once we have formed such a hypothesis, we need to check out if it is true of other data, and also see if it can bring other analytical consequences.

A little further thought allows us to find support for the two-way distinction for nouns. For example, consider the usage of *much* and *many*:

(18)   a.   much evidence, much equipment, much information, much advice
         b.   *much clue, *much tool, *much armchair, *much bags

(19)   a.   *many evidence, *many equipment, *many information, *many advice
         b.   many clues, many tools, many suggestions, many armchairs

As observed here, count nouns can occur only with *many*, whereas non-count nouns can combine with *much*. Similar support can be found from the usage of *little* and *few*:

(20)   a.   little evidence, little equipment, little advice, little information
         b.   *little clue, *little tool, *little suggestion, *little armchair

(21)   a.   *few evidence, *few equipment, *few furniture, *few advice, *few information
         b.   few clues, few tools, few suggestions, few armchairs

The word *little* can occur with non-count nouns like *evidence*, yet *few* cannot. Meanwhile, *few* occurs only with count nouns.

Given these data, it appears that the two-way distinction is quite plausible and persuasive. We can now ask if this distinction into just two groups is really enough for the classification of nouns. Consider the following examples with *cake*:

(22)   a.   The mayor gave John some good cakes.
         b.   The president was hoping for a good cake.
         c.   The cake that Jones got was more delicious than the one that Smith got.

Similar behavior can be observed with a noun like *beer*, too:

(23)   a.   The bartender gave John some good beers.
         b.   No one knows how to tell from a good beer to a bad one.

These data show us that *cake* and *beer* may be classified as count nouns. However, observe the following:

(24)   a.   My pastor says I ate too much cake.

    b.   The students drank too much beer last night.

(25)   a.   We recommend to eat less cake and pastry.

    b.   People now drink less beer.

The data mean that *cake* and *beer* can also be used as non-count nouns since that can be used with *less* or *much*.

[Step IV: Revising the Hypothesis] The examples in (24) and (25) imply that there is another group of nouns that can be used as both count and non-count nouns. This leads us to revise the hypothesis in (17) as follows:

(26)   Revised Hypothesis:

    There are at least three groups of nouns: Group 1 (count nouns), Group 2 (non-count nouns), and Group 3 (count and non-count).

We can expect that context will determine whether a Group 3 noun is used as count or as non-count.

    As we have observed so far, the process of finding finite grammar rules crucially hinges on finding data, drawing generalizations, making a hypothesis, and revising this hypothesis with more data.

1.3   Why Do We Study Syntax and What Is It Good for?

There are many reasons for studying syntax, from general humanistic or behavioral motivations to much more specific goals such as those in the following:

- To help us to illustrate the patterns of English more effectively and clearly.
- To enable us to analyze the structure of English sentences in a systematic and explicit way.

    For example, let us consider how we could use the syntactic notion of **head**, which refers to the essential element within a phrase. The following is a short and informal rule for English subject-verb agreement.[7]

(27)   In English, the main verb agrees with the head element of the subject.

This informal rule can pinpoint what is wrong with the following two examples:

(28)   a.   *The recent strike by pilots have cost the country a great deal of money on tourism and so on.

    b.   *The average age at which people begin to need eyeglasses vary considerably.

Once we have structural knowledge of such sentences, it is easy to see that the essential element of the subject in (28a) is not *pilots* but *strike*. This is why the main verb should be *has* but not *have* to observe the basic agreement rule in (27). Meanwhile, in (28b), the head is the noun *age*, and thus the main verb *vary* needs to agree with this singular noun. It would not do to simply talk about 'the noun' in the subject in the examples in (28), as there is more than one. We need

---

[7]The notion of 'subject' is further discussed in Chapter 3 and that of 'head' in Chapter 4.

to be able to talk about the one which gives its character to the phrase, and this is the head. If the head is singular, so is the whole phrase, and similarly for plural. The head of the subject and the verb (in the incorrect form) are indicated in (29):

(29)   a. *[The recent **strike** by pilots] **have** cost the country a great deal of money from tourism and so on.

   b. *[The average **age** at which people begin to need eyeglasses] **vary** considerably.

Either example can be made into a grammatical version by pluralizing the head noun of the subject.

Now let us look at some slightly different cases. Can you explain why the following examples are unacceptable?

(30)   a. *Despite of his limited educational opportunities, Abraham Lincoln became one of the greatest intellectuals in the world.

   b. *A pastor was executed, notwithstanding many petitions in favor of him.

To understand these examples, we first need to recognize that the words *despite* and *notwithstanding* are prepositions, and further that canonical English prepositions combine only with noun phrases. In (30), these prepositions combine with prepositional phrases again (headed by *of* and *on* respectively), violating this rule.

A more subtle instance can be found in the following:

(31)   a.   Visiting relatives can be boring.

   b.   I saw that gas can explode.

These examples each have more than one interpretation. The first one can mean either that the event of seeing our relatives is a boring activity, or that the relatives visiting us are themselves boring. The second example can either mean that a specific can containing gas exploded, which I saw, or it can mean that I observed that gas has a possibility of exploding. If one knows English syntax, that is, if one understands the syntactic structure of these English sentences, it is easy to identify these different meanings.

Here is another example which requires certain syntactic knowledge:

(32)   He said that that 'that' that that man used was wrong.

This is the kind of sentence one can play with when starting to learn English grammar. Can you analyze it? What are the differences among these five *that*s? Structural (or syntactic) knowledge can be used to diagnose the differences. Part of our study of syntax involves making clear exactly how each word is categorized, and how it contributes to a whole sentence.

When it comes to understanding a rather complex sentence, knowledge of English syntax can be a great help. Syntactic or structural knowledge helps us to understand simple as well as complex English sentences in a systematic way. There is no difference in principle between the kinds of examples we have presented above and (33):

(33)   The government's plan, which was elaborated in a document released by the Treasury yesterday, is the formal outcome of the Government commitment at the Madrid summit last year to put forward its ideas about integration.

Apart from having more words than the examples we have introduced above, nothing in this example is particularly more complex.

1.4   Exercises

1. For each of the following nouns, decide if it can be used as a count or as a non-count (mass) noun. In doing so, construct acceptable and unacceptable examples using the tests (plurality, indefinite article, pronoun *one*, *few/little*, *many/much* tests) we have discussed in this chapter.
    (i)   activity, art, cheese, discussion, baggage, luggage, suitcase, religion, sculpture, paper, difficulty, cheese, water, experience, progress, research, life

2. Check or find out whether each of the following examples is grammatical or ungrammatical. For each ungrammatical one, provide at least one (informal) reason for its ungrammaticality, according to your intuitions or ideas.
    (i) a.   Kim and Sandy is looking for a new bicycle.
         b.   I have never put the book.
         c.   The boat floated down the river sank.
         d.   Chris must liking syntax.
         e.   There is eager to be fifty students in this class.
         f.   What is John eager to do?
         g.   What is John easy to do?
         h.   Is the boy who holding the plate can see the girl?
         i.   Which chemical did you mix the hydrogen peroxide and?
         j.   There seem to be a good feeling developing among the students.
         k.   Strings have been pulled many times to get students into that university.

3. Consider the following set of data, focusing on the usage of 'self' reflexive pronouns and personal pronouns:
    (i) a.   He washed himself.
         b.   *He washed herself.
         c.   *He washed myself.
         d.   *He washed ourselves.
    (ii) a.   *He washed him. ('he' and 'him' referring to the same person)
         b.   He washed me.
         c.   He washed her.

    d. He washed us.

Can you make a generalization about the usage of 'self' pronouns and personal pronouns like *he* here? In answering this question, pay attention to what the pronouns can refer to. Also consider the following imperative examples:

(iii) a. Wash yourself.

     b. Wash yourselves.

     c. *Wash myself.

     d. *Wash himself.

(iv) a. *Wash you!

     b. Wash me!

     c. Wash him!

Can you explain why we can use *yourself* and *yourselves* but not *you* as the object of the imperatives here? In answering this, try to put pronouns in the unrealized subject position.

4.   Read the following passage and identify all the grammatical errors. If you can, discuss the relevant grammar rules that you can think of.

    (i)   Grammar is important because it is the language that make it possible for us to talk about language. Grammar naming the types of words and word groups that make up sentences not only in English but in any language. As human beings, we can putting sentences together even as children—we can all do grammar. People associate grammar for errors and correctness. But knowing about grammar also helps us understood what makes sentences and paragraphs clearly and interesting and precise. Grammar can be part of literature discussions, when we and our students closely reading the sentences in poetry and stories. And knowing about grammar means finding out that all language and all dialect follow grammatical patterns.[8]

---

[8] Adapted from "Why is Grammar Important?" by The Assembly for the Teaching of English Grammar

2

From Words to Major Phrase Types

2.1 Introduction

In Chapter 1, we observed that the study of English syntax is the study of rules which generate an infinite number of grammatical sentences. These rules can be inferred from observations about the English data. One simple mechanism we recognize is that in forming grammatical sentences, we start from words, or 'lexical' categories. These lexical categories then form a larger constituent 'phrase'; and phrases go together to form a 'clause'. A clause either is, or is part of, a well-formed sentence:

(1)

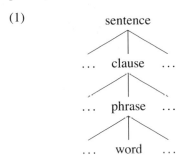

Typically we use the term 'clause' to refer to a complete sentence-like unit, but which may be part of another clause, as a subordinate or adverbial clause. Each of the sentences in (2b)–(2d) contains more than one clause, in particular, with one clause embedded inside another:

(2)   a.   The weather is lovely today.

   b.   I am hoping that [the weather is lovely today].

   c.   If [the weather is lovely today] then we will go out.

   d.   The birds are singing because [the weather is lovely today].

This chapter deals with what kind of combinatorial rules English employs in forming these phrases, clauses, and sentences.

2.2 Lexical Categories

2.2.1 Determining the Lexical Categories

The basic units of syntax are words. The first question is then what kinds of words (also known as parts of speech, or lexical categories, or grammatical categories) does English have? Are they simply *noun, verb, adjective, adverb, preposition*, and maybe a few others? Most of us would not be able to come up with simple definitions to explain the categorization of words. For instance, why do we categorize *book* as a noun, but *kick* as a verb? To make it more difficult, how do we know that *virtue* is a noun, that *without* is a preposition, and that *well* is an adverb (in one meaning)?

Words can be classified into different lexical categories according to three criteria: **meaning**, **morphological form**, and **syntactic function**. Let us check what each of these criteria means, and how reliable each one is.

At first glance, it seems that words can be classified depending on their **meaning**. For example, we could have the following rough semantic criteria for N (noun), V (verb), A (adjective), and Adv (adverb):

(3) a. N: referring to an individual or entity

  b. V: referring to an action

  c. A: referring to a property

  d. Adv: referring to the manner, location, time or frequency of an action

Though such semantic bases can be used for many words, these notional definitions leave a great number of words unaccounted for. For example, words like *sincerity, happiness*, and *pain* do not simply denote any individual or entity. *Absence* and *loss* are even harder cases.

There are also many words whose semantic properties do not match the lexical category that they belong to. For example, words like *assassination* and *construction* may refer to an action rather than an individual, but they are always nouns. Words like *remain, bother, appear*, and *exist* are verbs, but do not involve any action.

A more reliable approach is to characterize words in terms of their forms and functions. The 'form-based' criteria look at the **morphological form** of the word in question:

(4) a. N: __ + plural morpheme *-(e)s*

  b. N: __ + possessive *'s*

  c. V: __ + past tense *-ed -(e)s*

  d. V: __ + 3rd singular *-(e)s*

  e. A: __ + *-er/est* (or *more/most*)

  f. A: __ + *-ly* (to create an adverb)

According to these frames, where the word in question goes in the place indicated by __ , nouns allow the plural marking suffix *-(e)s* to be attached, or the possessive *'s*, whereas verbs can have the past tense *-ed* or the 3rd singular form *-(e)s*. Adjectives can take comparative and superlative endings -er or -est, or combine with the suffix -ly. (5) shows some examples derived from these frames:

(5)   a.   N: trains, actors, rooms, man's, sister's, etc.

       b.   V: devoured, laughed, devours, laughs, etc.

       c.   A: fuller, fullest, more careful, most careful, etc.

       d.   Adv: fully, carefully, diligently, clearly, etc.

The morphological properties of each lexical category cannot be overridden; verbs cannot have plural marking, nor can adjectives have tense marking. It turns out, however, that these morphological criteria are also only of limited value. In addition to nouns like *information* and *furniture* that we presented in Chapter 1, there are many nouns such as *love* and *pain* that do not have a plural form. There are adjectives (such as *absent* and *circular*) that do not have comparative -er or superlative -est forms, due to their meanings. The morphological (form-based) criterion, though reliable in many cases, is not a necessary and sufficient condition for determining the type of lexical categories.

The most reliable criterion in judging the lexical category of a word is based on its **syntactic function** or **distributional** possibilities. Let us try to determine what kind of lexical categories can occur in the following environments:

(6)   a.   They have no __ .

       b.   They can __ .

       c.   They read the __ book.

       d.   He treats John very __ .

       e.   He walked right __ the wall.

The categories that can go in the blanks are N, V, A, Adv, and P (preposition). As can be seen in the data in (7), roughly only one lexical category can appear in each position:

(7)   a.   They have no TV/car/information/friend.

       b.   They have no *went/*in/*old/*very/*and.

(8)   a.   They can sing/run/smile/stay/cry.

       b.   They can *happy/*down/*door/*very.

(9)   a.   They read the big/new/interesting/scientific book.

       b.   They read the *sing/*under/*very book.

(10)   a.   He treats John very nicely/badly/kindly.

       b.   He treats John very *kind/*shame/*under.

(11)   a.   He walked right into/on the wall.

       b.   He walked right *very/*happy/*the wall.

As shown here, only a restricted set of lexical categories can occur in each position; we can then assign a specific lexical category to these elements:

(12) a. N: TV, car, information, friend, . . .

    b. V: sing, run, smile, stay, cry, . . .

    c. A: big, new, interesting, scientific, . . .

    d. Adv: nicely, badly, kindly, . . .

    e. P: in, into, on, under, over, . . .

In addition to these basic lexical categories, does English have other lexical categories? There are a few more. Consider the following syntactic environments:

(13) a. __ student hits the ball.

    b. John sang a song, __ Mary played the piano.

    c. John thinks __ Bill is honest.

The only words that can occur in the open slot in (13a) are words like *the, a, this, that*, and so forth, which are determiner (Det). (13b) provides a frame for conjunctions (Conj) such as *and, but, so, for, or* and *yet*.[1] In (13c), we can have the category we call 'complementizer', here the word *that* – we return to these in (17) below.

Can we find any supporting evidence for such lexical categorizations? It is not so difficult to construct environments in which only these lexical elements appear. Consider the following:

(14) We found out that __ very lucrative jobs were in jeopardy.

Here we see that only words like *the, my, his, some, these, those*, and so forth can occur here. These articles, possessives, quantifiers, and demonstratives all 'determine' the referential properties of *jobs* here, and for this reason, they are called determiners. One clear piece of evidence for grouping these elements as the same category comes from the fact that they cannot occupy the same position at the same time:

(15) a. *[My these jobs] are in jeopardy.

    b. *[Some my jobs] are in jeopardy.

    c. *[The his jobs] are in jeopardy.

Words like *my* and *these* or *some* and *my* cannot occur together, indicating that they compete with each other for just one structural position.

Now consider the following examples:

(16) a. I think __ learning English is not easy at all.

    b. I doubt __ you can help me in understanding this.

    c. I am anxious __ you to study English grammar hard.

Once again, the possible words that can occur in the specific slot in (17) are strictly limited.

(17) a. I think *that* [learning English is not all that easy].

---

[1]These conjunctions are 'coordinating conjunctions' different from 'subordinating conjunctions' like *when, if, since, though*, and so forth. The former conjoins two identical phrasal elements whereas the latter introduces a subordinating clause as in *[Though students wanted to study English syntax], the department decided not to open that course this year.*

  b.   I doubt *if* [you can help me in understanding this].

  c.   I am anxious *for* [you to study English grammar hard].

The italicized words here are different from the other lexical categories that we have seen so far. They introduce a complement clause, marked above by the square brackets, and may be sensitive to the tense of that clause. A tensed clause is known as a 'finite' clause, as opposed to an infinitive. For example, *that* and *if* introduce or combine with a tensed sentence (present or past tense), whereas *for* requires an infinitival clause marked with *to*. We cannot disturb these relationships:

(18)   a.   *I think *that* [learning English to be not all that easy].

  b.   *I doubt *if* [you to help me in understanding this].

  c.   *I am anxious *for* [you should study English grammar hard].

The term 'complement' refers to an obligatory dependent clause or phrase relative to a head.[2] The italicized elements in (18) introduce a clausal complement and are consequently known as 'complementizers' (abbreviated as 'C'). There are only a few complementizers in English (*that*, *for*, *if*, and *whether*), but nevertheless they have their own lexical category.

   Now consider the following environments:

(19)   a.   John __ not leave.

  b.   John __ drink beer last night.

  c.   __ John leave for Seoul tomorrow?

  d.   John will study syntax, and Mary __ , too.

The words that can appear in the blanks are neither main verbs nor adjectives, but rather words like *will*, *can*, *shall* and *must*. In English, there is clear evidence that these verbs are different from main verbs, and we call them auxiliary verbs (Aux). The auxiliary verb appears in front of the main verb, which is typically in its citation form, which we call the 'base' form. Note the change in the main verb form in (20b) when the negation is added:

(20)   a.   He left.

  b.   He did not leave.

   There is also one type of *to* which is auxiliary-like. Consider the examples in (21) and (22):[3]

(21)   a.   Students wanted *to* write a letter.

  b.   Students intended *to* surprise the teacher.

(22)   a.   Students objected *to* the teacher.

  b.   Students sent letters *to* the teacher.

It is easy to see that in (22), *to* is a preposition. But how about the infinitival marker *to* in (21), followed by a base verb form? What lexical category does it belong to? Though the detailed

---

[2] See Chapter 4 for a fuller discussion of 'head' and 'complement'.

[3] See Chapter 8 for further discussion.

properties of auxiliary verbs will not be discussed until Chapter 8, we treat the infinitival marker *to* as an auxiliary verb. For example, we can observe that *to* behaves like an auxiliary verb *should*:

(23) a. It is crucial for John to show an interest.

  b. It is crucial that John should show an interest.

(24) a. I know I should [go to the dentist's], but I just don't want to.

  b. I don't really want to [go to the dentist's], but I know I should.

In (23), *to* and *should* introduce the clause and determines the tenseness of the clause. In (24), they both can license the ellipsis of its VP complement.[4]

Another property *to* shares with other auxiliary verbs like *will* is that it requires a base verb to follow. Most auxiliary verbs are actually finite (tensed) forms which therefore pattern with *that* in a finite clause, while the infinitival clause introduced by *for* is only compatible with *to*:

(25) a. She thought it was likely [that everyone *to/might/would fit into the car].

  b. She thought it was easy [for everyone to/*might/*would fit into the car].

Finally, there is one remaining category we need to consider, the 'particles' (Part), illustrated in (26):

(26) a. The umpire called *off* the game.

  b. The two boys looked *up* the word.

Words like *off* and *up* here behave differently from prepositions, in that they can occur after the object.

(27) a. The umpire called the game *off*.

  b. The two boys looked the word *up*.

Such distributional possibilities cannot be observed with true prepositions:

(28) a. The umpire fell *off* the deck.

  b. The two boys looked *up* the high stairs (from the floor).

(29) a. *The umpire fell the deck *off*.

  b. *The students looked the high stairs *up* (from the floor).

We can also find differences between particles and prepositions in combination with an object pronoun:

(30) a. The umpire called it *off*. (particle)

  b. *The umpire called *off* it.

(31) a. *The umpire fell it *off*.

  b. The umpire fell *off* it. (preposition)

---

[4]See Chapter 8 for detailed discussion on the ellipsis.

The pronoun *it* can naturally follow the preposition as in (31b), but not the particle in (30b). Such contrasts between prepositions and particles give us ample reason to introduce another lexical category Part (particle) which is differentiated from P (preposition). In the next section, we will see more tests to differentiate these two types of word.

2.2.2 Grammar with Lexical Categories

As noted in Chapter 1, the main goal of syntax is building a grammar that can generate an infinite set of well-formed, grammatical English sentences. Let us see what kind of grammar we can develop now that we have lexical categories. To start off, we will use the examples in (32):

(32)　a.　A man kicked the ball.

　　　b.　A tall boy threw the ball.

　　　c.　The cat chased the long string.

　　　d.　The happy student played the piano.

Given only the lexical categories that we have identified so far, we can set up a grammar rule for sentence (S) like the following:

(33)　S → Det (A) N V Det (A) N

The rule tells us what S can consist of: it must contain the items mentioned, except that those which are in parentheses are optional. So this rule characterizes any sentence which consists of a Det, N, V, Det, and N, in that order, possibly with an A in front of either N. We can represent the core items in a tree structure as in (34):

(34)

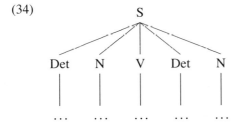

We assume a lexicon, a list of categorized words, to be part of the grammar along with the rule in (33):

(35)　a.　Det: a, that, the, this, ...

　　　b.　N: ball, man, piano, string, student, ...

　　　c.　V: kicked, hit, played, sang, threw, ...

　　　d.　A: handsome, happy, kind, long, tall, ...

By inserting lexical items into the appropriate pre-terminal nodes in the structure, where the labels above ... are, we can generate grammatical examples like those (32) as well as those like the following, not all of which describe a possible real-world situation:

(36)　a.　That ball hit a student.

    b.   The piano played a song.

    c.   The piano kicked a student.

    d.   That ball sang a student.

Such examples are all syntactically well-formed, even if semantically in some cases, implying that syntax is rather 'autonomous' from semantics. Note that any anomalous example can be preceded by the statement "Now, here's something hard to imagine: . . .".[5]

    Notice that even this simple grammar rule can easily extend to generate an infinite number of English sentences by allowing iteration of the A:[6]

(37)   S → Det A* N V Det A* N

The operator allows us to repeat any number of As, thereby generating sentences like (38). Note that the parentheses around 'A' in (34) are no longer necessary in this instance, for the Kleene Star operator means any number including zero.

(38)   a.   The tall man kicked the ball.

    b.   The tall, handsome man kicked the ball.

    c.   The tall, kind, handsome man kicked the ball.

One could even generate a sentence like (39):

(39)   The happy, happy, happy, happy, happy, happy man sang a song.

    A grammar using only lexical categories can be specified to generate an infinite number of well-formed English sentences, but it nevertheless misses a great deal of basic properties that we can observe. For example, this simple grammar cannot capture the agreement facts seen in examples like the following:

(40)   a.   The mother of the boy and the girl **is** arriving soon.

    b.   The mother of the boy and the girl **are** arriving soon.

Why do the verbs in these two sentences have different agreement patterns? Our intuitions tell us that the answer lies in two different possibilities for grouping the words:

(41)   a.   [The mother of [the boy and the girl]] is arriving soon.

    b.   [The mother of the boy] and [the girl] are arriving soon.

The different groupings shown by the brackets indicate who is arriving: in (41a), the mother, while in (41b) it is both the mother and the girl. The grouping of words into larger phrasal units which we call **constituents** provides the first step in understanding the agreement facts in (41).

    Now, consider the following examples:

(42)   a.   John saw the man with a telescope.

    b.   I like chocolate cakes and pies.

---

[5] See Exercise 9 of this chapter and the discussion of 'selectional restrictions' in Chapter 4.

[6] This iteration operator * is called the 'Kleene Star Operator', and is a notation meaning 'zero to infinitely many' occurrences. It should not be confused with the * prefixed to a linguistic example, indicating ungrammaticality.

c.   We need more intelligent leaders.

These sentences have different meanings depending on how we group the words. For example, (42a) will have the following two different constituent structures:

(43)   a.   John saw [the man with a telescope].
             (the man had the telescope)
       b.   John [[saw the man] with a telescope].
             (John used the telescope)

Even these very cursory observations indicate that a grammar with only lexical categories is not adequate for describing syntax. In addition, we need a notion of 'constituent', and need to consider how phrases may be formed, grouping certain words together.

2.3   Phrasal Categories

In addition to the agreement and ambiguity facts, our intuitions may also lead us to hypothesize constituency. If you were asked to group the words in (44) into phrases, what constituents would you come up with?

(44)   The student enjoyed his English syntax class last semester.

Perhaps most of us would intuitively assign the structure given in (45a), but not those in (45b) or (45c):

(45)   a.   [The student] [enjoyed [his English syntax class last semester]].
       b.   [The] [student enjoyed] [his English syntax class] [last semester].
       c.   [The student] [[enjoyed his English] [syntax class last semester]].

What kind of knowledge, in addition to semantic coherence, forms the basis for our intuitions of constituency? Are there clear syntactic or distributional tests which demonstrate the appropriate grouping of words or specific constituencies? There are certain salient syntactic phenomena which refer directly to constituents or phrases.

Cleft: The cleft construction, which places an emphasized or focused element in the X position in the pattern 'It is/was X that ... ', can provide us with simple evidence for the existence of phrasal units. For instance, think about how many different cleft sentences we can form from (46).

(46)   The policeman met several young students in the park last night.

With no difficulty, we can cleft almost all the constituents we can get from the above sentence:

(47)   a.   It was [the policeman] that met several young students in the park last night.
       b.   It was [several young students] that the policeman met in the park last night.
       c.   It was [in the park] that the policeman met several young students last night.
       d.   It was [last night] that the policeman met several young students in the park.

However, we cannot cleft sequences that do not form constituents:[7]

(48) a. *It was [the policeman met] that several young students in the park last night.

  b. *It was [several young students in] that the policeman met the park last night.

  c. *It was [in the park last night] that the policeman met several young students.

Constituent Questions and Stand-Alone Test: Further support for the existence of phrasal categories can be found in the answers to 'constituent questions', which involve a *wh*-word such as *who, where, when, how*. For any given *wh*-question, the answer can either be a full sentence or a fragment. This stand-alone fragment is a constituent:

(49) A: Where did the policeman meet several young students?

  B: In the park.

(50) A: Who(m) did the policeman meet in the park?

  B: Several young students.

This kind of test can be of use in determining constituents; we will illustrate with example (51):

(51)   John put old books in the box.

Are either *old books in the box* or *put old books in the box* a constituent? Are there smaller constituents? The *wh*-question tests can provide some answers:

(52) A: What did you put in your box?

  B: Old books.

  B: *Old books in the box.

(53) A: Where did you put the book?

  B: In the box.

  B: *Old books in the box.

(54) A: What did you do?

  B: *Put old books.

  B: *Put in the box.

  B: Put old books in the box.

Overall, the tests here will show that *old books* and *in the box* are constituents, and that *put old books in the box* is also a (larger) constituent.

The test is also sensitive to the difference between particles and prepositions. Consider the similar-looking examples in (55), including *looked* and *up*:

(55)   a. John looked up the inside of the chimney.

  b. John looked up the meaning of 'chanson'.

The examples differ, however, as to whether *up* forms a constituent with the following material or not. We can again apply the *wh*-question test:

---

[7]The verb phrase constituent *met . . . night* here cannot be clefted for independent reasons (see Chapter 12).

(56)   A: What did he look up?

     B: The inside of the chimney.

     B: The meaning of 'chanson'.

(57)   A: Where did he look?

     B: Up the inside of the chimney.

     B: *Up the meaning of 'chanson'.

(58)   A: Up what did he look?

     B: The inside of the chimney.

     B: *The meaning of 'chanson'.

What the contrasts here show is that *up* forms a constituent with *the inside of the chimney* in (55a) whereas it does not with *the meaning of 'chanson'* in (55b).

Substitution by a Pronoun: English, like most languages, has a system for referring back to individuals or entities mentioned by the use of pronouns. For instance, *the man who is standing by the door* in (59a) can be 'substituted' by the pronoun *he* in (59b).

(59)   a.   What do you think the man who is standing by the door is doing now?

     b.   What do you think *he* is doing now?

There are other pronouns such as *there, so, as*, and *which*, that also refer back to other constituents.

(60)   a.   Have you been [to Seoul]? I have never been *there*.

     b.   John might [go home], *so* might Bill.

     c.   John might [pass the exam], and *as* might Bill.

     d.   If John can [speak French fluently]   *which* we all know he can – we will have no problems.

A pronoun cannot be used to refer back to something that is not a constituent:

(61)   a.   John asked me to put the clothes in the cupboard, and to annoy him I really stuffed them *there* [there=in the cupboard].

     b.   John asked me to put the clothes in the cupboard, and to annoy him I stuffed *them* there [them=the clothes].

     c.   *John asked me to put the clothes in the cupboard, but I did *so* [=put the clothes] in the suitcase.

Both the pronoun *there* and *them* refer to a constituent. However, *so* in (61c), referring to a VP, refers only part of a constituent *put the clothes*, making it unacceptable.

Coordination: Another commonly-used test is coordination. Words and phrases can be co-ordinated by *conjunctions*, and each conjunct is typically the same kind of constituent as the other conjuncts:

(62) a. The girls [played in the water] and [swam under the bridge].

　　 b. The children were neither [in their rooms] nor [on the porch].

　　 c. She was [poor] but [quite happy].

　　 d. Many people drink [beer] or [wine].

If we try to coordinate unlike constituents, the results are typically ungrammatical.

(63) a. *Mary waited [for the bus] and [to go home].

　　 b. *Lee went [to the store] and [crazy].

　　 Even though such syntactic constituent tests are limited in certain cases, they are often adopted in determining the constituent of given expressions.

2.4   Phrase Structure Rules

We have seen evidence for the existence of phrasal categories. We say that phrases are projected from lexical categories, and hence we have phrases such as NP, VP, PP, and so on. As before, we use distributional evidence to classify each type, and then specify rules to account for the distributions we have observed.

2.4.1   NP: Noun Phrase

Consider (64):

(64) _ [liked ice cream].

The expressions that can occur in the blank position here are once again limited. The kinds of expression that do appear here include:

(65) Mary, I, you, students, the students, the tall students, the students from Seoul, the students who came from Seoul, etc.

If we look into the sub-constituents of these expressions, we can see that each includes at least an N and forms an NP (noun phrase). This leads us to posit the following rule:[8]

(66) NP → (Det) A* N (PP/S)

This rule characterizes a phrase, and is one instance of a phrase structure rule (PS rule). The rule indicates that an NP can consist of an optional Det, any number of optional A, an obligatory N, and then an optional PP or a modifying S.[9] The slash indicates different options for the same place in the linear order. These options in the NP rule can be represented in a tree structure:

---

[8]The relative clause *who came from Seoul* is kind of modifying sentence (S). See Chapter 11.

[9]To license an example like *the very tall man*, we need to make A* as AP*. For simplicity, we just use the former in the rule.

(67)

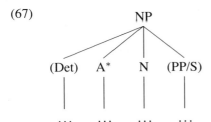

Once we insert appropriate expressions into the pre-terminal nodes, we will have well-formed NPs; and the rule will not generate the following NPs:

(68) *the whistle tune, *the easily student, *the my dog, ...

One important point is that as only N is obligatory in NP, a single noun such as *Mary, you,* or *students* can constitute an NP by itself. Hence the subject of the sentence *She sings* will be an NP, even though that NP consists only of a pronoun.

2.4.2 VP: Verb Phrase

Just as N projects an NP, V projects a VP. A simple test environment for VP is given in (69).

(69) The student __ .

(70) lists just a few of the possible phrases that can occur in the underlined position.

(70) snored, ran, sang, loved music, walked the dog through the park, lifted 50 pounds, thought Tom is honest, warned us that storms were coming, etc.

These phrases all have a V as their head – as projections of V, they form VP. VP can be characterized by the rule in (71), to a first level of analysis:

(71) VP → V (NP) (PP/S)

This simple VP rule says that a VP can consist of an obligatory V followed by an optional NP and then any number of PPs or an S. The rule thus does not generate ill-formed VPs such as these:

(72) *leave the meeting sing, *the leave meeting, *leave on time the meeting, ...

We can also observe that the presence of a VP is essential in forming a grammatical S, and the VP must be finite (present or past tense). Consider the following examples:

(73) a. The monkey wants to leave the meeting.
b. *The monkey eager to leave the meeting.

(74) a. The monkeys approved of their leader.
b. *The monkeys proud of their leader.

(75) a. The men practice medicine.
b. *The men doctors of medicine.

These examples show us that an English well-formed sentence consists of an NP and a (finite) VP, which can be represented as a PS rule:

(76)   S → NP VP

We thus have the rule that English sentences are composed of an NP and a VP, the precise structural counterpart of the traditional ideas of a sentence being 'a subject and predicate' or 'a noun and a verb'.

One more aspect to the structure of VP involves the presence of auxiliary verbs. Think of continuations for the fragments in (77):

(77)   a.   The students __ .

       b.   The students want __ .

For example, the phrases in (78a) and (78b) can occur in (77a) whereas those in (78c) can appear in (77b).

(78)   a.   run, feel happy, study English syntax, . . .

       b.   can run, will feel happy, must study English syntax, . . .

       c.   to run, to feel happy, to study English syntax, . . .

We have seen that the expressions in (78a) all form VPs, but how about those in (78b) and (78c)? These are also VPs, which happen to contain more than one V. In fact, the parts after the auxiliary verbs in (78b) and (78c) are themselves regular VPs. In the full grammar we will consider *to* and *can* and so on as auxiliary verbs, with a feature specification [AUX +] to distinguish them from regular verbs. Then all auxiliary verbs are simply introduced by a second VP rule:[10]

(79)   VP → V[AUX +]   VP

One more important VP structure involves the VP modified by an adverb or a PP:

(80)   a.   John [[read the book] loudly].

       b.   The teacher [[met his students] in the class].

In such examples, the adverb *loudly* and the PP *in the class* are modifying the preceding VP. To form such VPs, we need the PS rule in (81):

(81)   VP → VP Adv/PP

This rule, together with (76) will allow the following structure for (80b):[11]

(82)

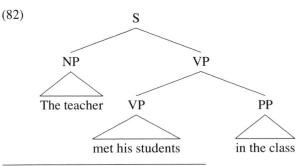

---

[10]The detailed discussion of English auxiliary verbs is found in Chapter 8.

[11]We use a triangle when we need not represent the internal structure of a phrase.

2.4.3   AP: Adjective Phrase

The most common environment where an adjective phrase (AP) occurs is in 'linking verb' constructions as in (83):

(83)   John feels __ .

Expressions like those in (84) can occur in the blank space here:

(84)   happy, uncomfortable, terrified, sad, proud of her, proud to be his student, proud that he passed the exam, etc.

Since these all include an adjective (A), we can safely conclude that they all form an AP. Looking into the constituents of these, we can formulate the following simple PS rule for the AP:[12]

(85)   AP → A (PP/VP/CP)

This simple AP rule can easily explain the following:

(86)   a.   John sounded [$_{AP}$ happy].
     b.   John sounded [$_{AP}$ proud [$_{PP}$ of her]].
     c.   John felt [$_{AP}$ proud [$_{CP}$ that his son won the game]].
     d.   John sounded [*happily/*very/*the student/*in the park].

The verb *sounded* requires an AP to be followed: (86a)–(86c) satisfies the rule in (85), but in (86c) we have no AP. In addition, observe the contrasts in the following examples:

(87)   a.   *The monkeys seem [want to leave the meeting].
     b.   The monkeys seem [eager to leave the meeting].

(88)   a.   *John seems [know about the bananas].
     b.   John seems [certain about the bananas].

These examples tell us that the verb *seem* combines with an AP, but not with a VP.

2.4.4   AdvP: Adverb Phrase

Another phrasal syntactic category is adverb phrase (AdvP), as exemplified in (89).

(89)   soundly, well, clearly, extremely, carefully, very soundly, almost certainly, very slowly, etc.

These phrases are often used to modify verbs, adjectives, and adverbs themselves, and they can all occur in principle in the following environments:

(90)   a.   He behaved very __ .
     b.   They worded the sentence very __ .
     c.   He treated her very __ .

---

[12]The phrase CP results from the combination of a complementizer like *that* and an S. See Chapter 4 for further discussion.

Phrases other than an AdvP cannot appear here. For example, an NP *the student* or AP *happy* cannot occur in these syntactic positions. Based on what we have seen so far, the AdvP rule can be given as follows:

(91)   AdvP → (AdvP) Adv

2.4.5   PP: Preposition Phrase

Another major phrasal category is preposition phrase (PP). PPs like those in (92), generally consist of a preposition plus an NP.

(92)   from Seoul, in the box, in the hotel, into the soup, with John and his dog, under the table, etc.

These PPs can appear in a wide range of environments:

(93)   a.   John came from Seoul.

b.   They put the book in the box.

c.   They stayed in the hotel.

d.   The fly fell into the soup.

One clear case in which only a PP can appear is the following:

(94)   The squirrel ran straight/right __ .

The intensifiers *straight* and *right* can occur neither with an AP nor with an AdvP:

(95)   a.   The squirrel ran straight/right up the tree.

b.   *The squirrel is straight/right angry.

c.   *The squirrel ran straight/right quickly.

From the examples in (92), we can deduce the following general rule for forming a PP:[13]

(96)   PP → P NP

The rule states that a PP consists of a P followed by an NP. We cannot construct unacceptable PPs like the following:

(97)   *in angry, *into sing a song, *with happily, . . .

2.5   Grammar with Phrases

We have seen earlier that the grammar with just lexical categories is not adequate for capturing the basic properties of the language. How much further do we get with a grammar which includes phrases? A set of PS rules, some of which we have already seen, is given in (98).[14]

---

[13]Depending on how we treat the qualifier *straight* and *right*, we may need to extend this PP rule as "PP → (Qual) P NP" so that the P may be preceded by an optional qualifier like *right* or *straight*. However, this means that we need to introduce another lexical category 'Qual'. Another direction is to take the qualifier categorically as an adverb carrying the feature QUAL while allowing only such adverbs to modify a PP.

[14]The grammar consisting of such form of rules is often called a 'Context Free Grammar', as each rule may apply any time its environment is satisfied, regardless of any other contextual restrictions.

(98) a. S → NP VP

    b. NP → (Det) A* N (PP/S)

    c. VP → V (NP) (PP/S/VP)

    d. AP → A (PP/S)

    e. AdvP → (AdvP) Adv

    f. PP → P NP

The rules say that a sentence is the combination of NP and VP, and an NP can be made up of a Det, any number of As, an obligatory N, and any number of PPs, and so on. Of the possible tree structures that these rules can generate, the following is one example:

(99)

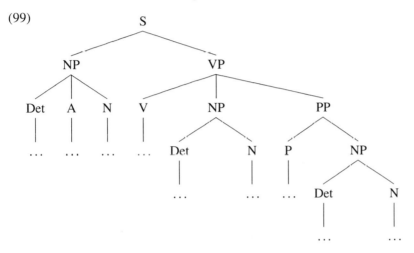

With the structural possibilities shown here, let us assume that we have the following lexical entries:

(100) a. Det: a, an, this, that, any, some, which, his, her, no, etc.

    b. A: handsome, tall, fat, large, dirty, big, yellow, etc.

    c. N: book, ball, hat, friend, dog, cat, man, woman, John, etc.

    d. V: kicked, chased, sang, met, believed, thinks, imagines, assumes etc.

Inserting these elements in the appropriate pre-terminal nodes (the places with dots) in (99), we are able to generate various sentences like those in (101):[15]

(101) a. This handsome man chased a dog.

    b. A man kicked that ball.

    c. That tall woman chased a cat.

    d. His friend kicked a ball.

---

[15]The grammar still generates semantically anomalous examples like #*The desk believed a man* or #*A man sang her hat*. For such semantically distorted examples, we need to refer to the notion of 'selectional restrictions' (see Chapter 7).

There are several ways to generate an infinite number of sentences with this kind of grammar. As we have seen before, one simple way is to repeat a category (e.g., adjective) infinitely as given in (98b). There are also other ways of generating an infinite number of grammatical sentences. Look at the following two PS rules from (98) again:

(102)   a.   S → NP VP

         b.   VP → V S

As we show in the following tree structure, we can 'recursively' apply the two rules, in the sense that one can feed the other, and then vice versa:

(103)

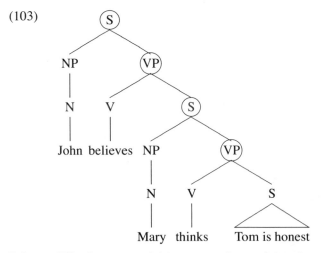

It is not difficult to expand this sentence by applying the two rules again and again:

(104)   a.   Bill claims John believes Mary thinks Tom is honest.

         b.   Jane imagines Bill claims John believes Mary thinks Tom is honest.

There is no limit to this kind of **recursive application** of PS rules: it proves that this kind of grammar can generate an infinite number of grammatical sentences.

   One structure which can be also recursive involves sentences involving auxiliary verbs. As noted before in (79), an auxiliary verb forms a larger VP after combining with a VP:

(105)

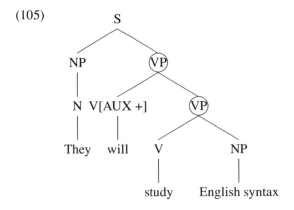

This means that we will also have a recursive structure like the following:[16]

(106)

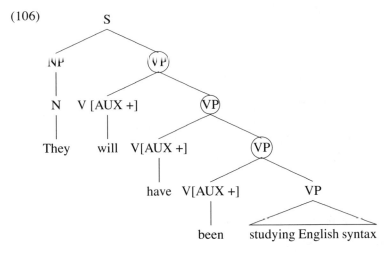

Another important property that PS rules bring us is the ability to make reference to **hierarchical structures** within given sentences, where parts are assembled into sub-structures of the whole. One merit of such hierarchical structural properties is that they enable us to represent the structural ambiguities of sentences we have seen earlier in (42). Let us look at more examples:

(107) a. The little boy hit the child with a toy.

   b. Chocolate cakes and pies are my favorite desserts.

Depending on which PS rules we apply, for the sentences here, we will have different hierarchical tree structures. Consider the possible partial structures of (107a) which the grammar can generate:[17]

(108) a.

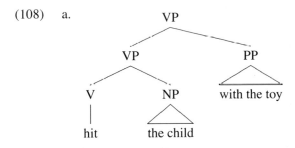

---

[16]Due to the limited number of auxiliary verbs, and restrictions on their cooccurrence, the maximum number of auxiliaries in a single English clause is 3. See Chapter 8.

[17]One can draw a slight different structure for (108b) with the introduction of the rule 'NP → NP PP'.

b.

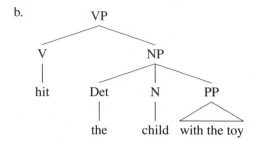

The structures clearly indicate what *with the toy* modifies: in (108a), it modifies the whole VP phrase whereas (108b) modifies just the noun *child*. The structural differences induced by the PS rules directly represent these meaning differences.

In addition, we can easily show why examples like the following are not grammatical:

(109)   a. *The children were in their rooms and happily.

　　　　b. *Lee went to the store and crazy.

We have noted that English allows two alike categories to be coordinated. This can be written as a PS rule, for phrasal conjunction, where XP is any phrase in the grammar.[18]

(110)   XP → XP$^+$ Conj XP

The 'coordination' rule says two identical XP categories can be coordinated and form the same category XP. Applying this PS rule, we will then allow (111a) but not (111b):

(111)   a.

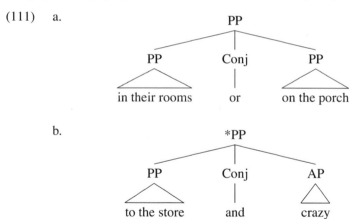

Unlike categories such as PP and AP may not be coordinated.

The PS rules further allow us to represent the difference between phrasal verb (e.g, *call off*) constructions and prepositional verb constructions (e.g. *rely on*), some of whose properties we have seen earlier. Consider a representative pair of contrasting examples:

(112)   a.   John suddenly got *off* the bus.

　　　　b.   John suddenly put *off* the customers.

---

[18]Different from the Kleene star operator *, the plus operator $^+$ here means the XP here occurs at least once.

By altering the position of *off*, we can determine that *off* in (112a) is a preposition whereas *off* in (112b) is a particle:

(113)　a.　*John suddenly got the bus off.

　　　　b.　John suddenly put the customers off.

This in turn means that *off* in (112a) is a preposition, forming a PP with the following NP, whereas *off* in (112b) is a particle that forms no constituent with the following NP *the customers*. This in turn means that in addition to the PP formation rule, the grammar needs to introduce the following VP rules:

(114)　a.　VP → V Part NP

　　　　b.　VP → V NP Part

　　　　c.　VP → V PP

Equipped with these rules, we then can easily represent the differences of these grammatical sentences (112a), (112b) and (113b) in tree structures:

(115)　a.

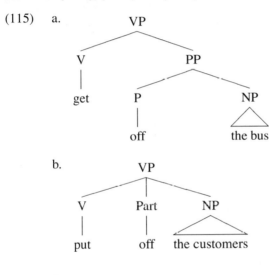

　　　b.

　　　c.

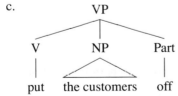

As represented here, the particle does not form a constituent with the following or preceding NP whereas the preposition does form a constituent with it.

In summary, we have seen that a grammar with lexical categories can not only generate an infinite number of grammatical English sentences, but also account for some fundamental properties, such as agreement and constituency.[19] This motivates the introduction of phrases into the grammar.

2.6 Exercises

1. Determine the lexical category of the italicized words in the following. In doing so, use the three criteria (morphological, semantic, and syntactic) to provide the evidence for your answer and state which one is the most reliable one.

   (i) a. His second *book* came out earlier this year and became an instant best-seller.
   b. When you *book* something such as a hotel room, you arrange to have it.
   c. Price quotes on selected categories *will* be sent out upon request.
   d. No doubt that he was forced to leave his family against his *will*.
   e. He intended to *will* the large amount of money to Frank.
   f. Jane stood aside to let her *pass*.
   g. He has a rail *pass* that's right for you.
   h. *Whose* book did you read last night?
   i. It is important *for* us to spend time with children.
   j. He was arrested *for* being drunk.
   k. I think *that* person we met last week is insane.
   l. We believe *that* he is quite reasonable.
   m. I forgot to return the book *that* I borrowed from the teacher.

2. Consider the following data carefully and describe the similarities and differences among *that, for, if* and *whether*. In so doing, first compare *that* and *for* and then see how these two are different from *if* and *whether*.

   (i) a. I am anxious that you should arrive on time.
   b. *I am anxious that you to arrive on time.
   (ii) a. I am anxious for you to arrive on time.
   b. *I am anxious for you should arrive on time.
   (iii) a. I don't know whether/if I should agree.
   b. I wonder whether/if you'd be kind enough to give us information.
   (vi) a. If students study hard, teachers will be happy.
   b. Whether they say it or not, most teachers expect their students to study hard.

3. Check if the italic parts form a constituent or not, using at least two constituenthood tests (e.g., cleft, pronoun substitution, stand-alone, etc.). Also provide tree structures for each of the following examples.

   (i) a. John bought *a book on the table*.

---

[19]In this chapter, we have not discussed the treatment of agreement with PS rules. Chapter 6 discusses the subject-verb agreement in detail.

   b. John put *a book on the table*.

(ii) a. She turned *down the side street*

   b. She turned *down his offer*.

(iii) a. He looked at *a book about swimming*.

   b. He talked to *a girl about swimming*.

   c. He talked with *a girl about swimming*.

(iv) a. I don't know *the people present*.

   b. John called *the president a fool*.

4. Explain why the examples in (i) are ungrammatical. As part of the exercise, first draw structure for each example and try to determine the applicability of the PS rules such as the coordination rule in (110), presented earlier in this chapter.

   (i) a. *Could you turn off the fire and on the light?

   b. *A nuclear explosion would wipe out plant life and out animal life.

   c. *He ran down the road and down the President.

   d. *I know the truth and that you are innocent.

   e. *Lee went to the store and crazy.

5. Provide a tree structure for each of the following sentences and suggest what kind of VP rules are necessary. In doing so, pay attention to the position of modifiers like *proudly*, *by the park*, and so forth.

   (i) a. John refused the offer proudly.

   b. I consider Telma the best candidate.

   c. I saw him leaving the main building.

   d. He took Masako to the school by the park.

   e. John sang a song and danced to the music.

   f. John wants to study linguistics in near future.

   g. They told Angelica to arrive early for the award.

   h. That Louise had abandoned the project surprised everyone.

6. Each of the following sentences is structurally ambiguous – it has at least two structures. Represent the structural ambiguities by providing different tree structures for each string of words.[20]

   (i) a. I know you like the back of my hand.

   b. I forgot how good beer tastes.

   c. I saw that gas can explode.

   d. Time flies like an arrow.

   e. I need to have that report on our webpage by tomorrow.

7. Provide tree structures for each of the following sentences and see if there are any new PS rules that we need to add, to supplement those we covered in this chapter. If there are

---

[20]For i-e, to help tease out the ambiguity, consider related potential interpretations like *Please put that book on my desk.* and *That report on our webpage alleges that it does not function well.*.

any places you cannot assign structures, please use triangles.

(i)   Different languages may have different lexical categories, or they might associate different properties to the same one. For example, Spanish uses adjectives almost interchangeably as nouns while English cannot. Japanese has two classes of adjectives whereas English has one; Korean, Japanese, and Chinese have measure words while European languages have nothing resembling them; many languages don't have a distinction between adjectives and adverbs, or adjectives and nouns, etc. Many linguists argue that the formal distinctions between parts of speech must be made within the framework of a specific language or language family, and should not be carried over to other languages or language families.[21]

---

[21] Adapted from `http://en.wikipedia.org/wiki/Part_of_speech`

3

Syntactic Forms, Grammatical Functions, and Semantic Roles

3.1 Introduction

In the previous chapter, we analyzed English sentences with PS rules. For example, the PS rule 'S → NP VP' represents the basic rule for forming well-formed English sentences. As we have seen, such PS rules allow us to represent the constituent structure of a given sentence in terms of lexical and phrasal **syntactic categories**. There are other dimensions of the analysis of sentences; one such way is using the notion of **grammatical functions** such as subject and object:

(1)   a.   Syntactic categories: N, A, V, P, NP, VP, AP, . . .

      b.   Grammatical functions: SUBJ (Subject), OBJ (Object), MOD (Modifier), PRED (Predicate), . . .

The notions such as SUBJ, OBJ and PRED represent the grammatical function each phrasal constituent plays in the given sentence. For example, consider one simple sentence:

(2)   The monkey scratched a boy on Monday.

This sentence can be structurally represented in terms of either syntactic categories or grammatical functions as in the following:

(3)   a.   [$_S$ [$_{NP}$ The monkey] [$_{VP}$ scratched [$_{NP}$ a boy] [$_{PP}$ on Monday]]].

      b.   [$_S$ [$_{SUBJ}$ The monkey] [$_{PRED}$ scratched [$_{OBJ}$ a boy] [$_{MOD}$ on Monday]]].

As shown here, *the monkey* is an NP in terms of its syntactic form, but is the SUBJ (subject) in terms of its grammatical function. The NP *a boy* is the OBJ (object) while the verb *scratched* functions as a predicator. More importantly, we consider the entire VP to be a PRED (predicate) which describes a property of the subject. *On Monday* is a PP in terms of its syntactic category, but serves as a MOD (modifier) here.

We also can represent sentence structures in terms of **semantic roles**. Constituents can be considered in terms of conceptual notions of semantic roles such as agent, patient, location, instrument, and the like. A semantic role denotes the underlying relationship that a participant has with the relation of the clause, expressed by the main verb. Consider the semantic roles of the NPs in the following two sentences:[1]

(4)   a.   John tagged the monkey in the forest.

        b.   The monkey was tagged in the forest by John.

Both of these sentences describe a situation in which someone named John tagged a particular monkey. In this situation, John is the agent and the monkey is the patient of the tagging event. This in turn means that in both cases, John has the semantic role of agent (*agt*), whereas the monkey has the semantic role of patient (*pat*), even though their grammatical functions are different. We thus can assign the following semantic role to each constituent of the examples:

(5)   a.   [[$_{agt}$ John] [$_{pred}$ tagged [$_{pat}$ the monkey] [$_{loc}$ in the forest]]].

        b.   [[$_{pat}$ The monkey] [$_{pred}$ was tagged [$_{loc}$ in the wood] [$_{agt}$ by John]]].

As noted here, in addition to agent and patient, we have the semantic predicate (*pred*), which governs the roles, and also the locative (*loc*) role. So we now can describe the semantic role that each phrase describes.

Throughout this book we will see that English grammar refers to these three different levels of information (syntactic category, grammatical function, and semantic role), and that they interact with each other. For now, it may appear that they are equivalent classifications: for example, an agent is a subject and an NP, and a patient is an object and an NP. However, as we get further into the details of the grammar, we will see many ways in which the three levels are not simply co-extensive.

3.2 Grammatical Functions

How can we identify the grammatical function of a given constituent? Several tests can be used to determine grammatical function, as we show here.

3.2.1 Subjects

Consider the following pair of examples:

(6)   a.   [The cat] [devoured [the rat]].

        b.   [The rat] [devoured [the cat]].

These two sentences have exactly the same words and have the same **predicator** *devoured*. Yet they are significantly different in meaning, and the main difference comes from what serves as **subject** or **object** with respect to the predicator. In (6a), the subject is *the cat*, whereas in (6b) it is *the rat*, and the object is *the rat* in (6a) but *the cat* in (6b).

The most common structure for a sentence seems to be the one in which the NP subject is the one who performs the action denoted by the verb (thus having the semantic role of agent). However, this is not always so:

---

[1] Semantic roles are also often called 'thematic roles' or 'θ-roles' ("theta roles") in generative grammar (Chomsky (1982, 1986)).

(7)   a.   My brother wears a green overcoat.

        b.   This car stinks.

        c.   It rains.

        d.   The committee disliked her proposal.

Wearing a green overcoat, stinking, raining, or disliking one's proposal is not an agentive activity; they indicate stative descriptions or situations. Such facts show that we cannot rely on the semantic roles of agent for determining subjecthood.

More reliable tests for subjecthood come from syntactic tests such as agreement, tag questions, and subject-auxiliary inversion.

Agreement: The main verb of a sentence agrees with the subject in English:

(8)   a.   She never writes/*write home.

        b.   These books *saddens/sadden me.

        c.   Our neighbor takes/*take his children to school in his car.

As we noted in Chapter 1, simply being closer to the main verb does not entail subjecthood:

(9)   a.   The book, including all the chapters in the first section, is/*are very interesting.

        b.   The effectiveness of teaching and learning *depend/depends on several factors.

        c.   The tornadoes that tear through this county every spring *is/are more than just a nuisance.

The subject in each example is *book*, *effectiveness*, and *tornadoes* respectively, even though there are nouns closer to the main verb. This indicates that it is not simply the linear position of the NP that determines agreement; rather, agreement shows us what the subject of the sentence is.

Tag questions: A tag question, a short question tagged onto the end of an utterance, is also a reliable subjecthood test:

(10)   a.   The lady singing with a boy is a genius, isn't she/*isn't he?

       b.   With their teacher, the kids have arrived safely, haven't they/ *hasn't he?

The pronoun in the tag question agrees with the subject in person, number, and gender – it refers back to the subject, but not necessarily to the closest NP, nor to the most topical one. The pronoun *she* in (10a) shows us that *lady* is the head of the subject NP in that example, and *they* in (10b) leads us to assign the same property to *kids*. The generalization is that a tag question must contain a pronoun which identifies the subject of the clause to which the tag is attached.

Subject-auxiliary inversion: In forming questions and other sentence-types, English has subject-auxiliary inversion, which applies only to the subject.

(11)   a.   This teacher is a genius.

       b.   The kids have arrived safely.

    c. It could be more detrimental.

(12) a. Is this teacher a genius?

       b. Have the kids arrived safely?

       c. Could it be more detrimental?

As seen here, the formation of 'Yes/No questions' such as these involves the first tensed auxiliary verb moving across the subject: more formally, the auxiliary verb is inverted with respect to the subject, hence the term 'subject-auxiliary inversion'. This is not possible with a non-subject:

(13) a. The kids in our class have arrived safely.

       b. *Have in our class the kids arrived safely?

Subject-auxiliary inversion provides another reliable subjecthood test.

3.2.2 Direct and Indirect Objects

A direct object (DO) is canonically an NP, undergoing the process denoted by the verb:

(14) a. His girlfriend bought this computer.

       b. That silly fool broke the teapot.

However, this is not a solid generalization. The objects (OBJ) in (15a) and (15b) are not really affected by the action. In (15a) the dog is experiencing something, and in (15b) the thunder is somehow causing some feeling in the dog:

(15) a. Thunder frightens [the dog].

       b. The dog fears [thunder].

Once again, the data show us that we cannot identify the object based on semantic roles. A much more firm criterion is the syntactic construction of **passivization**, in which a notional direct object appears as subject. The sentences in (16) can be turned into passive sentences in (17):

(16) a. His girlfriend bought this computer for him.

       b. The child broke the teapot by accident.

(17) a. This computer was bought for him by his girlfriend.

       b. The teapot was broken by the child by accident.

What we can notice here is that the objects in (16) are 'promoted' to subject in the passive sentences. The test comes from the fact that non-object NPs cannot be promoted to the subject:

(18) a. This item belongs to the student.

       b. *The student is belonged to by this item.

(19) a. He remained a good friend to me.

       b. *A good friend is remained to me (by him).

The objects that undergo passivization are direct objects.

An indirect object (IO) is an NP that occurs with a DO in a two-NP sequence, and it precedes the DO. The pattern is:

(20)   Subject – Verb – Indirect Object – Direct Object

The IO is the one to whom or for whom the action of the verb is done and who is receiving the direct object. It thus canonically has the semantic role of goal, recipient or benefactive:

(21)   a.   I threw [the puppy] [the ball]. (IO = goal)

      b.   John gave [the boys] [the CDs]. (IO = recipient)

      c.   My mother baked [me] [a birthday cake]. (IO = benefactive)

In each case, the DO has the semantic role of theme.

While we have used the terminology 'DO' and 'IO' here, in part to reflect the semantic roles of the different arguments, the passive rule that we introduce in Chapter 9 has the property of promoting the NP that would have immediately followed the verb to the subject position. This reflects the traditional intuition of how passive applies. Consequently, in the passives of examples like (21), the IO is now expressed as the subject.

(22)   a.   The boys were given the CDs (by John).

      b.   She was sent a review copy of the book (by the publisher).

Note that examples with the IO-DO order are different from those where the semantic role of the IO is expressed as an oblique PP, following the DO.[2]

(23)   a.   John gave the CDs to the boys.

      b.   The publisher sent a review copy of the book to her.

      c.   My mother baked a cake for me.

In this kind of example, it is the DO which passivizes, as it immediately follows the V in the active form, giving examples like the following:

(24)   a.   The CDs were given to the boys by John.

      b.   A review copy of the book was sent to her by the publisher.

      c.   This nice cake was baked for me by my mother.

The 'NP PP' expression is much more flexible than the 'NP NP' expression; the latter is restricted to the specific semantic roles mentioned above. So, for example, (25a) has no alternate expression where 'a frog' is an IO:

(25)   a.   The magician turned some feathers into a frog.

        *The magician turned a frog some feathers.

3.2.3   Predicative Complements

There also are NPs which follow a verb but which do not behave as DOs. Consider the following sentences:

---

[2]Strictly speaking, inside PP, the NP is the (direct) object of the preposition.

(26) a. This is *my ultimate goal*.

  b. Michelle became *an architect*.

(27) a. They elected Graham *chairman*.

  b. I consider Andrew *the best writer*

The italicized elements here are traditionally called 'predicative complements' in the sense that they function as the predicate of the subject or the object. However, even though they are NPs, they do not passivize:

(28) a. *Chairman was elected Graham.

  b. *The best writer was considered Andrew.

The difference between objects and predicative complements can also be seen in the following contrast:

(29) a. John made Kim *a great doll*.

  b. John made Kim *a great doctor.*

Even though the italicized expressions here are both NPs, they function differently. The NP *a great doll* in (29a) is the direct object, as in *John made a great doll for Kim*, whereas the NP *a great doctor* in (29b) cannot be an object: it serves as the predicate of the object *Kim*. If we think of part of the meaning informally, only in the second example would we say that the final NP describes the NP *Kim*.

(30) a. (29)a: Kim $\neq$ a great doll

  b. (29)b: Kim $=$ a great doctor

  In addition, phrases other than NPs can serve as predicative complements:

(31) a. The situation became *terrible*.

  b. This map is *what he wants*.

  c. The message was *that you should come on time*.

(32) a. I made Kim *angry*.

  b. I consider him *immoral*.

  c. I regard Andrew *as the best writer*.

  d. They spoil their kids *rotten*.

  The italicized complements function to predicate a property of the subject in (31) and of the object in (32).

3.2.4 Oblique Complements

Consider now the italicized expressions in (33):

(33) a. John put books *in the box*.

  b. John talked *to Bill about the exam*.

  c. She reminded him *of the last time they met*.

d. They would inform Mary *of any success they have made*.

These italicized expressions are neither objects nor predicative complements. Since their presence is obligatory, for syntactic well-formedness, they are called oblique complements. Roughly speaking, 'oblique' contrasts with the 'direct' functions of subject and object, and oblique phrases are typically expressed as PPs in English.

As we have seen before, most ditransitive verbs can also take oblique complements:

(34) a. John gave a book *to the student*.

b. John bought a book *for the student*.

The PPs here, which cannot be objects since they are not NPs, also do not serve as predicate of the subject or object – they relate directly to the verb, as oblique complements.

3.2.5 Modifiers

The functions of DO, IO, predicative complement, and oblique complement all have one common property: they are all selected by the verb, and we view them as being present to 'complement' the verb to form a legitimate VP. Hence, these are called **complements (COMPS)**, and typically they cannot be omitted.

Unlike these COMPS, there are expressions which do not complement the predicate in the same way, and which are truly optional:

(35) a. The bus stopped *suddenly*.

b. Shakespeare wrote his plays *a long time ago*.

c. They went to the theater *in London*.

d. He failed chemistry *because he can't understand it*.

The italicized expressions here are all optional and function as modifiers (also called 'adjuncts' or 'adverbial' expressions). These modifiers specify the manner, location, time, or reason, among many other properties, of the situations expressed by the given sentences – informally, they are the (*how, when, where*, and *why*) phrases.

One additional characteristic of modifiers is that they can be stacked up, whereas complements cannot.

(36) a. *John gave Tom [a book] [a record].

b. I saw this film [several times] [last year] [during the summer].

As shown here, temporal adjuncts like *several times* and *last year* can be repeated, whereas the two complements *a book* and *a record* in (36a) cannot. Of course, temporal adjuncts do not become the subject of a passive sentence, suggesting that they cannot serve as objects.

(37) a. My uncle visited today.

b. *Today was visited by my uncle.

3.3 Form and Function Together

We now can analyse each sentence in terms of grammatical functions as well as the structural constituents. Let us see how we can analyze a simple sentence along these two dimensions:

(38)

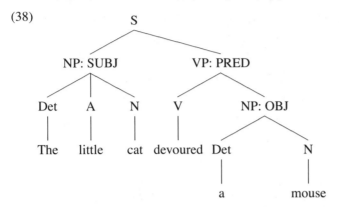

As represented here, the expressions *the little cat* and *a mouse* are both NPs, but they have different grammatical functions, SUBJ and OBJ. The VP as a whole functions as the predicate of the sentence, describing the property of the subject.[3]

Assigning grammatical functions within complex sentences is no different:

(39)

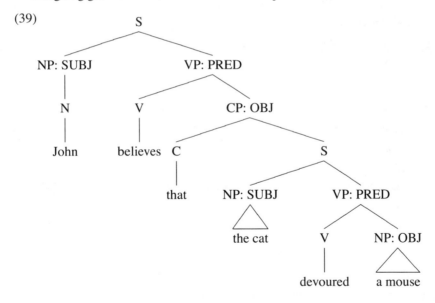

Each clause has its own SUBJ and PRED: *John* is the subject of the higher clause, whereas *the cat* is the subject of the lower clause. We also can notice that there are two OBJs: the CP is the

---

[3] A word of caution is in order here. We should not confuse the functional term 'adverbial' with the category term 'adverb'. The term 'adverbial' is used interchangeably with 'adjunct' or 'modifier', whereas 'adverb' only designates a part of speech. In English almost any kind of phrasal category can function as an adverbial element, but only a limited set of words are adverbs.

object of the higher clause whereas the NP is that of the lower clause.[4]

Every category in a given sentence has a grammatical function, but there is no one-to-one mapping between category such as NP or CP and its possible grammatical function(s). The following data set shows us how different phrase types can function as SUBJ or OBJ:[5]

(40)   a.   [$_{NP}$ The termites] destroyed the sand castle.

b.   [$_{VP}$ Being honest] is not an easy task.

c.   [$_{CP}$ That John passed] surprised her.

d.   [$_{VP}$ To finish this work on time] is almost unexpected.

e.   [$_{PP}$ Under the bed] is a safe place to hide.

(41)   a.   I sent [$_{NP}$ a surprise present] to John.

b.   They wondered [$_S$ what she did yesterday].

c.   They believed [$_{CP}$ that everybody would pass the test].

d.   Are you going on holiday before or after Easter? I prefer [$_{PP}$ after Easter].

As the examples in (40) and (41) show, not only NPs but also infinitival VPs and CPs can also function as SUBJ and OBJ. The following tag-question, subject-verb agreement, and subject-hood tests show us that an infinitival VP and CP can function as the subject.

(42)   a.   [That John passed] surprised her, didn't it?

b.   [[That the march should go ahead] and [that it should be cancelled]] have/*has been argued by different people at different times.

(43)   a.   [To finish it on time] made quite a statement, didn't it?

b.   [[To delay the march] and [to go ahead with it]] have/*has been argued by different people at different times.

The same goes for modifier (MOD), as noted before. Not only AdvP, but also phrases such as NP, S, VP, or PP can function as a modifier:

(44)   a.   The little cat devoured a mouse [$_{NP}$ last night].

b.   John left [$_{AdvP}$ very early].

c.   John has been at Stanford [$_{PP}$ for four years].

d.   John studied hard [$_{VP}$ to pass the exam].

e.   She disappeared [$_S$ when the main party arrived].

The sentence (44a) will have the following structure:

---

[4]The phrase CP is headed by the complementizer *that*.

[5]In due course, we will discuss in detail the properties of each phrase type here.

(45)

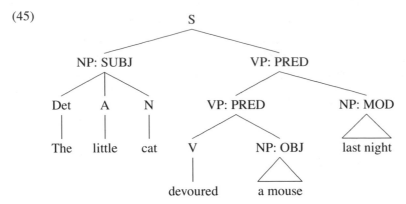

Here the expression *last night* is an adverbial NP in the sense that it is categorically an NP but functions as a modifier (adjunct) to the VP.

As we go through this book, we will see that the distinction between grammatical functions and categorical types is crucial in the understanding of English syntax.

3.4 Semantic Roles

As noted before, semantic roles were introduced as a way of classifying the arguments of predicators (mostly verbs and adjectives) into a closed set of participant types. Even though we cannot make any absolute generalizations about the relationship between grammatical functions and semantic roles, the properties of semantic roles do interact in regular ways with certain grammatical constructions. A list of the most relevant thematic roles and their associated properties is given below.[6]

- Agent: A participant which the meaning of the verb specifies as doing or causing something, possibly intentionally. Examples: subject of *eat, kick, hit, hammer*, etc.

(46) a. *John* ate his noodle quietly.
   b. *A boy* hit the ball.
   c. *A smith* hammered the metal.

- Patient: A participant which the verb characterizes as having something happen to it, and as being affected by what happens to it. Examples: object of *kick, hit, hammer*, etc.[7]

(47) a. A boy hit *the ball*.
   b. A smith hammered *the metal*.

- Experiencer: A participant who is characterized as aware of something. Examples: subject of perception verbs like *feel, smell, hear, see*, etc.

(48) a. *The students* felt comfortable in the class.

---

[6]The definition of semantic roles given here is adopted from Dowty (1989).

[7]Patient and theme are often unified into 'undergoer' in the sense that both the patient and theme individual undergo the action in question.

b. *The student* heard a strange sound.

• Theme: A participant which is characterized as changing its position or condition, or as being in a state or position. Examples: direct object of *give, hand*, subject of *come, happen, die*, etc.

(49) a. John gave *a book* to the students.

  b. *John* died last night.

• Benefactive: The entity that benefits from the action or event denoted by the predicator. Examples: oblique complement of *make, buy*, etc.

(50) a. John made a doll for *his son*.

  b. John bought a lot of books for *his sons*.

• Source: The one from which motion proceeds. Examples: object of *deprive, fell off, free, cure*, etc.

(51) a. John deprived *his sons* of game cards.

  b. John fell off *the chair*.

  c. John bought the book from

  d. Tom.

• Goal: The one to which motion proceeds. Examples: subject of *receive, buy*, indirect object of *tell, give*, etc.

(52) a. *Mary* received an award from the department.

  b. John told the rumor to *his friend*.

• Location: The thematic role associated with the NP expressing the location in a sentence with a verb of location. Examples: subject of *keep, own, retain*, locative PPs, etc.

(53) a. John put his books *in the attic*.

  b. *The government* kept all the money.

• Instrument: The medium by which the action or event denoted by the predicator is carried out. Examples: oblique complement of *hit, wipe, hammer*, etc.

(54) a. John hit the ball with *a bat*.

  b. John wiped the window with *a towel*.

An important advantage of having such semantic roles available to us is that they allow us to capture the relationship between two related sentences, as we have already seen. As another example, consider the following pair:

(55) a. [$_{agt}$ The cat] chased [$_{pat}$ the mouse].

b. [$_{pat}$ The mouse] was chased by [$_{agt}$ the cat].

Even though the above two sentences have different syntactic structures, they have essentially identical interpretations. The reason is that the same semantic roles assigned to the NPs: in both examples, the cat is the agent, and the mouse is the patient. Different grammatical uses of verbs may express the same semantic roles in different arrays.

The semantic roles also allow us to classify verbs into more fine-grained groups. For example, consider the following examples:

(56)　a.　There still remains an issue to be solved.

　　　b.　There lived a man with his grandson.

　　　c.　There arrived a tall, red-haired and incredibly well dressed man.

(57)　a.　*There sang a man with a pipe.

　　　b.　*There dances a man with an umbrella.

All the verbs are intransitive, but not all are acceptable in the *there*-construction. The difference can come from the semantic role of the postverbal NP, as assigned by the main verb. Verbs like *arrive, remain, live* are taken to assign the semantic role of 'theme' (see the list of roles above), whereas verbs like *sing, dance* assign an 'agent' role. We thus can conjecture that *there*-constructions do not accept the verb whose subject carries an agent semantic role.

While semantic roles provide very useful ways of describing properties across different constructions, we should point out that the theoretical status of semantic roles is still unresolved.[8] For example, there is no agreement about exactly which and how many semantic roles are needed. The problem is illustrated by the following simple examples:

(58)　a.　John resembles his mother.

　　　b.　A is similar to B.

What kind of semantic roles do the arguments here have? Both participants seem to be playing the same role in these examples – they both cannot be either agent or patient or theme. They are also cases where we might not be able to pin down the exact semantic role:

(59)　a.　John runs into the house.

　　　b.　Mary looked at the sky.

The subject John in (59a) is both agent and theme: it is agent since it initiates and sustains the movement but also theme since it is the object that moves.[9] Also, the subject Mary in (59b) can either be an experiencer or an agent depending on her intention – one can just look at the sky with no purpose at all.[10]

---

[8] See Levin and Rappaport Hovav (2005) for further discussion of this issue.

[9] Jackendoff (1990) develops an account of thematic roles in which agency and motion are two separate dimensions, so, in fact, a single NP can be agent and theme.

[10] To overcome the problem of assigning the correct semantic role to an argument, one can assume that each predicator has its own (individual) semantic roles. For example, the verb *kick*, instead of having an agent and a patient, has two individualized semantic roles 'kicker' and 'kicked'. See Pollard and Sag (1987).

Even though there are theoretical issues involved in adopting semantic roles in the grammar, there are also many advantages of using them. We can make generalizations about the grammar of the language: typically the 'agent' takes the subject position, while an NP following the word *from* is serving as the 'source'. As we will see in the next chapter, semantic roles are also recognized as the standard concepts used for organizing predicate-argument structures for predicates within the lexicon. In the subsequent chapters, we will refer to semantic roles in various places.

3.5   Exercises

1. Construct sentences containing the following grammatical functions:
    (i) a. subject, predicator, direct object
        b. subject, predicator, indirect object, direct object
        c. subject, predicator, adjunct
        d. adjunct, subject, predicator
        e. adjunct, subject, predicator, direct object
        f. subject, predicator, direct object, oblique complement
        g. subject, predicator, predicative complement
        h. subject, predicator, direct object, predicative complement
        i. subject, predicator, predicative complement, adjunct
        j. subject, predicator, direct object, predicative complement, adjunct

2. Give the grammatical function of the italicized phrases in the following examples:
    (i) a. *All of his conversation* was reported to me.
        b. Sandy removed *her ballet shoes.*
        c. The school awarded *a few of the girls in Miss Kim's class* scholarships.
        d. She was *the nicest teacher in the Senior School.*
        e. They elected him *America's 31st President.*
        f. *The next morning* we set out for Seoul.
        g. *Doing syntax* is not easy.
        h. This is the place *to go to.*
        i. He saw the man *with the stick.*
        j. *This week* will be a difficult one for us.
        k. We need to finish the project *this week.*

3. Draw tree structures for the following sentences and then assign an appropriate grammatical function to each phrase.
    (i) a. They parted the best of friends.
        b. In the summer we always go to France.

    c.   Benny worked in a shoe factory when he was a student.

    d.   Last year I saw this film several times.

    e.   He baked Tom the bread last night.

    f.   That they have completed the course is amazing.

    g.   Everyone hoped that she would sing.

    h.   The gang robbed her of her necklace.

    i.   They helped us edit the script.

    j.   The teacher made students happy.

    k.   We reminded him of the agreement.

4.   Consider the following examples:

   (i) a.   There is/*are only one chemical substance involved in nerve transmission.

       b.   There *is/are more chemical substances involved in nerve transmission.

With respect to the grammatical function of *there*, what can we infer from these data? Try out more subjecthood tests such as the tag-question test to determine the grammatical function of *there* in these examples. In addition, try to decide what is the subject in the following so-called 'locative inversion' examples and provide at least three different locative inversion examples that you can find from naturally-occurring material.

   (ii) a.   In the garden stands/*stand a statue.

       b.   Among the guests was/*were sitting my friend Louise.

5.   Determine the grammatical function of the italicized phrase, providing at least one syntactic test we have discussed in the chapter.[11]

   (i) a.   This proved *a decisive factor*.

       b.   This proved *my hypothesis*.

       c.   The students all enjoyed *that summer*.

       d.   The students all worked *that summer*.

       e.   The scientist made her *a robot*.

       f.   The students called me *a teacher*.

6.   Assign a semantic role to each argument in the following sentences.

   (i) a.   A big green insect flew into the soup.

       b.   John's mother sent a letter to Mary.

       c.   John smelled the freshly baked bread.

       d.   We placed the cheese in the refrigerator.

       e.   Frank threw himself into the sofa.

       f.   The crocodile devoured the doughnut.

       g.   John came from Seoul.

       h.   John is afraid of Bill.

       i.   The ice melted.

---

[11] This exercise is adopted from Huddleston and Pullum (2002).

j.   The vacuum cleaner terrifies the child.

7.   Determine the grammatical functions for the underlined expressions in the following text.

(i)   Scientists found that the birds sang well in the evenings, but performed badly
in the mornings. After being awake several hours, however, the young males
regained their mastery of the material and then improved on the previous day's
accomplishments. To see whether this dip in learning was caused by the same
kind of pre-coffee fog that many people feel in the morning, the researchers
prevented the birds from practicing first thing in the morning. They also tried
keeping the birds from singing during the day, and they used a chemical called
melatonin to make the birds nap at odd times. The researchers concluded that
their study supports the idea that sleep helps birds learn. Studies of other animals
have also suggested that sleep improves learning.[12]

---

[12]From *Science News Online*, Feb 2, 2007

4

Head, Complements, and Modifiers

4.1 Projections from Lexical Heads to Phrases

4.1.1 Internal vs. External Syntax

As we have seen in the previous chapters, both syntactic categories (NP, AP, VP, PP, etc.) and grammatical functions (subject, complement, and modifier) play important roles in the analysis of English sentences. We have also observed that the grammatical function and form of each constituent depend on where it occurs or what it combines with.

The combinatory properties of words and phrases involve two aspects of syntax: **internal** and **external** syntax.[1] **Internal syntax** deals with how a given phrase itself is constructed in a well-formed manner whereas **external syntax** is concerned with how a phrase can be used in a larger construction. Observe the following examples:

(1)   a. *John [put his gold].

        b. *John [put under the bathtub].

        c. *John [put his gold safc].

        d. *John [put his gold to be under the bathtub].

        e. John [put his gold under the bathtub].

Why is only (1e) acceptable? Simply, because only it satisfies the condition that the verb *put* selects an NP and a PP as its complements, and it combines with them in the VP. In the other examples, this condition is not fulfilled. This combinatory requirement starts from the internal (or lexical) properties of the verb *put*, and is not related to any external properties of the VP.

In contrast, the external syntax is concerned with the external environment in which a phrase occurs. Some of the unacceptable examples in (1) can be legitimate expressions if they occur in the proper (syntactic) context.

(2)   a.   This is the box in which John [put his gold]. (cf. (1a))

        b.   This is the gold that John [put under the bathtub]. (cf. (1b))

---

[1]The terms 'internal' and 'external' syntax are from Baker, C.L. (1995).

Meanwhile, the well-formed VP in (1e) can be unacceptable, depending on external contexts. For example, consider the frame induced by the governing verb *kept* in (3):

(3)   a.   *The king kept [put his gold under the bathtub].

         b.   The king kept [putting his gold under the bathtub].

The VP *put his gold under the bathtub* is a well-formed phrase, but cannot occur in (3a) since this is not the environment where such a finite VP occurs. That is, the verb *kept* requires the presence of a gerundive VP like *putting his gold under the bathtub*, and therefore imposes an external constraint on VPs.

4.1.2   Notion of Head, Complements, and Modifiers

One important property we observe in English phrase-internal syntax is that in building up any phrase, there is one obligatory element in each phrase. That is, each phrase has one essential element as represented in the diagrams in (4):

(4)   a.   b.   c.

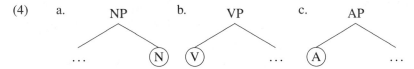

The circled element here is the essential, obligatory element within the given phrase. We call this essential element the **head** of the phrase.[2] The head of each phrase thus determines its 'projection' into a larger phrasal constituent. The head of an NP is thus N, the head of a VP is V, and the head of an AP is A.

The notion of **headedness** plays an important role in the grammar. For example, the verb *put*, functioning as the head of a VP, dictates what it must combine with – two complements, NP and PP. Consider other examples:

(5)   a.   The defendant denied the accusation.

         b.   *The defendant denied.

(6)   a.   The teacher handed the student a book.

         b.   *The teacher handed the student.

The verb *denied* here requires an NP object whereas *handed* requires two NP complements, in this use. The properties of the head verb itself determine what kind of elements it will combine with. As noted in the previous chapter, the elements which a head verb should combine with are called **complements**. The complements include direct object, indirect object, predicative complement, and oblique complement since these are all potentially required by some verb or other.

The properties of the head become properties of the whole phrase. Why are the examples in (7b) and (8b) ungrammatical?

(7)   a.   They [want to leave the meeting].

---

[2]See section 1.3 in Chapter 1 also.

     b. *They [eager to leave the meeting].

(8)   a.   The senators [know that the president is telling a lie].

     b.   *The senators [certain that the president is telling a lie].

The examples in (7b) and (8b) are unacceptable because of the absence of the required head. The unacceptable examples lack a finite (tensed) VP as the bracketed part, but we know that English sentences require a finite VP as their immediate constituent, as informally represented as in (9):

(9)   English Declarative Sentence Rule:
         Each declarative sentence must contain a finite VP as its head.

Each finite VP is headed by a finite verb. If we amend the ungrammatical examples above to include a verb but not a finite one, they are still ungrammatical:

(10)   a. *They [(to) be eager to leave the meeting].

     b. *The senators [(to) be certain that the president is telling a lie].

The VP is considered to be the (immediate) head of the sentence, with the verb itself as the head of the VP. In this way, we can talk about a finite or non-finite sentence, one which is ultimately headed by a finite or nonfinite verb, respectively.[3]

   In addition to the complements of a head, a phrase may also contain **modifiers** (or also called adjuncts):

(11)   a. Tom [$_{VP}$ [$_{VP}$ offered advice to his students] *in his office*].

     b. Tom [$_{VP}$ [$_{VP}$ offered advice to his students] *with love*].

The PPs *in his office* or *with love* here provide further information about the action described by the verb, but are not required as such by the verb. These phrases are optional and function as modifiers, and they function to augment the minimal phrase projected from the head verb *offered*. The VP which includes this kind of modifier forms a *maximal phrase*. We might say that the inner VP here forms a 'minimal' VP which includes all the 'minimally' required complements, and the outer VP is the 'maximal' VP which includes optional modifiers.

   What we have seen can be summarized as follows:

(12)   a. **Head**: A lexical or phrasal element that is essential in forming a phrase.

     b. **Complement**: A phrasal element that a head must combine with or a head selects. This includes direct object, indirect object, predicative complement, and oblique complement.

     c. **Modifier**: A phrasal element not selected by the verb functions as a modifier to the head phrase.

     d. **Minimal Phrase**: A minimal phrase is the phrase including a head and all of its complements.

---

[3] See Chapter 5.2 for the detailed discussion of English verb form (VFORM) values including finite and nonfinite.

e. **Maximal Phrase**: A maximal phrase is the phrase that includes complements as well as modifiers.

4.2 Differences between Complements and Modifiers

Given these notions of complements and modifiers, the question that follows is then how we can distinguish between complements and modifiers. There are several tests to determine whether a phrase is a complement or a modifier.[4]

Obligatoriness: As hinted at already, complements are strictly-required phrases whereas modifiers are not. The examples in (13)–(15) show that the verb *placed* requires an NP and a PP as its complements, *kept* an NP and a PP or an AP, and *stayed* a PP.

(13) a. John placed Kim behind the garage.
       b. John kept him behind the garage.
       c. *John stayed Kim behind the garage.

(14) a. *John placed him busy.
       b. John kept him busy.
       c. *John stayed him busy.

(15) a. *John placed behind the counter.
       b. *John kept behind the counter.
       c. John stayed behind the counter.

In contrast, modifiers are optional. Their presence is not required by the grammar:

(16) a. John deposited some money in the bank.
       b. John deposited some money in the bank on Friday.

In (16b), the PP *on Friday* is optional here, serving as a modifier.

Iterability: The possibility of iterating identical types of phrase can also distinguish between complements and modifiers. In general two or more instances of the same modifier type can occur with the same head, but this is impossible for complements.

(17) a. *The UN blamed global warming [on humans] [on natural causes].
       b. Kim and Sandy met [in Seoul] [in the lobby of the Lotte Hotel] in March.

In (17a) *on humans* is a complement and thus the same type of PP *on natural causes* cannot co-occur. Yet *in Seoul* is a modifier and we can repeatedly have the same type of PP.

---

[4]Most of the criteria we discuss here are adopted from Pollard and Sag (1987).

Do-so Test: Another reliable test often used to distinguish complements from modifiers is the *do so* or *do the same thing* test. As shown in (18), we can use *do the same thing* to avoid repetition of an identical VP expression:

(18) a. John deposited some money in the checking account and Mary did the same thing (too).

     b. John deposited some money in the checking account on Friday and Mary did the same thing (too).

What we can observe in (18b) is that the VP *did the same thing* can replace either the minimal phrase *deposited some money in the checking account* or the maximal phrase including the modifier *on Friday*. Notice that this VP can replace only the minimal phrase, leaving out the modifier.

(19) John deposited some money in the checking account on Friday and Mary did the same thing on Monday.

From these observations, we can draw the conclusion that if something can be replaced by *do the same thing*, then it is either a minimal or a maximal phrase. This in turn means that this 'replacement' VP cannot be understood to leave out any complement(s). This can be verified with more data:

(20) a. *John [deposited some money in the checking account] and Mary did the same thing in the savings account.

     b. *John [gave a present to the student] and Mary did the same thing to the teacher.

Here the PPs *in the checking account* and *to the student* are both complements, and thus they should be included in the *do the same thing* phrase. This gives us the following informal generalization:

(21) *Do-so* Replacement Condition:
The phrase *do so* or *do the same thing* can replace a verb phrase which includes at least all the complements of the verb.

This condition explains why we cannot have another locative complement phrase *in the savings account* or *to the teacher* in (20). The unacceptability of the examples in (22) also supports this generalization about English grammar.

(22) a. *John locked Fido in the garage and Mary did so in the room.

     b. *John ate a carrot and Mary did so a radish.

Constancy of semantic contribution: An adjunct can cooccur with a relatively broad range of heads whereas a complement is typically limited in its distribution. Note the following contrast:

(23) a. Kim camps/jogs/mediates on the hill.

    b.   Kim jogs on the hill/under the hill/over the hill.

(24)   a.   Kim depends/relies on Sandy.

    b.   Kim depends on Sandy/*at Sandy/*for Sandy.

The semantic contribution of the adjunct *on the hill* in (23a) is independent of the head whereas that of the complement *on Sandy* is idiosyncratically dependent upon the head.

Structural Difference: We could distinguish complements and modifiers by tree structures, too: complements combine with a lexical head (not a phrase) to form a minimal phrase whereas modifiers combine with a phrase to form a maximal phrase. This means that we have structures of the following forms:

(25)

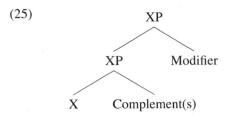

As represented in the tree structures, complements are sisters of the lexical head X, whereas modifiers are sisters of a phrasal head. This structural difference between complements and modifiers provides a clean explanation for the contrast in *do-so* test. Given that the verb *ate* takes only an NP complement whereas *put* takes an NP and a PP complement, we will have the difference in the two structures shown in (26):

(26)   a.

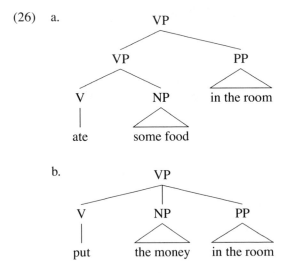

    b.

In this way, we represent the difference between complements and modifiers.

Ordering Difference: Another difference that follows from the structural distinction between complements and modifiers is an ordering difference. As a complement needs to combine with a lexical head first, modifiers follow complements:

(27)　a.　John met [a student] [in the park].

　　　b.　*John met [in the park] [a student].

A similar contrast can be observed in the following contrast:

(28)　a.　the student [of linguistics] [with long hair]

　　　b.　*the student [with long hair] [of linguistics]

The PP *with long hair* is a modifier whereas the *of linguistics* is the complement of *student*. This is why *with long hair* cannot occur between the head *student* and its complement *of linguistics*.[5]

　　As such, observed ordering restrictions can provide more evidence for the distinction between complements and modifiers.

4.3　PS Rules, X′-Rules, and Features

We have seen in Chapter 2 that PS rules can describe how English sentences are formed. However, two main issues arise with the content of PS rules.[6] The first is related to the **headedness** of each phrase, often called the 'endocentricity' property of each phrase.

　　Let us consider the PS rules that we saw in the previous chapters. We have seen that PS rules such as those in (29) can characterize well-formed phrases in English, together with an appropriate lexicon:

(29)　a.　S → NP VP

　　　b.　NP → Det AdjP* N

　　　c.　VP → V (NP) (VP)

　　　d.　VP → V NP AP

　　　e.　VP → V NP NP

　　　f.　VP　›　V S

　　　g.　AP → A VP

　　　h.　PP → P NP

　　　i.　VP → Adv VP

One common property of all these rules is, as we have discussed, that every phrase has its own head. In this sense, each phrase is the projection of a head, and thereby has the endocentricity. However, we can ask the theoretical question of whether or not we can have rules like the following, in which the phrase has no head at all:

(30)　a.　VP → P NP

---

[5] See (49) for the structural differences between *with long hair* and *of linguistics*.

[6] The discussion of this section is based on Sag et al. (2003).

b. NP → PP S

Nothing in the grammar makes such PS rules unusual, or different in any way from the set in (29). Yet, if we allow such 'non-endocentric' PS rules in which a phrase does not have a lexical head, the grammar would then be too powerful to generate only the grammatical sentences of the language.

Another limit that we can find from the simple PS rules concerns an issue of **redundancy**. Observe the following:

(31) a. *The problem disappeared the accusation.

  b. The problem disappeared.

(32) a. *The defendant denied.

  b. The defendant denied the accusation.

(33) a. *The boy gave the book.

  b. The boy gave the baby the book.

What these examples show is that each verb has its own requirement for its complement(s). For example, *deny* requires an NP, whereas *disappear* does not, and *gave* requires two NPs as its complements. The different patterns of complementation are said to define different subcategories of the type verb. The specific pattern of complements is known as the 'subcategorization' requirement of each verb, which can be represented as following (IV: intransitive, TV: transitive, DTV: ditransitive):

(34) a. disappear: IV, __

  b. deny: TV, __ NP

  c. give: DTV, __ NP NP

In addition, in order to license the grammatical sentences in (31)–(33), we need to have the following three VP rules:

(35) a. VP → IV

  b. VP → TV NP

  c. VP → DTV NP NP

We can see here that in each VP rule, only the appropriate verb can occur. That is, a DTV cannot form a VP with the rules in (35a) or (35b): It forms a VP only according to the last PS rule. Each VP rule thus also needs to specify the kind of verb that can serve as its head.

Taking these all together, we see that a grammar of the type just suggested must redundantly encode the subcategorization information both in the lexical type of each verb (e.g., DTV) and in the PS rule for that type of verb.

A similar issue of redundancy arises in accounting for subject-verb agreement:

(36) a. The bird devours the worm.

  b. The birds devour the worm.

To capture the fact that the subject NP agrees with the predicate VP, we need to differentiate the S rule into the following two:

(37) a. $S \rightarrow NP_{sing}\ VP_{sing}$ (for (36)a)

     b. $S \rightarrow NP_{pl}\ VP_{pl}$ (for (36)b)

The two PS rules ensures that the singular (*sing*) subject combines with a singular VP whereas the plural (*pl*) subject NP with a plural VP.

Descriptively, there is no problem with a grammar with many specific parts. From a theoretical perspective, though, we have a concern about the the endocentricity and redundancy issues. A more particular related question is that of how many PS rules English has. For example, how many PS rules do we need to characterize English VPs?—Presumably there are as many rules as there are subcategories of verb.

We need to investigate the abstract content of PS rules, in order to develop a theoretical view of them. For example, it seems to be the case that each PS rule must have a 'head'. This will disallow many possible PS rules which we can write using the rule format, from being actual rules of any language.

In order to understand more about the structures that rules describe, we need two more notions, 'intermediate category/phrase' and '**specifier (SPR)**'. We motivate the idea of the intermediate category, and then specifier is a counterpart of it. Consider the examples in (38):

(38) a. Every photo of Max and sketch by his students appeared in the magazine.

     b. No photo of Max and sketch by his students appeared in the magazine.

What are the structures of these two sentences? Do the phrases *every photo of Max* and *sketch by his students* form NPs? It is not difficult to see *sketch by his students* is not a full NP by itself, for if it was, it should be able to appear as subject by itself.

(39)   *Sketch by his students appeared in the magazine.

In terms of the semantic units, we can assign the following structures to the above sentences, in which *every* and *no* operate over the meaning of the rest of the phrase:

(40) a. [Every [[photo of Max] and [sketch by his students]]] appeared in the magazine.

     b. [No [[photo of Max] and [sketch by his students]]] appeared in the magazine.

The expression *photo of Max* and *sketch by his students* are phrasal elements but not full NPs — so what are they? We call these 'intermediate phrases', notationally represented as N-bar or N′. The phrase N′ is thus intuitively bigger than a noun, but smaller than a full NP, in the sense that it still requires a determiner from the class *the, every, no, some*, and the like.

The complementary notion that we introduce at this point is 'specifier' (SPR), which can include the words just mentioned as well as phrases, as we illustrate in (41):

(41) a. [the enemy's] [$_{N'}$ destruction of the city]

     b. [The enemy] [$_{VP}$ destroyed the city].

The phrase *the enemy's* in (41a) and the subject *the enemy* in (41b) are semantically similar in the sense that they complete the specification of the event denoted by the predicate. These phrases are treated as the specifiers of N′ and of VP, respectively.

As for the possible specifiers of N′, observe the following:

(42)   a.   *a* little dog, *the* little dogs (indefinite or definite article)

   b.   *this* little dog, *those* little dogs (demonstrative)

   c.   *my* little dogs, *their* little dog (possessive adjective)

   d.   *every* little dog, *each* little dog, *some* little dog, *either* dog, *no* dog (quantifying)

   e.   *my friend's* little dog, *the Queen of England's* little dog (possessive phrase)

The italicized expressions here all function as the specifier of N′. However, notice that though most of these specifiers are determiners, some consist of several words as in (42e) (*my friend's, the Queen of England's*) . This motivates us to introduce the new phrase type DP (determiner phrase) that includes the possessive phrase (NP + 's) as well as determiners. This new phrase then will give us the generalization that the specifier of N′ is a DP.[7]

Now let us compare the syntactic structures of (41a) and (41b):

(43)

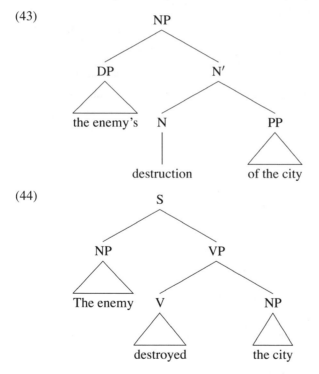

(44)

Even though the NP and S are different phrases, we can notice several similarities. In the NP structure, the head N *destruction* combines with its complement and forms an intermediate

---

[7]Some analyses take the whole expression in (43) to be a DP (e.g., a little dog, my little dogs) in which expressions like *little dog* is not an N′ but an NP.

phrase N′ which in turn combines with the specifier DP *the enemy's*. In the S structure, the head V combines with its complement *the city* and forms a VP. This resulting VP then combines with the subject *the enemy*, which is also a specifier. In a sense, the VP is an intermediate phrase that requires a subject in order to be a full and complete S.

Given these similarities between NP and S structures, we can generalize over them as in (45), where X is a variable over categories such as N, V, P, and other grammatical categories:[8]

(45)

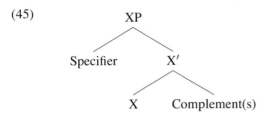

This structure in turn means the grammar now includes the following two rules:[9]

(46)   a.   XP → Specifier, X′ (Head-Specifier Rule)

b.   XP → X, YP* (Head-Complement Rule)

These Head-Specifier and Head-Complement Rules, which form the central part of 'X′-theory', account for the core structure of NP as well as that of S. In fact, these two general rules can also represent most of the PS rules we have seen so far. In addition to these two, we just need one more rule:[10]

(47)   XP → Modifier, X′ (Head-Modifier Rule)

This Head-Modifier Rule allows a modifier to combine with its head as in the PS rule VP → VP Adv/PP, as presented in the following:

(48)

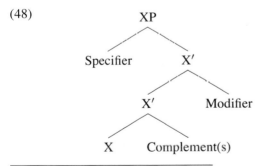

---

[8]We can assume that the head of S is VP and that VP is an intermediate phrase in the sense that it still requires a subject as its specifier.

[9]Unlike the PS rules we have seen so far, the rules here are further abstracted, indicated by the comma notation between daughters on the right-hand side. We assume that the relative linear order of a head and complements etc. is determined by a combination of general and language-specific ordering principles, while the hierarchical X′-structures themselves are universal.

[10]The comma indicates that the modifier can appear either before the head or after the head as in *always read books* or *read books always*.

One thing to notice in the Head-Complement Rule is that the head must be a lexical element. This in turn means that we cannot apply the Head-Modifier Rule first and then the Head-Complement Rule. This explains the following contrast:

(49) a. the king [of Rock and Roll] [with a hat]

b. *the king [with a hat] [of Rock and Roll]

The badness of (49b) is due to the fact that the modifier *with a hat* is combined with the head *king* first.

(50) a.

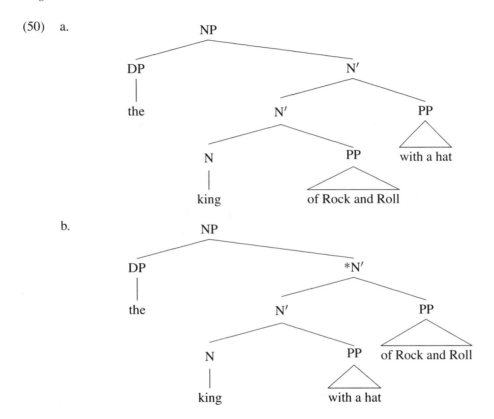

b.

We can observe in (50b) that the combination of *king* with *with a hat* forms an N′, but the combination of the complement *of Rock and Roll* with this N′ will not satisfy the Head-Complement Rule.

The existence and role of the intermediate phrase N′, which is a larger than a lexical category but still not a fully-fledged phrase, can be further supported from the pronoun substitution examples in (51):

(51) a. The present king of country music is more popular than the last *one*.

b. *The king of Rock and Roll is more popular than the *one* of country music.

Why do we have the contrast here? One simple answer is that the pronoun *one* here replaces an N′ but not an N or an NP. This will also account for the following contrast, too:

(52) A· Which student were you talking about?

 B: The one with long hair.

 B: *The one of linguistics with long hair.

The phrase *of linguistics* is the complement of *student*. This means the N-bar pronoun *one* should include this. However, the modifier *with long hair* cannot be within the N'.

There are several more welcome consequences that the three X' rules bring to us. The grammar rules can account for the same structures as all the PS rules we have seen so far: with those rules we can identify phrases whose daughters are a head and its complement(s), or a head and its specifier, or a head and its modifier. The three X' rules thereby greatly minimize the number of PS rules that need to characterize well-formed English sentences.

In addition, these X' rules directly solve the endocentricity issue, for they refer to 'Head'. Assume that X is N, then we will have N, N', and NP structures. We can formalize this more precisely by introducing the feature POS (part of speech), which has values such as *noun, verb, adjective*. The structure (53) shows how the values of the features in different parts of a structure are related:

(53)

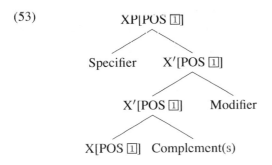

The notation ① shows that whatever value the feature has in one place in the structure, it has the same value somewhere else. This is a representational tag, in which the number ① has no significance: it could as easily be ⑦ or ④³⁷. We provide more details of the formal feature system in the following section.

So (53) indicates that the phrase's POS value is identical to its head daughter, capturing the headedness of each phrase: the grammar just does not allow any phrase without a head. The redundancy issue mentioned above for agreement is now a matter of introducing another feature, NUMBER. That is, with the new feature NUMBER, with values *singular* and *plural*, we can add a detail to the Head-Specifier Rule as following:

(54)   XP → Specifier[NUMBER ①], X'[NUMBER ①]

The rule states that the subject's NUMBER value is identical with that of the predicate VP's NUMBER value. The two rules in (37) are both represented in (54).

4.4 Lexicon and Feature Structures

In the previous section, we have seen that the properties of a lexical head determine the components of the minimal phrase, in terms of complements, and that other properties of the head are directly properties of the phrase. This information is encoded in a lexical entry, for each word in the lexicon.

Every lexical entry at least includes phonological (but in practice, orthographic), morphological, syntactic, and semantic information. For example, the word *puts* will have at least the following information:

(55)   Minimal Lexical Information for *puts*:

    a. phonological information: <puts>

    b. syntactic information: verb, finite, 3rd singular

    c. argument information: $<agent_i, theme_j, location_k>$

    d. semantic information: $put'(i,j,k)$

The phonological information is the information about how the word is pronounced; the syntactic information indicates that this particular word is a verb and is in the 3rd singular present (finite) form. The argument structure represents the number of arguments which the verb selects, to indicate the participants that are minimally involved in the event expressed by the verb. This argument information is linked to its more precise meaning as indicated by the indexes *i*, *j* and *k*. These indexes refer to the participants denoted by the arguments. Finally, the semantic structure represents that the verb's meaning relates three participants – someone *i* who is doing the action of putting, something *j* being put in a place, and someplace *k* it is put in. These lexical entries can be represented in a more systematic and precise way with the system of feature structures, which we now introduce.

4.4.1 Feature Structures and Basic Operations

Most modern grammars rely on a representation of lexical information in terms of features and their values.[11] We present here a formal and explicit way of representing it with **feature structures**. Each feature structure is an attribute-value matrix (AVM):

(56) $\begin{bmatrix} \text{Attribute1} & value1 \\ \text{Attribute2} & value2 \\ \text{Attribute3} & value3 \\ \dots & \dots \end{bmatrix}$

The value of each attribute can be an atomic element, a list, a set, or a feature structure:

---

[11] In particular, grammars such as Head-driven Phrase Structure Grammar (HPSG) and Lexical Functional Grammar (LFG) are couched upon mathematically well-defined feature structure systems. The theory developed in this textbook heavily relies upon the feature structure system of HPSG. See Sag et al. (2003).

(57)
$$\begin{bmatrix} \text{Attribute1} & atomic \\ \text{Attribute2} & \langle \quad \rangle \\ \text{Attribute3} & \{ \quad \} \\ \text{Attribute4} & [\dots] \end{bmatrix}$$

One important property of every feature structure is that it is *typed*.[12] That is, each feature structure is relevant only for a given type. A simple illustration can show why feature structure needs to be typed. The upper left declaration in italics is the *type* of the feature structure:

(58) a.
$$\begin{bmatrix} university \\ \text{NAME} & kyunghee\ univ. \\ \text{LOCATION} & seoul \end{bmatrix}$$

  b. *
$$\begin{bmatrix} university \\ \text{NAME} & kyunghee\ univ. \\ \text{MAYOR} & kim \end{bmatrix}$$

The type *university* may have many properties, including its name and location, but having a MAYOR (though it can have president) is inappropriate. In the linguistic realm, we might declare that TENSE is appropriate only for *verb*, for example.

Now consider the following example of a typed feature structure, information about one author of this book:

(59)
$$\begin{bmatrix} author \\ \text{NAME} & kim \\ \text{SONS} & \langle Edward,\ Richard \rangle \\ \text{HOBBIES} & \{ swimming,\ jogging,\ reading, \dots \} \\ \text{ADVANCED-DEGREE} & \begin{bmatrix} \text{FIELD} & linguistics \\ \text{AREA} & syntax\text{-}semantics \\ \text{YEAR} & 1996 \end{bmatrix} \end{bmatrix}$$

This illustrates the different types of values that attributes (feature names) may have. Here, the value of the attribute NAME is atomic, whereas the value of SONS is a list which represents something relative about the two values, in this case that one is older than the other. So, for example 'youngest son' would be the right-most element in the list value of SONS. Meanwhile, the value of HOBBIES is a set, showing that there is no significance in the relative ordering. Finally, the value of the feature ADVANCED-DEGREE is a feature structure which in turn has three attributes.

One useful notion in the feature structure is **structure-sharing**, which we have already seen above in terms of the ☐ notation (see (53)). This is to represent cases where two features (or

---

[12]Even though every feature structure is *typed* in the present grammar, we will not specify the type of each feature structure unless it is necessary for the discussion.

attributes) have an identical value:

(60)

$$\begin{bmatrix} individual \\ \text{NAME} \quad kim \\ \text{TEL} \quad \boxed{1} \\ \text{SONS} \quad \left\langle \begin{bmatrix} individual \\ \text{NAME} \quad richard \\ \text{TEL} \quad \boxed{1} \end{bmatrix}, \begin{bmatrix} individual \\ \text{NAME} \quad edward \\ \text{TEL} \quad \boxed{1} \end{bmatrix} \right\rangle \end{bmatrix}$$

For the type *individual*, attributes such as NAME and TEL and SONS are appropriate. (60) represents a situation in which the particular individual *kim* has two sons, and their TEL attribute has a value which is the same as the value of his TEL attribute, whatever the value actually is.

In addition to this, the notion of **subsumption** is also important in the theoretical use of feature structures; the symbol $\sqsupseteq$ represents subsumption. The subsumption relation concerns the relationship between a feature structure with general information and one with more specific information. In such a case, the general one subsumes the specific one. Put differently, a feature structure A subsumes another feature structure B if A is not more informative than B.

(61)

$$\text{A:} \begin{bmatrix} individual \\ \text{NAME} \quad kim \end{bmatrix} \sqsupseteq \text{B:} \begin{bmatrix} individual \\ \text{NAME} \quad kim \\ \text{TEL} \quad 961\text{-}0892 \end{bmatrix}$$

In (62), A represents more general information than B. This kind of subsumption relation is used to represent 'partial' information, for in fact we cannot represent the total information describing all possible worlds or states of affairs. In describing a given phenomenon, it will be more than enough just to represent the particular or general aspects of the facts concerned. Each small component of feature structure will provide partial information, and as the structure is built up, the different pieces of information are put together.

The most crucial operation in feature structures is **unification**, represented by $\sqcup$. Feature unification means that two compatible feature structures are unified, conveying more coherent and rich information. Consider the feature structures in (62); the first two may unify to give the third:

(62)

$$\begin{bmatrix} individual \\ \text{NAME} \quad kim \end{bmatrix} \sqcup \begin{bmatrix} individual \\ \text{TEL} \quad 961\text{-}0892 \end{bmatrix} \rightarrow$$

$$\begin{bmatrix} individual \\ \text{NAME} \quad kim \\ \text{TEL} \quad 961\text{-}0892 \end{bmatrix}$$

The two feature structures are unified, resulting in a feature structure with both NAME and TEL information. However, if two feature structures have incompatible feature values, they cannot be unified:

(63) $\begin{bmatrix} individual \\ \text{NAME} \quad edward \end{bmatrix} \sqcup \begin{bmatrix} individual \\ \text{NAME} \quad richard \end{bmatrix}$ /̣

$* \begin{bmatrix} individual \\ \text{NAME} \quad edward \\ \text{NAME} \quad richard \end{bmatrix}$

Since the two smaller feature structures here have different NAME values, they cannot be unified. Unification will make sure that information is consistent as it is built up in the analysis of a phrase or sentence.

4.4.2 Feature Structures for Linguistic Entities

Any individual or entity including a linguistic expression can be represented by a feature structure. For example, the word *puts*, whose general type is *verb*, can have a feature structure like the following:[13]

(64) $\begin{bmatrix} verb \\ \text{PHON} \quad \langle puts \rangle \\ \text{SYN} \quad \begin{bmatrix} \text{POS} \quad verb \\ \text{VFORM} \quad fin \end{bmatrix} \\ \text{ARG-ST} \quad \langle [agt]_i, [th]_j, [loc]_k \rangle \\ \text{SEM} \quad \begin{bmatrix} \text{PRED} \quad put\text{-}relation \\ \text{AGENT} \quad i \\ \text{THEME} \quad j \\ \text{LOCATION} \quad k \end{bmatrix} \end{bmatrix}$

This feature structure has roughly the same information as the informal representation in (55). The verb *puts*, like any verb, has its own phonological (PHON) value, syntactic (SYN), argument structure (ARG-ST), and semantic (SEM) information. The SYN attribute indicates that the POS (part of speech) value is *verb*, that it has a finite verbal inflectional form value (VFORM). The ARG-ST attribute indicates that the verb selects three arguments (with thematic roles agent, theme, location), which will be realized as the subject and two complements in the full analysis. The SEM feature represents the information this verb denotes the predicate relation *put-relation*, whose three participants are linked to the elements in the ARG-ST via the indexing values *i, j,* and *k*.

One thing to note here is that since there are some cases where we have difficulties in assigning a specific named semantic role to a selected argument discussed in Chapter 3, we typically just indicate the number of arguments each predicate is selecting in ARG-ST: we underspecify

---

[13]Later on, we will not represent the PHON and SEM values unless relevant to the discussion at hand.

the information unless it is necessary to show more details. So, for example, verbs like *smile,*
devour and *give* will have the following ARG-ST representations, respectively:

(65) a. $\left[\text{ARG-ST} \langle [\quad] \rangle \right]$

b. $\left[\text{ARG-ST} \langle [\quad], [\quad] \rangle \right]$

c. $\left[\text{ARG-ST} \langle [\quad], [\quad], [\quad] \rangle \right]$

One-place predicates like *smile* subcategorizes for just one argument, two-place predicates like
devour take two arguments, and three-place predicates take three arguments. Eventually, the
arguments selected by each predicate are linked to grammatical functions, to the core semantic
properties, and to other parts of the representation of the grammatical properties.

The arguments in the ARG-ST follow this ordering:[14]

(66) Subject > Direct Object > Indirect Object > Oblique

4.4.3 Argument Realization

Each element on the ARG-ST list is realized as SPR (specifier) or COMPS (complements),
through one of the rules in (46).[15] In general, the basic pattern is that the first element on the list
is realized as subject and the rest as complements:

(67) Argument Realization Constraint (ARC, first approximation):
      The first element on the ARG-ST list is realized as SPR, the rest as COMPS in
      syntax.

This realization is obligatory in English; for example, the three arguments of *put* are realized as
subject and complements, with the putter (agent) as subject:[16]

(68) a. John put the book in the box.

b. *John put in the box.

c. *In the box put John the book.

d. #The book put John in the box.

We see that the arguments selected by a lexical head should be all realized as SPR and COMPS,
which are combined in the notion of valence (VAL) features.[17] More formally, we can represent
this constraint as applied to *put* as the following feature structure:

---

[14]This ordering, tracing back to the accessibility hierarchy of Keenan and Comrie (1977), reflects a cross-linguistic
property regarding what functions are most easily relativized. The same ordering relations also play an important role
in explaining binding facts (see Pollard and Sag 1994 and Sag et al. (2003).

[15]Once again, remember that the term SPR includes subject as well as the noun's specifier.

[16]The notation # indicates that the structure is technically well-formed from a syntactic perspective, but semantically
anomalous.

[17]The term 'valence' refers to the number of arguments that a lexical item can combine with, to make a syntactically
well-formed sentence, often along with a description of the categories of those constituents. It is inspired by the notion
of valence as used in atomic theory in chemistry.

(69)
$$\begin{bmatrix} \text{VAL} & \begin{bmatrix} \text{SPR} & \langle \boxed{1}\text{NP} \rangle \\ \text{COMPS} & \langle \boxed{2}\text{NP}, \boxed{3}\text{PP} \rangle \end{bmatrix} \\ \text{ARG-ST} & \langle \boxed{1}, \boxed{2}, \boxed{3} \rangle \end{bmatrix}$$

The boxed tags show the different identities in the overall structure. For example, the first element of ARG-ST and of SPR have the boxed tag $\boxed{1}$, ensuring that the two are identical. The general ARC constraint blocks examples like (68c) in which the location argument is realized as the subject, as shown in (70):

(70)
$$*\begin{bmatrix} \text{VAL} & \begin{bmatrix} \text{SPR} \ \langle \boxed{3}\text{PP} \rangle \\ \text{COMPS} \ \langle \boxed{1}\text{NP}, \boxed{2}\text{NP} \rangle \end{bmatrix} \\ \text{ARG-ST} & \langle \boxed{1}, \boxed{2}, \boxed{3} \rangle \end{bmatrix}$$

This violates the ARC, which requires the first element of ARG-ST be realized as the SPR (the subject of a verb or the specifier of a noun).

Notice that the arguments can be realized into different categories, depending on the properties of the given verb:

(71)   a.   The election results surprised everybody.

   b.   That he won the election surprised everybody.

The data indicate that verbs like *surprise* will take two arguments, but the first argument can be realized either as an NP subject as in (71a) or a CP subject as in (71b). This difference in the argument realization can be represented as the following, respectively:

(72)   a.
$$\begin{bmatrix} \text{VAL} & \begin{bmatrix} \text{SPR} \ \langle \boxed{1}\text{NP} \rangle \\ \text{COMPS} \ \langle \boxed{2}\text{NP} \rangle \end{bmatrix} \\ \text{ARG-ST} & \langle \boxed{1}, \boxed{2} \rangle \end{bmatrix}$$

   b.
$$\begin{bmatrix} \text{VAL} & \begin{bmatrix} \text{SPR} \ \langle \boxed{1}\text{CP} \rangle \\ \text{COMPS} \ \langle \boxed{2}\text{NP} \rangle \end{bmatrix} \\ \text{ARG-ST} & \langle \boxed{1}, \boxed{2} \rangle \end{bmatrix}$$

Though there is no difference in terms of the number of arguments that *surprise* select, the arguments can be realized in a different phrase. As the book goes on, we will see how the argument realization is further constrained by the lexical properties of the verb in question or by other grammatical components.

4.4.4   Verb Types and Argument Structure

As mentioned earlier, lexical elements in the classes V, A, N, and P, select one or more complement(s) to form a minimal phrase. With the construct of ARG-ST, we know that every lexical element has ARG-ST information which will be realized in surface form through the SPR and COMPS values. Verb types can be differentiated by looking only at the COMPS value since every verb will have one SPR (subject) element. This is exactly the way that verbs are differentiated using the traditional notion of subcategorization.

Intransitive: This is a type of verb that does not have any COMPS:

(73) a. John disappeared.

      b. *John disappeared Bill.

(74) a. John sneezed.

      b. *John sneezed the money.

These verbs have no COMPS element—the list is necessarily empty. Such a verb will have just one argument that is realized as subject:[18]

(75)
$$
\begin{bmatrix}
\langle \text{disappear} \rangle \\
\text{VAL} \quad \begin{bmatrix} \text{SPR} & \langle \boxed{1}\text{NP} \rangle \\ \text{COMPS} & \langle \ \rangle \end{bmatrix} \\
\text{ARG-ST} \quad \langle \boxed{1} \rangle
\end{bmatrix}
$$

Linking verbs: Verbs such as *look*, *seem*, *remain*, and *feel* require different complements that are typically of category AP:

(76) a. The president looked [weary].

      b. The teacher became [tired of the students].

      c. The lasagna tasted [scrumptious].

      d. John remained [somewhat calm].

      e. The jury seemed [ready to leave].

These verbs also can select other phrases (here, NP):

(77) a. John became a success.

      b. John seemed a fool.

      c. John remained a student.

Though each verb may select different types of phrases, they all at least select a predicative complement, where a property is ascribed to the subject. (Compare *John remained a student* and *John revived a student*.) This subcategorization requirement can be represented as follows:[19]

(78)
$$
\begin{bmatrix}
\langle \text{become} \rangle \\
\text{VAL} \quad \begin{bmatrix} \text{SPR} & \langle \boxed{1}\text{NP} \rangle \\ \text{COMPS} & \langle \boxed{2}\text{AP} \mid \text{NP[PRD +]} \rangle \end{bmatrix} \\
\text{ARG-ST} \quad \langle \boxed{1}, \boxed{2} \rangle
\end{bmatrix}
$$

---

[18]For convenience we omit the PHON value of each lexical entry; instead we just list its spelling value on the left top corner.

[19]While the term PRED is given as a function name to a predicate, the attribute PRD (predicative) is used when a phrase functions as a predicate.

This kind of verb selects two arguments: one is canonically an NP to be realized as the subject and the other is any phrase (XP) that can function as a predicate (PRD +) (see also the examples in (85)). Of course, this presupposes an accurate characterization of which phrases can be [PRD +], which we simply assume here.

Transitive verbs: Unlike linking verbs, pure transitive verbs select a referential, non-predicative NP as their complement, functioning as direct object:

(79) a. John saw Fred.

b. Alice typed the letter.

c. Clinton supported the health care bill.

d. Raccoons destroyed the garden.

Such verbs will have the following lexical information:

$$(80) \quad \begin{bmatrix} \langle \text{destroy} \rangle \\ \text{VAL} \quad \begin{bmatrix} \text{SPR} & \langle \boxed{1}\text{NP} \rangle \\ \text{COMPS} & \langle \boxed{2}\text{NP} \rangle \end{bmatrix} \\ \text{ARG-ST} \quad \langle \boxed{1}, \boxed{2} \rangle \end{bmatrix}$$

Ditransitive: Similar to such monotransitive verbs like *destroy*, English also has what are called 'ditransitive' verbs. These verbs take an IO followed by a DO:

(81) a. The school board leader asked the students a question.

b. The parents bought the children non-fiction novels.

c. John taught new students English Syntax.

As we have seen in Chapter 3.2, such verbs have three arguments: the subject and two complement NPs which function as indirect and direct object, respectively:

$$(82) \quad \begin{bmatrix} \langle \text{teach} \rangle \\ \text{VAL} \quad \begin{bmatrix} \text{SPR} & \langle \boxed{1}\text{NP} \rangle \\ \text{COMPS} & \langle \boxed{2}\text{NP}, \boxed{3}\text{NP} \rangle \end{bmatrix} \\ \text{ARG-ST} \quad \langle \boxed{1}, \boxed{2}[\textit{goal}], \boxed{3}[\textit{theme}] \rangle \end{bmatrix}$$

The resulting structure with such verbs like *give, bring, tell, show, offer* is typically referred to as the 'double object' construction. As we noted in Chapter 3.2, these verbs typically have related verbs in which the semantic role of the IO is realized instead as an oblique PP complement:

(83) a. The school board leader asked a question of the students.

b. The parents bought non-fiction novels for the children.

c. John taught English Syntax to new students.

In this realization, unlike the uses in (81), the second argument has the theme role while the third one has some other role; we illustrate here with goal:

(84)

$$\begin{bmatrix} \langle \text{teach} \rangle \\ \text{VAL} \begin{bmatrix} \text{SPR} & \langle \boxed{1}\text{NP} \rangle \\ \text{COMPS} & \langle \boxed{2}\text{NP}, \boxed{3}\text{PP} \rangle \end{bmatrix} \\ \text{ARG-ST} \quad \langle \boxed{1}, \boxed{2}[\textit{theme}], \boxed{3}[\textit{goal}] \rangle \end{bmatrix}$$

The structures with such verbs, often called 'prepositional object' constructions, thus share some properties with the double object constructions in (81).[20]

Complex Transitive: There is another type of transitive verb which selects two complements, one functioning as a direct object and the other as a predicative phrase (NP, AP, or VP), describing the object:

(85) a. John regards Bill as a good friend.

b. The sexual revolution makes some people uncomfortable.

c. Ad agencies call young people Generation X-ers.

d. Historians believe FDR to be our most effective president.

In (85a), the predicative PP *as a good friend* follows the object *Bill*; in (85b), the AP *uncomfortable* serves as a predicate phrase of the preceding object *some people*. In (85c), the NP *Generation X-ers* is the predicative phrase. In (85d), the predicative phrase is an infinitive VP. Just like linking verbs, these verbs require a predicative ([PRD +]) XP as complement:

(86)

$$\begin{bmatrix} \langle \text{call} \rangle \\ \text{VAL} \begin{bmatrix} \text{SPR} & \langle \boxed{1}\text{NP} \rangle \\ \text{COMPS} & \langle \boxed{2}\text{NP}, \boxed{3}\text{XP} \rangle \end{bmatrix} \\ \text{ARG-ST} \quad \langle \boxed{1}, \boxed{2}, \boxed{3}[\text{PRD} +] \rangle \end{bmatrix}$$

This means that the verbs in (85) all select an object NP and an XP phrase that function as a predicate.

Even though these five types of verb that we have seen so far represent many English verb types, there are other verbs that do not fit into these classes; for instance, the use of the verb *carry* in (87).

(87) a. *John carried to the door.

b. John carried her on his back.

The examples in (87) illustrate that *carried* requires an NP and a PP, as represented in the feature structure:

---

[20]There are also differences between the two, for example, with respect to information structure (see Goldberg (2006) and the references cited therein). The similarities and differences between the two constructions have raised the question of whether one can be generated from the other (Larson (1988), Baker (1997)) or whether the two should be treated independently (Jackendoff (1990), Goldberg (2006)).

(88)
$$
\begin{bmatrix}
\langle \text{carry} \rangle \\
\text{VAL} \begin{bmatrix} \text{SPR} & \langle \boxed{1}\text{NP} \rangle \\ \text{COMPS} & \langle \boxed{2}\text{NP}, \boxed{3}\text{PP} \rangle \end{bmatrix} \\
\text{ARG-ST} \ \langle \boxed{1}[agt], \boxed{2}[th], \boxed{3}[loc] \rangle
\end{bmatrix}
$$

The PP here cannot be said to be predicate of the object *her*; it denotes the location to which John carries her.

Of course, there are various other verb types that we have not described here, in terms of complementation patterns. As the book goes on, we will see yet more different types of verbs.

4.5   Exercises

1. Do the following as an exercise for understanding the notion of feature structures.

   (i) a. Describe yourself as a feature structure as far as you can. Try to introduce feature attributes which have different value types such as atomic, list, set, or another feature structure (e.g., NAME, SIBLINGS, EMAIL, HOBBIES, etc).

   b. Provide two examples which illustrate the feature structure operations, structure sharing, subsumption, and unification. Use the attributes you used for describing yourself.

2. For each of the verbs below, use it in a grammatical example; write down the example and provide its lexical entry including the COMPS value.

   (i)   appear, consider, award, borrow, owe, explain, introduce, discuss, tell, say

3. Find out how each of these three groups are different in terms of subcategorization patterns (COMPS) value. In doing so, construct grammatical and ungrammatical examples for each verb.

   (i) a. bring, cook, teach, build, make

   b. donate, describe, report, purchase, obtain

   c. bet, cost, fine, spare, forgive

4. Provide tree structures for the following pairs of sentences while checking the grammatical function of each phrase with valid distributional tests. In doing so, state what differences we need to represent for the underlined expressions.

   (i) a. Tom locked Fido *in the garage.*
       b. Tom bathed Fido *in the garage.*

   (ii) a. Tom placed it *under the table.*
        b. Tom played it *under the table.*

   (iii) a. I wonder *if you will come back tomorrow.*
         b. You would have a reply *if you come back tomorrow.*

5. For each example below, draw its structure and then give the lexical entry (SPR and COMPS value) of the main verb.

   (i) a. Tom hid the manuscript in the cupboard.
       b. Fred hired Sharon to change the oil.
       c. They pushed the prisoners into the truck.
       d. Frank hopes to persuade Harry to make the cook wash the dishes.
       e. George mailed the attorney his photograph of the accident.
       f. Tom keeps asking Karen's sister to buy the car.
       g. Jane left the book on the table.
       h. We have not confirmed whether the flight had been booked.
       i. We saw him beaten by the champion.
       j. They confined his remarks to the matter under discussion.

6. The verbs in the following examples are used incorrectly. Correct the errors or replace the verb with another one, and write out each new example. In addition, provide the COMPS value for each verb (in its use in your grammatical examples).

   (i) a. *Oliver ascribed his longevity there.
        b. *Oliver mentioned Charles the problem.
        c. *Oliver fined ten pounds to the prisoner.
        d. *Oliver drove me a lunatic.
        e. *Oliver addressed the king the letter.
        f. *Oliver absented his brother from the meeting.

7. Draw tree structures for the following two sentences. In particular, provide detailed NP structures using the intermediate phrase N′:

   (i) a. The students of English from Seoul faced many issues in the process of interpreting, transcribing, and editing the poems.
        b. The love of my life and father of my children would never do such a thing.
        c. The museum displayed no painting by Miro or drawing by Klee.
        d. By law, every dog and cat in the area has to be spayed or neutered.

8. Read the following texts and provide the ARG-ST, SPR and COMPS values of the underlined expressions.

   (i) Learning to <u>use</u> a language freely and fully is a lengthy and effortful process. Teachers cannot <u>learn</u> the language for their students. They can <u>set</u> their students on the road, <u>helping</u> them to develop confidence in their own learning powers. Then they must <u>wait</u> on the sidelines, <u>ready</u> to encourage and assist.

   (ii) Deep ecologists <u>put</u> a reign on human exploitation of natural "resources" except to <u>satisfy</u> vital needs. Thus, the use of a field by an African tribe to <u>grow</u> grain for survival is an example of a vital need whereas the <u>conversion</u> of a swamp to an exclusive golf course would not. Rest <u>assured</u> that much of the mining, harvesting, and development of our technological age would not <u>meet</u> the requirement of this principle. Rather than being <u>concerned</u> about how to <u>raise</u> automobile production, this ethic would be <u>interested</u> in solving the problem of human mobility in a way that would not *require* the disruption of highways, roads, and parking lots. It <u>rebels</u> against an industrialist world view: "Before it is possessed and used, every plant is a weed and every mineral is just another rock."[21]

---

[21] From http://www.unitedearth.com.au/deepecology.html

5

More on Subjects and Complements

5.1 Grammar Rules and Principles

As we have seen in the previous chapter, the arguments in ARG-ST are realized as the syntactic elements SPR (subject of a verb and determiner of a noun) and COMPS. The X′ rules control their combination with a relevant head:

(1) a. XP → Specifier, Head
  b. XP → Head, Complement(s)
  c. XP → Modifier, Head

The rule (1a) represents the case where a head combines with its specifier (e.g., a VP with its subject and an N′ with its determiner), whereas (1b) says that a head combines with its complement(s) and forms a phrase. (1c) allows a combination of a head with its modifier. As noted earlier, in order to guarantee that the head's POS (part of speech) value is identical with its mother phrase, we need to introduce the category variable X and the feature POS:

(2) a. Head-Specifier Rule:
    $\text{XP}\begin{bmatrix} \text{POS } \boxed{1} \end{bmatrix} \rightarrow \text{Specifier, X}'\begin{bmatrix} \text{POS } \boxed{1} \end{bmatrix}$

  b. Head-Complement Rule:
    $\text{XP}\begin{bmatrix} \text{POS } \boxed{1} \end{bmatrix} \rightarrow \text{X}\begin{bmatrix} \text{POS } \boxed{1} \end{bmatrix}, \text{Complement(s)}$

  c. Head-Modifier Rule:
    $\text{XP}\begin{bmatrix} \text{POS } \boxed{1} \end{bmatrix} \rightarrow \text{Modifier, XP}\begin{bmatrix} \text{POS } \boxed{1} \end{bmatrix}$

The POS feature is thus a head feature which passes up to a 'mother' phrase from its head 'daughter', as shown in (3):

(3)

VP[POS *verb*]

V[POS *verb*]   PP

77

This percolation from a head to its mother is ensured by the following Head Feature Principle:

(4)   The Head Feature Principle (HFP):
        A phrase's head feature (e.g., POS, VFORM, etc.) is identical with that of its head.

The HFP thus ensures that every phrase has its own lexical head with the identical POS value. The HFP will apply to any features that we declare to be 'head features', VFORM being another. The grammar does not allow hypothetical phrases like the following:

(5)   *VP[POS *verb*]
                    _____/_____
            A[POS *adj*]   PP

We have not yet spelled out clearly what ensures a lexical head to combine not just with one of its complements but with all of its COMPS elements. Consider the following examples:

(6)   a. Kim put the book in the box.

        b. *Kim put the book.

        c. *Kim put in the box.

As seen from the contrast here and as noted in the lexical entry in (7), the verb *put* selects two complements and must combine with all of its complements.

(7) $\begin{bmatrix} \text{HEAD} \mid \text{POS } verb \\ \text{VAL} \begin{bmatrix} \text{SPR } \langle \text{NP} \rangle \\ \text{COMPS } \langle \text{NP, PP} \rangle \end{bmatrix} \end{bmatrix}$

We can also see that a finite verb must combine with its subject:

(8)   a. *Is putting the book in the box.

        b. *Talked with Bill about the exam.

Such combinatorial requirements can be formally stated in the revised grammar rules as given in (9):

(9)   a. Head-Specifier Rule:
            $\text{XP}\left[\text{SPR } \langle \quad \rangle\right] \rightarrow \boxed{1}, \textbf{H}[\text{SPR } \langle \boxed{1} \rangle]$

        b. Head-Complement Rule:
            $\text{XP}\left[\text{COMPS } \langle \quad \rangle\right] \rightarrow \textbf{H}[\text{COMPS } \langle \boxed{1},\dots,\boxed{n} \rangle], \boxed{1},\dots,\boxed{n}$

        c. Head-Modifier Rule:
            $\text{XP} \rightarrow [\text{MOD } \langle \boxed{1} \rangle], \boxed{1}\textbf{H}$

The grammar rules here are well-formedness conditions on possible phrases in English, indicating what each head combines with and then what happens as the result of the combination.

For example, in (9a) when a head, requiring an SPR, combines with it, we have a well-formed head-specifier phrase with the SPR value discharged; in (9b), a head combines with all of its COMPS value, it forms a Head-Complement phrase with no further COMPS value; in (9c), when a modifier combines (carrying the MOD feature) with the head it modifies, the resulting phrase forms a well-formed head-modifier phrase.[1]

These three grammar rules, interacting with the general principles such as the HFP, license grammatical sentences in English. Let us consider one example in a little more detail:[2]

(10)

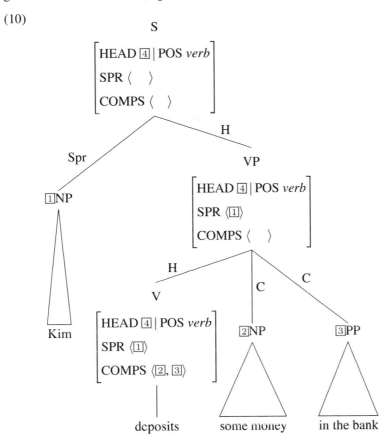

The finite verb *deposits* selects a subject (a specifier) and two complements. The HFP ensures that the head feature POS values of the verb, its mother VP and S are all identical. When the lexical head combines with its two complements, the COMPS value becomes empty, forming a VP in accordance with the Head-Complement Rule. This VP will still need to combine with its SPR in order to form a complete sentence. This kind of 'discharging' mechanism is further

---

[1]In addition to these three grammar rules, English employs the Head-Filler Rule that licenses the combination of a head missing one phrasal element with a filler that matches this missing element, as in *What did John eat __ ?* See Chapter 10 for discussion of this rule.

[2]For convenience reason, we adopt a shorthand system in representing feature structures, suppressing unrelated features. For example, the fully specified feature structure in (10) will include VAL as well as PHON, SYN, SEM, etc.

ensured by the following general principle:

(11)   The Valence Principle (VALP):
       The mother's SPR and COMPS value is identical with its head daughters minus the discharged value(s).

This principle thus ensures that when the VP in (10) combines with the subject SPR, it forms a complete S in accordance with the Head-Specifier Rule. More generally, the VALP ensures that each verb combines in the syntactic structure with exactly all and only the syntactic dependents that its SPR and COMPS values indicate.

5.2   Feature Specifications on the Complement Values

5.2.1   Complements of Verbs

Intuitively, English verbs have 6 grammatical forms. For example, the verb *drive* can take these forms: *drives, drove, drive, driving, driven, to drive*, in addition to the citation form. The present and past tense forms are usually classified together as *fin(ite)*, with all the rest being *nonfin(ite)* in some way. Using this division, we might lay out the forms as in (12):

(12)   Types of English Verb Forms:

Finiteness	Verb forms	Example
fin	*es*	He *drives* a car.
	ed	He *drove* a car.
	pln	They *drive* a car.
nonfin	*bse*	He wants to *drive* a car.
	ing	*Driving* a car, he sang a song.
		He was *driving*.
		He is proud of *driving* a car.
	en	*Driven* by the mentor, he worked.
		The car was *driven* by him.
		He has *driven* the car.
	inf	He has to *drive*.

The *fin* forms have three subtypes *es*, *pst*, and *pln* (plain). Notice that there might be mismatch between the form and function: although the *ed* verb canonically describes a past event as in (13a), while the *es* and *pln* verb represents a present event as in (13b), this is not always true.[3] For example, the *es* in (13c) describes a future event:

(13)   a.   John called me yesterday.

       b.   John smiles a lot because of his two sons.

       c.   John leaves town tomorrow.

---

[3]More specifically, the plain form, though identical to the citation form, is used for present tense when the subject is anything other than 3rd person singular.

English also has a 'historic present', as in *So last night I get home from work and for the first time all summer there is an ice cream truck driving around by my house*. The mapping between a VFORM value and tense (present, past, future) is not one-to-one.

The *nonfin* forms have the basic forms of *bse* (base), *ing* (present participle), and *en* (past participle), and *inf* (infinitive). This classification means that the plain and base forms are identical with the lexical base (or citation) of the lexeme.[4] Even though the two forms are identical in most cases, substitution tests by the past form or by the verb *be* can show us a clear difference:

(14) a. They write/wrote to her.

  b. They are/*be kind to her.

(15) a. They want to write/*wrote to her.

  b. They want to be/*are kind to her.

The verbs *write* and *are* in (14) are plain forms whereas *write* and *be* in (15) are base forms with no tense information.

All these verbal forms are all generated from the citation form (the lexeme) by English inflectional lexical rules. For example, the *es* form will be derived by a rule like this:

(16) Present Inflectional Lexical Rule:

$$\begin{bmatrix} lexeme \\ \text{FORM } \boxed{1} \\ \text{HEAD} \begin{bmatrix} \text{POS} & verb \end{bmatrix} \end{bmatrix} \Rightarrow \begin{bmatrix} \text{FORM } F_{pres}(\boxed{1}) \\ \text{HEAD} \begin{bmatrix} \text{POS} & verb \\ \text{VFORM} & es \end{bmatrix} \end{bmatrix}$$

The rule states that given a verb lexeme we derive its *es* form by applying the F_{pres} function whose value can be either '(e)s' (for 3rd singular as in *He drives a car*) or none as in *They drive a car*, or even a suppletive form (e.g, *is*).

We also follow the fairly standard generative grammatical analysis of English 'infinitives' in which the infinitive part is a head (*to*) which takes as its complement a verb in the *bse* form. With these classifications, we propose the following hierarchy for the values of the attribute VFORM:

(17)

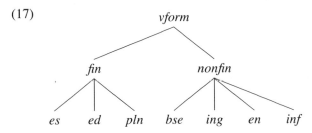

The classification of VFORM values here means that the values of VFORM can be typed, and those types have different subtypes. Sometimes we want to be able to refer to the type of a value, as in (18a), and sometimes to a particular form, as in (18b).

---

[4]A lexeme is thus an abstract unit of morphological analysis. For example, *drive, drives, driving, drove, drive* are forms of the same lexeme DRIVE. In this sense, we can take a lexicon to consist of lexemes as headwords.

(18)   a.   [VFORM *fin*]

      b.   [VFORM *ing*]

The need to distinguish between *fin* and *nonfin* is easily determined. Every declarative sentence in English needs to have a finite verb with tense information:

(19)   a.   The student [knows the answers].

      b.   The student [knew the answers].

      c.   The students [know the answers].

(20)   a.   *The student [knowing the answers].

      b.   *The student [known the answers].

The unacceptability of the examples in (20) is due to the fact *knowing* and *known* have no expression of tense – they are not finite. This in turn shows us that only finite verb forms can be used as the head of the highest VP in a declarative sentence, satisfying a basic requirement placed on English declarative sentences:

(21)   English Declarative Sentence Rule:
        For an English declarative sentence to be well-formed, its verb form value (VFORM) must be finite.

The finiteness of a sentence or a VP comes from the head verb, showing that the finiteness of the VFORM value is a head feature:

(22)

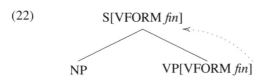

One thing we need to remember is that the two participle forms (present and past) have many different uses, in different constructions, as partially exemplified in (23) and (24).

(23)   Usages of the present participle (*ing*) form:

      a.   He is <u>writing</u> another long book about beavers.
          (part of the the progressive aspect construction)

      b.   Broadly <u>speaking</u>, the project was successful.
          (used as a sentence modifier)

      c.   He is proud of his son's <u>passing</u> the bar exam.
          (used in a gerundive construction)

(24)   Usages of the past participle (*en*) form:

      a.   The chicken has <u>eaten</u>.
          (part of the perfect aspect construction)

      b.   The chicken was <u>eaten</u>.
          (part of the passive voice construction)

    c.   <u>Seen</u> from this perspective, there is no easy solution.

        (used as a sentence modifier)

Some of these usages have been introduced as VFORM values for the ease of exposition (cf. Gazdar et al. (1985) or Ginzburg and Sag (2000)) though strictly speaking, there are only two participle **forms** in English, which each have several functions or constructional usages.

    Every verb will be specified for a value of the head feature VFORM. For example, let us consider a simple example like *The student knows the answer*. Here the verb *knows* will have the following lexical information:

(25)

$$\begin{bmatrix} \langle \text{knows} \rangle \\ \text{HEAD} \begin{bmatrix} \text{POS} & verb \\ \text{VFORM} & es \end{bmatrix} \\ \text{VAL} \begin{bmatrix} \text{SPR} & \langle \boxed{1}\text{NP} \rangle \\ \text{COMPS} & \langle \boxed{2}\text{NP} \rangle \end{bmatrix} \\ \text{ARG-ST} \langle \boxed{1}, \boxed{2} \rangle \end{bmatrix}$$

This [VFORM *es*] value will be projected to the S in accordance with the HFP, as represented in the following:

(26)

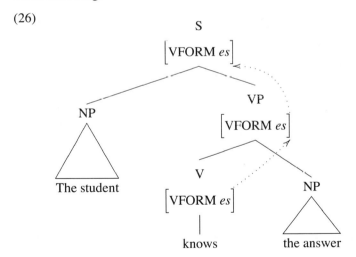

It is easy to verify that if we have *knowing* instead of *knows* here, the S would have the [VFORM *ing*] and the result could not be a well-formed declarative sentence. This is simply because the value *ing* is a subtype of *nonfin*.

    There are various constructions in English where we need to refer to VFORM values, such as:

(27)   a.   The monkeys kept [forgetting/*forgot/*forgotten their lines]. (*ing*)

   b.   We caught them [eating/*ate/*eat/*eaten the bananas]. (*ing*)

   c.   John made Mary [cook/*to cook/*cooking Korean food]. (*bse*)

Even though each main verb here requires a VP as its complement (the part in brackets), the required VFORM value could be different, as illustrated by the following lexical entries:

(28)   a.
$$
\begin{bmatrix}
\langle\text{keep}\rangle \\
\text{HEAD} \mid \text{POS} \quad verb \\
\text{COMPS} \qquad \langle\text{VP}[ing]\rangle
\end{bmatrix}
$$

      b.
$$
\begin{bmatrix}
\langle\text{make}\rangle \\
\text{HEAD} \mid \text{POS} \qquad verb \\
\text{COMPS} \qquad \langle\text{NP, VP}[bse]\rangle
\end{bmatrix}
$$

Such lexical specifications on the VP's VFORM value will make sure that these verbs only combine with a VP complement with the appropriate VFORM value. The following structure represents one example:

(29)

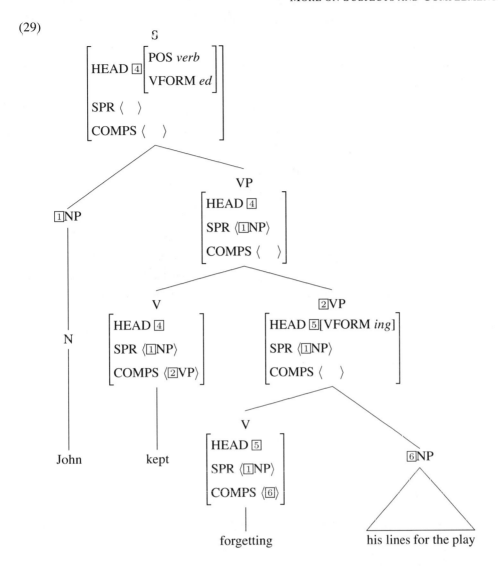

The finite verb *kept* selects as its complement a VP whose VFORM value is *ing*. The verb *forgetting* has this VFORM value which is passed up to its mother VP in accordance with the HFP. The Head-Complement Rule allows the combination of the head verb *kept* with this VP. In the upper part of the structure, the VFORM value of the verb *kept* is also passed up to its mother node VP, ensuring that the VFORM value of the S is a subtype of *fin*, satisfying the basic English rule for declarative sentences.

5.2.2 Complements of Adjectives

There are at least two types of adjectives in English in terms of complement selection: those selecting no complements at all, and those taking complements. As shown in the following examples, an adjective like *despondent* optionally takes a complement, while *intelligent* does not take any complements:

(30) a. The monkey seems despondent (that it is in a cage).

  b. He seems intelligent (*to study medicine).

Adjectives such as *eager, fond* and *compatible* each select a complement, possibly of different categories (for example, VP or PP).

(31) a. Monkeys are eager [to leave/*leaving the compound].

  b. The chickens seem fond [of/*with the farmer].

  c. The foxes seem compatible [with/*for the chickens].

  d. These are similar [to/* with the bottles].

  e. The teacher is proud [of/*with his students].

  f. The contract is subject [to/*for approval by my committee].

One thing we can note again is that the complements also need to be in a specific VFORM and PFORM value, where PFORM indicates the form of a specific preposition, as illustrated in examples (31b–f). Just like verbs, adjectives also place restrictions on the VFORM or PFORM value of their complement. Such restrictions are also specified in the lexical information, for example:

(32) a.
$$\begin{bmatrix} \langle \text{eager} \rangle \\ \text{HEAD} \,|\, \text{POS} \quad adj \\ \text{SPR} \qquad\qquad \langle \text{NP} \rangle \\ \text{COMPS} \qquad\; \langle \text{VP[VFORM } inf] \rangle \end{bmatrix}$$

  b.
$$\begin{bmatrix} \langle \text{fond} \rangle \\ \text{HEAD} \,|\, \text{POS} \quad adj \\ \text{SPR} \qquad\qquad \langle \text{ NP } \rangle \\ \text{COMPS} \qquad\; \langle \text{PP[PFORM } of] \rangle \end{bmatrix}$$

Such lexical entries will project sentences like the following:

(33)

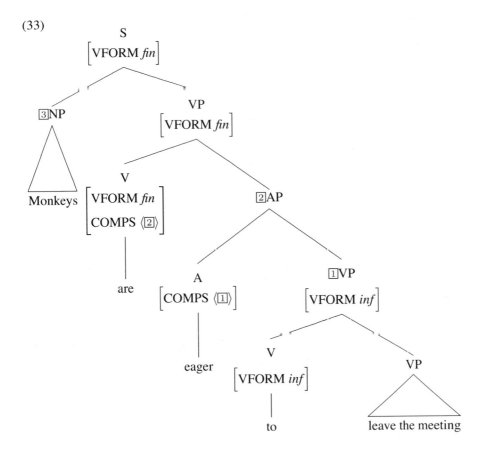

As represented in this simplified tree structure, the adjective *eager* combines with its VP[*inf*] complement in accordance with the Head-Complement Rule. In addition, this rule also licenses the combination of the infinitival marker *to* with its VP[*bse*] complement (see also section 8.3.4) and the combination of the copula *are* with its AP complement. The HFP ensures the HEAD features, POS and VFORM, are passed up to the final S. Each structure will satisfy all the relevant constraints and principles.

5.2.3 Complements of Common Nouns

Nouns do not usually select complements, though they often may have specifiers. For example, common nouns such as *idea, book, beer* require only a specifier, but no complement. Yet there also are nouns which do require a specific type of complement, such as *proximity, faith, king, desire*, and *bottom*:

(34) a.   their proximity to their neighbors/*for their neighbors

      b.   Bill's faith in/*for Fred's sister

      c.   the king of/*in English

      d.   the desire to become famous/*for success

      e.   the bottom of/*in the barrel

Although these complements can be optional in the right context (as marked with parentheses in (35)), they are grammatically classified as complements of the nouns, and are represented in the following simplified lexical entries:[5]

(35)   a. $\begin{bmatrix} \langle\text{proximity}\rangle \\ \text{HEAD}\,|\,\text{POS} \quad noun \\ \text{SPR} \qquad\qquad \langle \boxed{1}\text{DP} \rangle \\ \text{COMPS} \qquad \langle (\boxed{2}\text{PP[PFORM } to]) \rangle \end{bmatrix}$

       b. $\begin{bmatrix} \langle\text{faith}\rangle \\ \text{HEAD}\,|\,\text{POS} \quad noun \\ \text{SPR} \qquad\qquad \langle \boxed{1}\text{DP} \rangle \\ \text{COMPS} \qquad \langle (\boxed{2}\text{PP[PFORM } in]) \rangle \end{bmatrix}$

In these particular entries, both the SPR and COMPS are indicated as required; in other words, these represent the uses of these nouns in examples like those in (34).

Though many more details remain to be covered for the various complement types of lexical categories, the discussion so far has given an idea of what kinds of complements different categories select for.

5.3   Feature Specifications for the Subject

In general, most verbs select a regular NP as subject:

(36)   a.   John/Some books/The spy disappeared.

       b.   The teacher/The monkey/He fooled the students.

However, as noted in the previous chapter, certain English verbs select only *it* or *there* as subject:

(37)   a.   It/*John/*There rains.

       b.   There/*The spy lies a man in the park.

The pronouns *it* and *there* are often called 'expletives', indicating that they do not have or contribute any meaning. The use of these expletives is restricted to particular contexts or verbs, though both forms have regular pronoun uses as well. One way to specify such lexical specifications for subjects is to make use of a form value specification for nouns: all regular nouns [NFORM *norm(al)*] as default specification; overall we classify nouns as having three different NFORM values: *normal, it,* and *there.* Given the NFORM feature, we can have the following lexical entries for the verbs above:

---

[5]DP covers not only simple determiners like *a, the,* and *that,* but also includes a possessive phrase like *John's.* In Chapter 6 we cover NP structures in detail.

(38) a.
$$\begin{bmatrix} \langle\text{rained}\rangle \\ \text{SPR} \quad\quad \langle\text{NP[NFORM } it]\rangle \\ \text{COMPS} \quad \langle \quad \rangle \end{bmatrix}$$

b.
$$\begin{bmatrix} \langle\text{fooled}\rangle \\ \text{SPR} \quad\quad \langle\text{ NP[NFORM } norm\rangle \\ \text{COMPS} \quad \langle\text{ NP }\rangle \end{bmatrix}$$

We can also observe that only a limited set of verbs require their subject to be [NFORM *there*]:[6]

(39) a. There exists only one truly amphibian mammal.

   b. There arose a great storm.

(40) a. There exist few solutions which are cost-effective.

   b. There is a riot in the park.

   c. There remained just a few problems to be solved.

The majority of verbs do not allow *there* as subject:

(41) a. *There runs a man in the park.

   b. *There sings a man loudly.

For the sentences with *there* subjects, we first consider the verb forms which have regular subjects. A verb like *exist* in (39a) takes one argument when used in an example like *Only one truly amphibian mammal exists*, and the argument will be realized as the SPR, as dictated by the entry in (42a). In addition, such verbs can introduce *there* as the subject, through the Argument Realization option given in (42b), which is the form that occurs in the structure of (39a).

(42) a.
$$\begin{bmatrix} \langle\text{exists}\rangle \\ \text{SPR} \quad\quad \langle\boxed{1}\text{NP}\rangle \\ \text{COMPS} \quad \langle \quad \rangle \\ \text{ARG-ST} \quad \langle\boxed{1}\text{NP} \quad \rangle \end{bmatrix}$$

b.
$$\begin{bmatrix} \langle\text{exists}\rangle \\ \text{SPR} \quad\quad \langle\boxed{1}\text{NP[NFORM } there]\rangle \\ \text{COMPS} \quad \langle\boxed{2}\text{NP} \rangle \\ \text{ARG-ST} \quad \langle\boxed{1}\text{NP}, \boxed{2}\text{NP}\rangle \end{bmatrix}$$

---

[6]Some verbs such as *arise* or *remain* sound a little archaic in these constructions.

5.4 Clausal Complement or Subject

5.4.1 Verbs Selecting a Clausal Complement

We have seen that the COMPS list includes predominantly phrasal elements. However, there are verbs selecting not just a phrase but a whole clause as a complement, either finite or nonfinite. For example, consider the complements of *think* or *believe*:

(43)   a.   I think (that) the press has a check-and-balance function.

b.   They believe (that) Charles Darwin's theory of evolution is just a scientific theory.

The C (complementizer) *that* here is optional, implying that this kind of verb selects for a finite complement clause of some type, which we will notate as a [VFORM *fin*] clause. That is, these verbs will have one of the following two COMPS values:

(44)   a. $\left[\text{COMPS} \quad \left\langle \text{S[VFORM } \textit{fin}] \right\rangle \right]$

b. $\left[\text{COMPS} \quad \left\langle \text{CP[VFORM } \textit{fin}] \right\rangle \right]$

If the COMPS value only specifies a VFORM value, the complement can be either S or CP. This means that we can subsume these two uses into the following single lexical entry, suppressing the category information of the sentential complement:[7]

(45) $\begin{bmatrix} \langle \text{believe} \rangle \\ \text{HEAD | POS} \quad \textit{verb} \\ \text{COMPS} \quad \left\langle \text{[VFORM } \textit{fin}] \right\rangle \end{bmatrix}$

This lexical entry then will allow both of the following structures in which *believe* combines with a finite S or a finite CP:

(46)

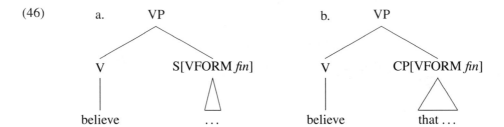

We can also find somewhat similar verbs like *demand* and *require* with the difference in the VFORM value on its sentential complement:

(47)   a.   John demanded [that she stop phoning him].

b.   The rules require [that the executives be polite].

---

[7]Although the categories V or VP are also potentially specified as [VFORM *fin*], such words or phrases cannot be complements of verbs like *think* or *believe*. This is because complements are typically saturated phrases, with no unsatisfied requirements for complements or specifiers. While S and CP are *saturated* categories projected from V, VP and V are not saturated.

Unlike *think* or *believe*, these verbs which introduce a subjunctive clause typically only take a CP[VFORM *bse*] as their complement: the finite verb itself is actually in the *bse* form. Observe the structure of (47b):

(48)

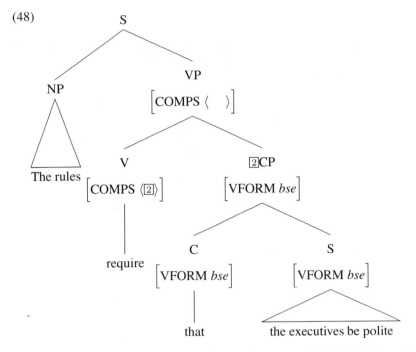

The verb *require* selects a *bse* CP or S complement, and this COMPS requirement is discharged at its mother VP: this satisfies the Head-Complement Rule. There is one issue here with respect to the percolation of the VFORM value: the CP must be *bse*, and this information must come from the head C, not from its complement S. One way to make sure this is so is to assume that the VFORM value of C is identical with that of its complement S, as in this lexical entry:

(49)
$$
\begin{bmatrix}
\langle\text{that}\rangle \\[4pt]
\text{HEAD} \quad \begin{bmatrix} \text{POS } comp \\ \text{VFORM } \boxed{1} \end{bmatrix} \\[8pt]
\text{SPR} \quad \langle\ \rangle \\[4pt]
\text{COMPS} \quad \langle \text{S[VFORM } \boxed{1}]\rangle
\end{bmatrix}
$$

This lexical information will then allow us to pass on the VFORM value of S to the head C and then percolate up to the CP according to the HFP. This encodes the intuition that a complementizer 'agrees' in VFORM value with its complement sentence.

There are also verbs which select a sequence of an NP followed by a CP as complements. NP and CP are abbreviations for feature structure descriptions that include the information [POS *noun*] and [POS *comp*], respectively:

(50) a. Joe warned the class that the exam would be difficult.

b. We told Tom that he should consult an accountant.

c. Mary convinced me that the argument was sound.

The COMPS value of such verbs will be as in (51):

(51) $\left[\text{COMPS} \langle \text{NP, CP[VFORM } fin]\rangle\right]$

In addition to the *that*-type of CP, there is an infinitive type of CP, headed by the complementizer *for*. Some verbs select this nonfinite CP as the complement:

(52) a. Tom intends for Sam to review that book.

b. John would prefer for the children to finish the oatmeal.

The data show that verbs like *intend* and *prefer* select an infinitival CP clause. The structure of (52a) is familiar, but now has a nonfinite VFORM value within it:

(53)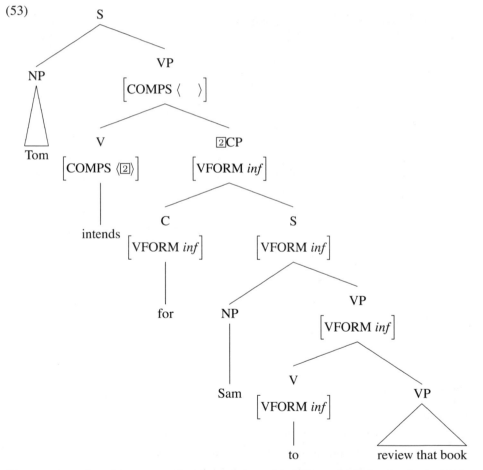

The structure given here means that the verb *intends* will have the following lexical information:

(54)
$$
\begin{bmatrix}
\langle intends \rangle \\[4pt]
\text{HEAD} \begin{bmatrix} \text{POS} & verb \\ \text{VFORM} & es \end{bmatrix} \\[10pt]
\text{COMPS} \ \langle \text{CP[VFORM } inf] \rangle
\end{bmatrix}
$$

To fill out the analysis, we need explicit lexical entries for the complementizer *for* and for *to*, which we treat as an (infinitive) auxiliary verb. In fact, *to* has a distribution very similar to the finite modal auxiliaries such as *will* or *must*, differing only in the VFORM value (see section 8.3.4).

(55) a.
$$
\begin{bmatrix}
\langle for \rangle \\[4pt]
\text{HEAD} \begin{bmatrix} \text{POS} & comp \\ \text{VFORM} & inf \end{bmatrix} \\[10pt]
\text{COMPS} \ \langle \text{S[VFORM } inf] \rangle
\end{bmatrix}
$$

    b.
$$
\begin{bmatrix}
\langle to \rangle \\[4pt]
\text{HEAD} \begin{bmatrix} \text{POS} & verb \\ \text{VFORM} & inf \end{bmatrix} \\[10pt]
\text{COMPS} \ \langle \text{VP[VFORM } bse] \rangle
\end{bmatrix}
$$

Just like the complementizer *that*, the complementizer *for* selects an infinitival S as its complement, inheriting its VFORM value too. The evidence that the complementizer *for* requires an infinitival S can be found from coordination data:

(56) a. For John to either [make up such a story] or [repeat it] is outrageous.
       (coordination of *bse* VPs)

    b. For John either [to make up such a story] or [to repeat it] is outrageous.
       (coordination of *inf* VPs)

    c. For [John to tell Bill such a lie] and [Bill to believe it] is outrageous.
       (coordination of *inf* Ss)

Given that only like categories (constituents with the same label) can be coordinated, we can see that base VPs, infinitival VPs, and infinitival Ss are all constituents.[8]

One thing to note here is that the verbs which select a CP[VFORM *inf*] complement can also take a VP[VFORM *inf*] complement:

(57) a. John intends to review the book.

    b. John would prefer to finish the oatmeal.

By underspecifying the category information of complements, we can generalize this subcategorization information:

---

[8]Tensed VPs can be coordinated regardless of their different tense values as in *Kim [alienated cats] and [loves his dog]*.

(58)
$$\begin{bmatrix} \langle \text{intend} \rangle \\ \text{HEAD} \,|\, \text{POS} \quad verb \\ \text{COMPS} \,\langle [\text{VFORM} \quad inf] \rangle \end{bmatrix}$$

Since the specification [VFORM *inf*] is quite general, it can be realized either as CP[VFORM *inf*] or VP[VFORM *inf*].

However, this does not mean that all verbs behave alike: not all verbs can take variable complement types such as an infinitival VP or S. For examples, *try, tend, hope*, and others select only a VP[*inf*] as attested by the data:

(59) a. Tom tried to ask a question.

b. *Tom tried for Bill to ask a question.

(60) a. Tom tends to avoid confrontations.

b. *Tom tends for Mary to avoid confrontations.

(61) a. Joe hoped to find a solution.

b. *Joe hoped for Beth to find a solution.

Such subcategorization differences are hard to predict just from the meaning of verbs: they are simple lexical specifications which language users need to learn.

There is another generalization that we need to consider with respect to the property of verbs that select a CP: most verbs that select a CP can at first glance select an NP, too:

(62) a. John believed it/that he is honest.

b. John mentioned the issue to me/mentioned to me that the question is an issue.

Should we have two lexical entries for such verbs or can we have a simple way of representing such a pattern? To reflect such lexical patterns, we can assume that English parts of speech come in families and can profitably be analyzed in terms of a type hierarchy as following:[9]

(63)

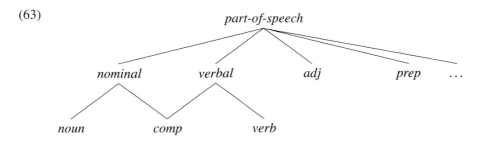

According to the hierarchy, the type *nominal* is a supertype of both *noun* and *comp*. In accordance with the basic properties of systems of typed feature structures, an element specified as [POS *nominal*] can be realized either as [POS *noun*] or [POS *comp*]. These will correspond to the phrasal types NP and CP, respectively.[10]

---

[9]This type hierarchy is adopted from Kim and Sag (2005).

[10]For the function of *verbal*, see Chapter 12.

The hierarchy implies that the subcategorization pattern of English verbs will refer to (at least) each of these types. Consider the following patterns:

(64)   a.   She pinched [his arm] as hard as she could.

   b.   *She pinched [that he feels pain].

(65)   a.   We hope [that such a vaccine could be available in ten years].

   b.   *We hope [the availability of such a vaccine in ten years].

(66)   a.   Cohen proved [the independence of the continuum hypothesis].

   b.   Cohen proved [that the continuum hypothesis was independent].

The *part-of-speech* type hierarchy in (63) allows us to formulate simple lexical constraints that reflect these subcategorization patterns, making reference to *noun*, *verbal*, and *nominal*:

(67)   a. $\left[\text{ARG-ST} \quad \langle \text{ NP, NP[POS } noun], \dots \rangle \right]$

   b. $\left[\text{ARG-ST} \quad \langle \text{ NP, CP[POS } comp], \dots \rangle \right]$

   c. $\left[\text{ARG-ST} \quad \langle \text{ NP, [POS } nominal], \dots \rangle \right]$

In each class, the ARG-ST list specifies the argument elements that the verbs select (in the order ⟨ Subject, Direct Object, ... ⟩). The POS value of a given element is the part-of-speech type that a word passes on to the phrases it projects. These three patterns illustrate that English transitive verbs come in at least three varieties.

5.4.2   Verbs Selecting a Clausal Subject

In addition to CP as a complement, we also find some cases where a CP is the subject of a verb:

(68)   a.   [John] bothers me.

   b.   [That John snores] bothers me.

(69)   a.   [John] loves Bill

   b.   *[That John snores] loves Bill.

The contrast here means that verbs like *bother* can have two realizations of the ARG-ST, whereas those like *love* allow only one:

(70)   a. $\begin{bmatrix} \langle \text{bothers} \rangle \\ \text{SPR} \quad \langle \boxed{1}[\text{POS } nominal] \rangle \\ \text{COMPS} \quad \langle \boxed{2}\text{NP} \rangle \\ \text{ARG-ST} \quad \langle \boxed{1}, \boxed{2} \rangle \end{bmatrix}$

   b. $\begin{bmatrix} \langle \text{loves} \rangle \\ \text{SPR} \quad \langle \boxed{1}\text{NP} \rangle \\ \text{COMPS} \quad \langle \boxed{2}\text{NP} \rangle \\ \text{ARG-ST} \quad \langle \boxed{1}, \boxed{2} \rangle \end{bmatrix}$

These different realizations all hinge on the lexical properties of the given verb, and only some verbs allow the dual realization described by (70a).

A clausal subject is not limited to a finite *that*-headed CP, but there are other clausal types:

(71) a. [That John sold the ostrich] surprised Bill.
          (*that*-clause CP subject)

      b. [(For John) to train his horse] would be desirable.
          (infinitival CP or VP subject)

      c. [That the king or queen be present] is a requirement on all Royal weddings.
          (subjunctive *that*-clause CP subject)

      d. [Which otter you should adopt first] is unclear.
          (*wh*-question CP subject)

Naturally, each particular predicate dictates which kinds of subjects are possible, as in (71), and which are not, as in (72):

(72) a. *That Fred was unpopular nominated Bill.

      b. *That Tom missed the lecture was enjoyable.

      c. *For John to remove the mother is undeniable.

      d. *How much money Gordon spent is true.

For example, the difference between the two verbs *nominate* and *surprise* can be seen in these partial lexical entries:

(73) a.
$$\begin{bmatrix} \langle\text{nominate}\rangle \\ \text{SPR} \quad\quad\quad \langle\boxed{1}\text{NP}\,\rangle \\ \text{COMPS} \quad\quad \langle\,\boxed{2}\text{NP}\,\rangle \\ \text{ARG-ST}\ \langle\boxed{1},\boxed{2}\rangle \end{bmatrix}$$

      b.
$$\begin{bmatrix} \langle\text{surprise}\rangle \\ \text{SPR} \quad\quad\quad \langle\boxed{1}[\text{POS } nominal]\,\rangle \\ \text{COMPS} \quad\quad \langle\,\boxed{2}\text{NP}\,\rangle \\ \text{ARG-ST}\ \langle\boxed{1},\boxed{2}\rangle \end{bmatrix}$$

Unlike *nominate*, the first argument of *surprised* can be a *nominal*. This means that its subject can be either an NP or a CP.

5.4.3 Adjectives Selecting a Clausal Complement

Like verbs, certain adjectives can also select CPs as their complements. For example, *confident* and *insistent* select a finite CP, whereas *eager* selects an infinitival CP:

(74) a. Tom is confident [that the elephants respect him].

      b. Tom is insistent [that the witnesses be truthful].

(75) a. Tom seems eager [for her brother to catch a cold].

b. Tom seems eager [to catch a cold].

We can easily find more adjectives which select a CP complement:

(76) a. I am ashamed that I neglected you.

b. I am delighted that Mary finished his thesis.

c. We are content for the cleaners to return the drapes next week.

d. We were thankful that no one had been hurt.

e. We were glad it was over.

The lexical entries for some adjectives are given in (77):

(77) a. $\begin{bmatrix} \langle \text{confident} \rangle \\ \text{HEAD} \mid \text{POS} \quad adj \\ \text{COMPS} \qquad \langle \text{CP[VFORM } fin] \rangle \end{bmatrix}$

b. $\begin{bmatrix} \langle \text{insistent} \rangle \\ \text{HEAD} \mid \text{POS} \quad adj \\ \text{COMPS} \qquad \langle \text{CP[VFORM } bse] \rangle \end{bmatrix}$

c. $\begin{bmatrix} \langle \text{eager} \rangle \\ \text{HEAD} \mid \text{POS} \quad adj \\ \text{COMPS} \qquad \langle \text{[VFORM } inf] \rangle \end{bmatrix}$

Such lexical entries, interacting with the Head-Complement Rule, the Head-Specifier Rule, and the HFP, can license analyses such as (78), for (75b):

(78)

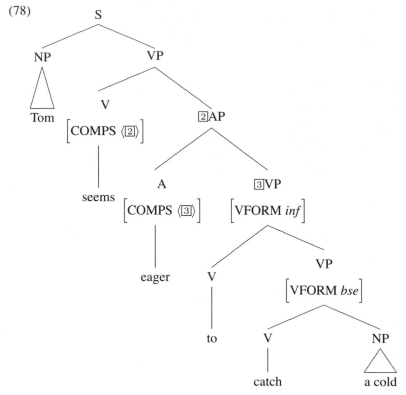

When the head adjective *eager* combines with its complement, VP[*inf*], it satisfies the Head-Complement Rule. The same rule allows the combination of the verb *seem* with its AP complement.

5.4.4 Nouns Selecting a Clausal Complement

Nouns can also select a CP complement, for example, *eagerness*:

(79) a. (John's) eagerness [for Harry to win the election]

     b. (John's) eagerness [to win the election]

These examples imply that *eagerness* will have the following lexical information:

(80) $\begin{bmatrix} \langle \text{eagerness} \rangle \\ \text{HEAD} \mid \text{POS} \quad noun \\ \text{COMPS} \qquad \langle [\text{VFORM } inf] \rangle \end{bmatrix}$

This lexical entry will allow a structure like the following:

(81)

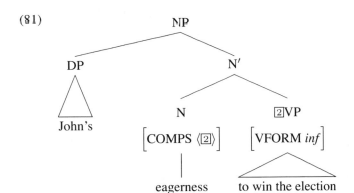

One pattern that we can observe is that when a verb selects a CP complement, if there is a corresponding noun, it also selects a CP:

(82)   a.   Bill alleged that Fred signed the check.

       b.   We believe that the directors were present.

       c.   We convinced him that the operation is safe.

(83)   a.   the allegation that Fred signed the check

       b.   the belief that the directors were present

       c.   his conviction that the operation is safe

This shows us that the derivational process which derives a noun from a verb preserves the COMPS value of that verb.

   Not surprisingly, not all nouns select a CP complement:

(84)   a.   *his attention that the earth is round

       b.   *his article that the earth is flat

       c.   *the ignorance that James can play the flute

       d.   *the expertise that she knows how to bake croissants

These nouns cannot combine with a CP, indicating that they do not have CP in the value of COMPS.

5.4.5   Prepositions Selecting a Clausal Complement

In general, prepositions in English cannot select a CP complement.

(85)   a.   *Alan is thinking about [that his students are eager to learn English].

       b.   *Fred is counting on [for Tom to make an announcement].

However, *wh*-CPs, sometimes known as indirect questions, may serve as prepositional complements.

(86)   a.   The outcome depends on [how many candidates participate in the election].

       b.   Fred is thinking about [whether he should stay in Seoul].

These facts show us that indirect questions have some feature which distinguishes them from canonical *that-* or *for*-CPs, and makes them somehow closer to true nouns (for NP is the typical complement for a preposition).

5.5 Exercises

1. Check if each of the following expressions selects for a clausal complement:

    (i)   ignore, doubt, deny, prefer, intend, glad, unsure, confident, allegation, ignorance

    Write out the examples which justify your classifications.

2. Check if each of the following expressions selects a clausal subject or not.

    (i)   annoy, vanish, remain, admire, select, mandatory, enjoyable, apparent

    Write out the examples which justify your classifications.

3. For each sentence, draw a tree structure and then give the COMPS value (including VFORM and PFORM value) for the italicized word.

    (i) a.   The offer *made* Smith admire the administrators.

         b.   John tried to make Sam *let* George ask Bill to keep delivering the mail.

         c.   The soldiers must *enforce* Bill to make the baby be quiet.

         d.   John *enjoyed* drawing trees for his syntax homework.

         e.   The picture on the wall *reminded* him of his country.

         f.   Free enterprise is *compatible* with American values and traditions.

         g.   They were taking a hard *look* at possible FTA.

         h.   We need to be in frequent *contact* with the clients.

         i.   The contract is *subject* to approval by my committee.

         j.   *Acknowledge* that everyone has limits.

         k.   We are *aware* of the existing problems.

4. Identify errors in the following sentences, focusing on the form values of verbs, adjectives, and nouns, and/or their COMPs values.

    (i) a.   *Why don't you leaving me concentrate on my work?

         b.   *The general commended that all troops was in dress uniform.

         c.   *My morning routine features swim free styles slowly for one hour.

         d.   *You should avoid to travel in the rush hour.

         e.   *You should attempt answering every question.

         f.   *The authorities blamed Greenpeace with the bombing.

         g.   *The authorities charged the students of the cheating.

         h.   *Sharon has been eager finishing the book.

         i.   *We respect Mary's desire for becoming famous.

         j.   *John referred from the building.

         k.   *John died to heart disease.

         l.   *John paid me against the book.

         m.   *We were glad what to do.

         n.   *She was busy to make lunch.

5. Draw trees for the following examples with detailed NP structures.

    (i) a.   The constant rain forced the abandonment of the next day's competitions.

    b.   The committee will study the feasibility of setting up a national computer network.

    c.   Aloe may have an analgesic effect on inflammation and minor skin irritations.

    d.   The public never had faith in his ability to handle the job.

    e.   He repeated his claim that the people backed his action.

6. In general the present and base forms of a main verb are identical, but can be distinguished in the case of *be*, with its present form *are*:

    (i) a.   We made them *take the money*.

        b.   *We made them *are* rude.

        c.   We made them *be* rude.

Do the same substitution test for the following sentences and determine whether the italicized verb is the base or present form.

    (ii) a.   Do not *use* these words in the beginning of a sentence.

        b.   We know the witnesses *seem* eager to testify against the criminal.

        c.   Jane isn't sure whether the students *keep* the books.

        d.   Why not *try* to catch the minnows?

7. Read the following text and provide the lexical entries for the underlined words. In doing so, try to specify the VFORM or PFORM value of the complement(s).

    (i)   The study of grammar <u>helps</u> us to communicate more effectively. Quite simply, if we know how English works, then we can <u>make</u> better use of it. For most purposes, we need to be able to construct sentences which are far more complicated than *David plays the piano*. A <u>knowledge</u> of grammar enables us to evaluate the choices which are <u>available</u> to us during composition. In practice, these choices are never as simple as the choice between *David plays the piano* and **plays David piano the*. If we understand the relationship between the parts of a sentence, we can <u>eliminate</u> many of the ambiguities and misunderstandings which <u>result</u> from poor construction. In the interpretation of writing, too, grammatical knowledge is often crucially important. The <u>understanding</u> of literary texts, for example, often <u>depends</u> on careful grammatical analysis. Other forms of writing can be equally <u>difficult</u> to interpret. Scientific and academic writing, for instance, may be complex not just in the ideas they convey, but also in their syntax. These types of writing can be difficult to understand easily without some <u>familiarity</u> with how the parts <u>relate</u> to each other. The study of grammar <u>enables</u> us to go beyond our instinctive, native-speaker knowledge, and to use English in an intelligent, informed way.[11]

---

[11] From 'Introducing the Internet Grammar of English' at `http://www.ucl.ac.uk/internet-grammar/intro/intro.htm`.

6

Noun Phrases and Agreement

6.1 Classification of Nouns

Nouns not only represent entities like people, places, or things, but also denote abstract and intangible concepts such as *happiness, information, hope*, and so on. Such diversity of reference renders it difficult to classify nouns solely according to their meanings. The following chart shows the canonical classification of nouns taking into account semantic differences, but also considering their formal and grammatical properties:

(1)   Types of Nouns in English:

common noun	countable	desk, book, difficulty, remark, etc.
	uncountable	butter, gold, music, furniture, laziness, etc.
proper noun		Seoul, Kyung Hee, Stanford, Palo Alto, January, etc.
pronoun	personal	he, she, they, his, him, etc.
	relative	that, which, what, who, whom, etc.
	interrogative	who, where, how, why, when, etc.
	indefinite	anybody, everybody, somebody, nobody, anywhere, etc.

We see that nouns fall into three major categories: common nouns, proper nouns, and pronouns. One important aspect of common nouns is that they are either count or non-count. Whether a noun is countable or not does not fully depend on its reference; examples like *difficulty* which is mass (non-count) but *difficulties* which is count, show how subtle the distinction can be, and nouns like *furniture/*furnitures* are only mass while *a chair/chairs* are only count.

Proper nouns denote specific people or places and are typically uncountable. Common nouns and proper nouns display clear contrasts in terms of the combinatorial possibilities with determiners as shown in the following chart:[1]

---

[1] Some of the forms shown in the table as ungrammatical do have different grammatical uses: *He's some Einstein!* and stressed *some* as in *In every class you have to read at least SOME book or other.*

(2)   Combinatory Possibilities with Determiners:

	Proper N	Common N		
		countable	uncountable	neutral
Only N	Einstein	*book	music	cake
the + N	*the Einstein	the book	the music	the cake
a + N	*an Einstein	a book	*a music	a cake
some + N	*some Einstein	*some book	some music	some cake
N + s	*Einsteins	books	*musics	cakes

Proper nouns do not combine with any determiner, as can be seen from the chart. Meanwhile, count nouns have singular and plural forms (e.g., *a book* and *books*), whereas uncountable nouns combine only with *some* or *the*. As noted in Chapter 1, some common nouns may be either count or non-count, depending on the kind of reference they have. For example, *cake* can be countable when it refers to a specific one as in *I made a cake*, but can be noncountable when it refers to 'cake in general' as in *I like cake*.

Together with verbs, nouns are of pivotal importance in English, forming the semantic and structural components of sentences. This chapter deals with the structural, semantic, and functional dimensions of NPs, with focus on the agreement relationships of nouns with determiners and of subjects with verbs.

6.2 Syntactic Structures

6.2.1 Common Nouns

As noted before, common nouns can have a determiner as a specifier, unlike proper and pronouns. In particular, count nouns cannot be used without a determiner when they are singular:

(3)   a. *Book is available in most countries.

       b. *Student studies English for 4 hours a day.

(4)   a. Rice is available in most countries.

       b. Students study English for 4 hours a day.

We can see here that mass nouns, or plural count nouns, are fully grammatical as bare nouns phrases.[2]

This has the consequence for our grammatical analysis that singular countable nouns like *student* must select a determiner as specifier. As we have seen in Chapters 2 and 4, there are various kinds of expressions which can serve as determiners including *a, an, this, that, any, some, his, how, which, some, no, much, few, . . .* as well as a possessive phrase:

(5)   a. His friend learned dancing.

       b. My bother's friend learned dancing.

---

[2]The style of English used in headlines does not have this restriction, e.g., *Student discovers planet, Army receives high-tech helicopter.*

    c.   The president's bodyguard learned surveillance.

    d.   The King of Rock and Roll's records led to dancing.

These possessive NPs *my brother's* or *the president's* are not determiners, because they are phrases. We take such phrases as DPs headed by the Det *'s* (cf. Abney (1987)). Let's consider the lexical entries for the relevant words:

(6)

a.
$$\begin{bmatrix} \langle my \rangle \\ \text{HEAD} \mid \text{POS} \quad det \\ \text{SPR} \qquad\qquad \langle \quad \rangle \\ \text{COMPS} \qquad\quad \langle \quad \rangle \end{bmatrix}$$

b.
$$\begin{bmatrix} \langle 's \rangle \\ \text{HEAD} \mid \text{POS} \quad det \\ \text{SPR} \qquad\qquad \langle \text{NP} \rangle \\ \text{COMPS} \qquad\quad \langle \quad \rangle \end{bmatrix}$$

c.
$$\begin{bmatrix} \langle brother \rangle \\ \text{HEAD} \mid \text{POS} \quad noun \\ \text{SPR} \qquad\qquad \langle \text{DP} \rangle \\ \text{COMPS} \qquad\quad \langle \quad \rangle \end{bmatrix}$$

c.
$$\begin{bmatrix} \langle friend \rangle \\ \text{HEAD} \mid \text{POS} \quad noun \\ \text{SPR} \qquad\qquad \langle \text{DP} \rangle \\ \text{COMPS} \qquad\quad \langle \quad \rangle \end{bmatrix}$$

As given here, determiners like *my* and uncountable nouns like *rice* select neither specifier nor complement whereas the possessive marker *'s* and the countable noun *friend* requires a NP and DP specifier, respectively. Meanwhile, countable noun *brother* requires a DP as its specifier. This means that not only a simple determiner but also a possessive NP can function as a specifier. Reflecting this generalization, we can assume that a countable noun selects not a simple determiner but a DP (determiner phrase) as its specifier: These lexical entries will project NP structures like the following for (5b):

(7)

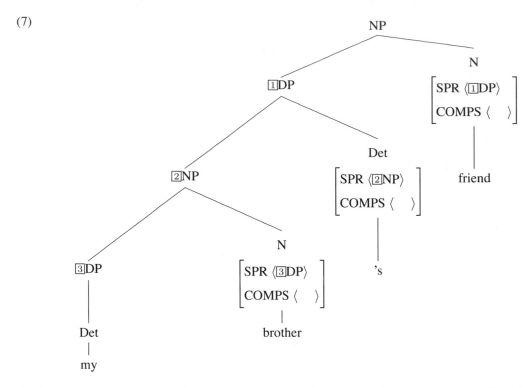

As shown here, the noun *friend* does not select a complement, and thus projects to an NP with its specifier DP *my brother's*. The head of this DP is the possessive determiner selecting an NP as given in (6b). The expression *my brother* is also a full NP just like the whole phrase *my brother's friend*. The common noun *brother* as given in (6c) requires a DP as its specifier: a determiner like *the, my, his* or *their* will be able to project into a DP but not a pronoun like *I, he* or *they*, so that the grammar rules out examples like **I brother* (see Chapter 2.2).

6.2.2 Pronouns

The core class of pronouns in English includes at least three main subgroups:

(8) a. Personal pronouns: I, you, he, she, it, they, we

  b. Reflexive pronouns: myself, yourself, himself, herself, itself

  c. Reciprocal pronoun: each other

Personal pronouns refer to specific persons or things and take different forms to indicate person, number, gender, and case. They participate in agreement relations with their **antecedent**, the phrase which they are understood to be referring to (indicated by the underlined parts of the examples in (9)).

(9) a. President Lincoln delivered his/*her Gettysburg Address in 1863.

  b. After reading the pamphlet, Judy threw it/*them into the garbage can.

  c. I got worried when the neighbors let their/*his dogs out.

Reflexive pronouns are special forms which typically are used to indicate a reflexive activity or action, which can include mental activities.

(10) a. After the party, I asked <u>myself</u> why I had faxed invitations to everyone in my office building.

  b. <u>Edward</u> usually remembered to send a copy of his e-mail to <u>himself</u>.

As noted earlier, these personal or reflexive pronouns neither take a determiner nor combine with an adjective except in very restricted constructions.[3].

6.2.3 Proper Nouns

Since proper nouns usually refer to something or someone unique, they do not normally take a plural form and cannot occur with a determiner:

(11) a. John, Bill, Seoul, January, . . .

  b. *a John, *a Bill, *a Seoul, *a January, . . .

However, proper nouns can be converted into countable nouns when they refer to a particular individual or type of individual:

(12) a. No John Smiths attended the meeting.

  b. This John Smith lives in Seoul.

  c. There are three Davids in my class.

  d. It's nothing like the America I remember.

  e. My brother is an Einstein at maths.

In such cases, proper nouns are converted into common nouns, may select a specifier, and take other nominal modifiers. This means that a proper noun will have a lexical entry like (13a) but can be related to one like (13b):[4]

(13)

a.
$$\begin{bmatrix} prpn \\ \langle John \rangle \\ \text{HEAD} | \text{POS} \quad noun \\ \text{SPR} \qquad \langle \quad \rangle \\ \text{COMPS} \quad \langle \quad \rangle \end{bmatrix}$$

b.
$$\begin{bmatrix} cn\text{-}prpn \\ \langle John \rangle \\ \text{HEAD} | \text{POS} \quad noun \\ \text{SPR} \qquad \langle DP \rangle \\ \text{COMPS} \quad \langle \quad \rangle \end{bmatrix}$$

6.3 Agreement Types and Morpho-syntactic Features

6.3.1 Noun-Determiner Agreement

Common nouns in English participate in three types of agreement. First, they are involved in determiner-noun agreement. All countable nouns are used either as singular or plural. When they combine with a determiner, there must be an agreement relationship between the two:

---

[3]These restricted constructions involve some indefinite pronouns (e.g., *a little something, a certain someone*)

[4]Once again, the italic part at the top of the feature structure denotes the type of the expression described. For example, *prpn* here means *proper-noun* and *cn-prpn* means *common-noun-prpn* derived from a proper noun.

(14) a. this book/that book

    b. *this books/*that books/these books/those books

    c. *few dog/few dogs

The data in turn means that the head noun's number value should be identical to that of its specifier, leading us to revise the Head-Specifier Rule:

(15) Head-Specifier Rule:

$$XP \rightarrow SPR\begin{bmatrix} AGR & \boxed{1} \end{bmatrix}, \mathbf{H}\begin{bmatrix} AGR & \boxed{1} \end{bmatrix}$$

This revised rule guarantees that English head-specifier phrases require their head and specifier to share agreement features, implying that determiners and nouns have NUM (number) information as their syntactic AGR (agreement) value:

(16)

a.
$$\begin{bmatrix} \langle a \rangle \\ HEAD \begin{bmatrix} POS\ det \\ AGR \mid NUM\ sing \end{bmatrix} \\ SPR \quad \langle \quad \rangle \\ COMPS \langle \quad \rangle \end{bmatrix}$$

b.
$$\begin{bmatrix} \langle book \rangle \\ HEAD \begin{bmatrix} POS\ noun \\ AGR \mid NUM\ sing \end{bmatrix} \\ SPR \quad \langle DP[NUM\ sing] \rangle \\ COMPS \langle \quad \rangle \end{bmatrix}$$

Common nouns thus impose a specific NUM value on the specifier:[5]

(17)

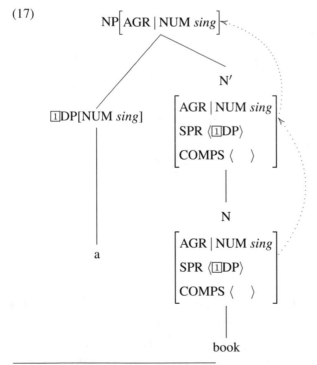

---

[5]Keen readers may have noticed that we allow a vacuous projection from N to N′ and to NP when no specifier or complement is combined. We can also allow an N to directly project into an NP.

The singular noun *book* selects a singular determiner like *a*. Notice that the AGR value on the head noun *book* is passed up to the whole NP, marking the whole NP as singular, so that it can combine with a singular VP, if it is the subject.

In addition, there is nothing preventing a singular noun from combining with a determiner which is not specified at all for a NUM value:

(18)   a. *those book, *these book, ...

      b. no book, the book, my book, ...

Determiners like *the, no* and *my* are not specified for a NUM value. Formally, their NUM value is underspecified as *num(ber)*. That is, the grammar of English has the underspecified value *num* for the feature NUM, with two subtypes *sing(ular)* and *pl(ural)*:

(19)

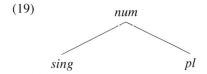

Given this hierarchy, nouns like *book* requiring a singular Det can combine with determiners like *the* whose AGR value is *num*. This is in accord with the grammar since the value *num* is a supertype of *sing*.

6.3.2   Pronoun-Antecedent Agreement

As noted earlier, a second type of agreement is pronoun-antecedent agreement, as indicated in (20).

(20)   a. In the book, he talks about his ups and downs at McLaren. Throughout **it** all he seeks to answer the questions about himself.

      b. If John wants to succeed in corporate life, **he/*she** has to know the rules of the game.

      c. The critique of Plato's *Republic* was written from a contemporary point of view. **It** was an in-depth analysis of Plato's opinions about possible governmental forms.

The pronoun *he* or *it* here needs to agree with its antecedent not only with respect to the number value but also with respect to person (1st, 2nd, 3rd) and gender (masculine, feminine, or neuter) values too. This shows us that nouns have also information about person and gender as well as number in the AGR values:

(21)

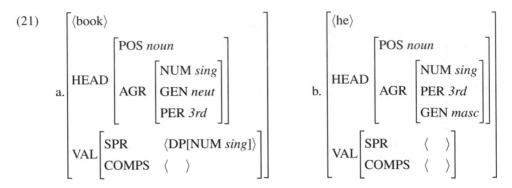

As we have briefly shown, nouns have NUM, PER(SON), and GEN(DER) for their AGR values. The PER value can be *1st, 2nd* or *3rd*; the GEN value can be *masc(uline)*, *fem(inine)* or *neut(er)*. The NUM values are shown in (19) above.

6.3.3 Subject-Verb Agreement

The third type of agreement is subject-verb agreement, which is one of the most important phenomena in English syntax. Let us look at some slightly complex examples:

(22)   a.   The <u>characters</u> in Shakespeare's *Twelfth Night* ***lives/live** in a world that has been turned upside-down.

      b.   <u>Students</u> studying English **read/*reads** Conrad's *Heart of Darkness* while at university.

As we can see here, the subject and the verb need to have an identical number value; and the person value is also involved in agreement relations, in particular when the subject is a personal pronoun:

(23)   a.   <u>You</u> **are/*is** the only person that I can rely on.

      b.   <u>He</u> **is/*are** the only person that I can rely on.

These facts show us that a verb lexically specifies the information about the number as well as person values of the subject that it selects for.

To show how the agreement system works, we will use some simpler examples:

(24)   a.   The boy swims/*swim.

      b.   The boys swim/*swims.

English verbs will have at least the following selectional information:

(25)
$$\begin{bmatrix} \langle swims \rangle \\ \\ HEAD \quad \begin{bmatrix} POS \; verb \\ VFORM \; es \end{bmatrix} \\ \\ VAL \mid SPR \quad \left\langle NP \begin{bmatrix} PER \; 3rd \\ NUM \; sing \end{bmatrix} \right\rangle \end{bmatrix}$$

The present-tense verb *swims* thus specifies that its subject (SPR's value) carries a 3rd singular AGR information. This lexical information will license a structure like the following:

(26)

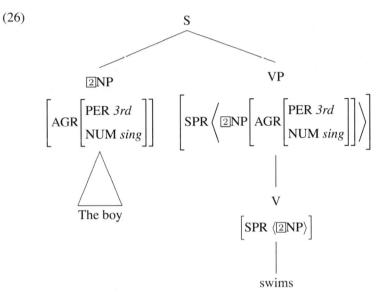

Only when the verb combines with a subject satisfying its AGR requirement will we have a well-formed head-subject phrase. In other words, if this verb were to combine with a subject with an incompatible agreement value, we would generate an ungrammatical example like **The boys swims* in (24b). In this system, what subject-verb agreement is is structure-sharing between the AGR value of the subject (SPR value of the verb) and that of the NP that the VP combines with.

The acute reader may have noticed that there are similarities between noun-determiner agreement and subject-verb agreement, that is, in the way that agreement works inside NP and inside S. Both NP and S require agreement between the head and the specifier, as reflected in the revised Head-Specifier Rule in (15).

6.4 Semantic Agreement Features

What we have seen so far is that the morphosyntactic AGR values of noun or verb can be specified, and may be inherited by phrases built out of them. However, consider now the following examples adopted from Nunberg (1995):

(27)   a.   [The hash browns at table nine] are/*is getting cold.

       b.   [The hash browns at table nine] is/*are getting angry.

When (27b) is spoken by a waiter to another waiter, the subject refers to a person who ordered hash browns. A somewhat similar case is found in (28):

(28)   King prawns cooked in chili salt and pepper was very much better, a simple dish succu-
      lently executed.

Here the verb form *was* is singular to agree with the dish being referred to, rather than with a plurality of prawns. If we simply assume that the subject phrase inherits the morphosyntactic agreement features of the head noun *(hash) browns* in (27b) and *(King) prawns* in (28), and requires that these features match those of the verb, we would not expect the singular verb form to be possible at all in these examples. In the interpretation of a nominal expression, it must be anchored to an individual in the situation described. We call this anchoring value the noun phrase's 'index' value. The index of *hash browns* in (27a) must be anchored to the plural entities on the plate, whereas that of *hash browns* in (27b) is anchored to a customer who ordered the food.

    English agreement is not purely morpho-syntactic as described in the sections above, but context-dependent in various ways, via the notion of 'index' that we have just introduced. Often what a given nominal refers to in the real world is important for agreement – index agreement. Index agreement involves sharing of referential indexes, closely related to the semantics of a nominal, and somewhat separate from the syntactic agreement feature AGR. This then requires us to distinguish the morphological AGR value and semantic (SEM(ANTIC)) IND(EX) value. So, in addition to the morphological AGR value introduced above, each noun will also have a semantic IND value representing what the noun refers to in the actual world.

(29)   a.
$$
\begin{bmatrix}
\langle \text{boy} \rangle \\
\text{SYN} \mid \text{HEAD} \begin{bmatrix} \text{POS } noun \\ \text{AGR} \mid \text{NUM } sing \end{bmatrix} \\
\text{SEM} \mid \text{IND} \mid \text{NUM } sing
\end{bmatrix}
$$

      b.
$$
\begin{bmatrix}
\langle \text{boys} \rangle \\
\text{SYN} \mid \text{HEAD} \begin{bmatrix} \text{POS } noun \\ \text{AGR} \mid \text{NUM } pl \end{bmatrix} \\
\text{SEM} \mid \text{IND} \mid \text{NUM } pl
\end{bmatrix}
$$

The lexical entry for *boy* indicates that it is syntactically a singular noun (through the feature AGR) and semantically also denotes a singular entity (through the feature IND). And the verb will place a restriction on its subject's IND value rather than its morphological AGR value:[6]

(30)
$$\begin{bmatrix} \langle \text{swims} \rangle \\ \text{SYN} \begin{bmatrix} \text{HEAD} \begin{bmatrix} \text{POS } verb \\ \text{AGR} \mid \text{NUM } sing \end{bmatrix} \\ \text{VAL} \mid \text{SPR} \left\langle \text{NP[IND} \mid \text{NUM } sing] \right\rangle \end{bmatrix} \\ \text{SEM} \mid \text{IND } s0 \end{bmatrix}$$

The lexical entry for *swims* here indicates that it is morphologically marked as singular (the AGR feature) and selects a subject to be linked to a singular entity in the context (by the feature IND). Different from nouns, the verb's own IND value is a situation index (s0) in which the individual referred to through the SPR value is performing the action of swimming. If the referent of this subject (its IND value) does not match, we would generate an ungrammatical example like **The boys swims*:

(31)

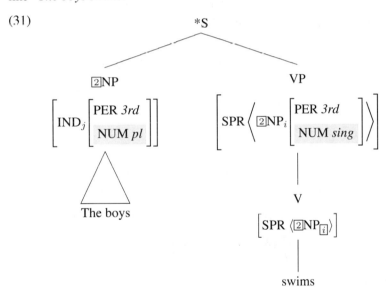

As we can see here, the required subject has the IND value *i*, but the subject has a different IND value *j*.

In the most usual cases, the AGR and IND value are identical, but they can be different, as in examples like (27b). This means that depending on the context, *hash browns* can have different IND values:[7]

---

[6]The IND value of a noun will be an individual index (*i, j, k*, etc) whereas that of a verb or predicative adjective will be a situation index such as *s0, s1, s2*, etc.

[7]As indicated here, the lexical expression now has two features SYN (SYNTAX) and SEM (SEMANTICS). The feature SYN includes HEAD and SPR and COMPS. The feature SEM is for semantic information. As our discussion goes on, we will add more to this part.

(32)

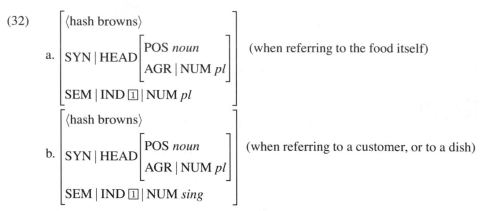

a. (when referring to the food itself)

b. (when referring to a customer, or to a dish)

In the lexical entry (32b), the AGR's NUM value is plural but its IND's NUM value is singular. As shown by (27), the reference *hash browns* can be transferred from cooked potatoes to the customer who ordered it. This means that given an appropriate context, there could be a mismatch between the morphological form of a noun and the index value that the noun refers to.

What this indicates is that subject-verb agreement and noun-specifier agreement are different. In fact, English determiner-noun agreement is only a reflection of morpho-syntactic agreement features between determiner and noun, whereas both subject-verb agreement and pronoun-antecedent agreement are index-based agreement. This is represented in (33).

(33)   Morpho-syntactic agreement (AGR)

Det   head-noun   verb   . . .

Index agreement (IND)

Such agreement patterns can be clearly found in examples like the following where the underlined parts have singular agreement with *four pounds*, which is internally plural.

(34)   [Four pounds] <u>was</u> quite a bit of money in 1950 and <u>it</u> was not easy to come by.

Given the separation of the morphological AGR value and the semantic IND value, nothing blocks mismatches between the two (AGR and IND) as long as all the other constraints are satisfied. Observe further examples in the following:

(35)   a.   [Five pounds] is/*are a lot of money.

b.   [Two drops] deodorizes/*deodorize anything in your house.

c.   [Fifteen dollars] in a week is/*are not much.

d.   [Fifteen years] represents/*represent a long period of his life.

e.   [Two miles] is/*are as far as they can walk.

In all of these examples with measure nouns, the plural subject combines with a singular verb. An apparent conflict arises from the agreement features of the head noun. For proper agreement inside the noun phrase, the head noun has to be plural, but for subject-verb agreement the noun has to be singular. Consider the example in (35a). The nouns *pounds* and *drops* here are morphologically plural and thus must select a plural determiner, as argued so far. But when these nouns are anchored to the group as a whole – that is, conceptualized as referring to a single measure, the index value has to be singular, as represented in (36).

(36)
$$
\begin{bmatrix}
\langle\text{pounds}\rangle \\[4pt]
\text{SYN}\begin{bmatrix}
\text{HEAD}\begin{bmatrix} \text{POS } noun \\ \text{AGR } \boxed{1}\,|\ \text{NUM } pl \end{bmatrix} \\[10pt]
\text{SPR}\left\langle \text{DP}\big[\text{AGR } \boxed{1}\big] \right\rangle
\end{bmatrix} \\[10pt]
\text{SEM}\,|\,\text{IND}\,|\ \textbf{NUM } sing
\end{bmatrix}
$$

As indicated in the lexical entry (36), the morpho-syntactic number value of *pounds* is plural whereas the index value is singular. In the present analysis, this would mean that *pounds* will combine with a plural determiner but with a singular verb. This is possible, as noted earlier in section 2, since the index value is anchored to a singular individual in the context of utterance. The present analysis thus generates the following structure for the sentence (35a):

(37)

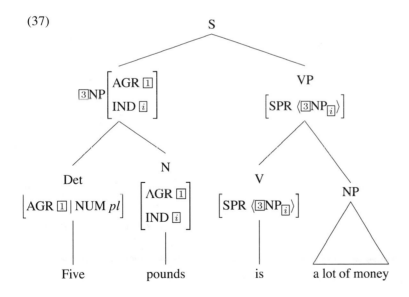

As we can see here, the present analysis takes determiner-head agreement to be morpho-syntactic agreement, and so the head *pounds* needs to refer to only the AGR feature value. This way of looking at English agreement will enable us to explain the following:

(38)   a. *These dollars is what I want to donate to the institute.

     b. *These pounds is a lot of money.

There is nothing wrong in forming *these dollars* or *these pounds* since *dollars* and *pounds* can combine with a plural DP (or determiner). The issue is the agreement between the subject *these dollars* and the verb *is*. Unlike *five dollars* or *five pounds*, *these dollars* and *these pounds* are semantically not taken to refer to a single unit: they always refer to plural entities. Thus no mismatch is allowed in these examples.

However, a similar mismatch between subject and verb is also found in cases with terms for social organizations or collections, as in the following authentic examples:[8]

(39) a. This Government have/has been more transparent in the way they have dealt with public finances than any previous government.

 b. In preparation for the return fixture this team have/has trained more efficiently than they had in recent months.

The head noun *government* or *team* is singular so that it can combine with the singular determiner *this*. But the conflicting fact is that the singular noun phrase can combine even with a plural verb *have* as well as with a singular verb *has*. This is possible since the index value of the subject can be anchored either to a singular or to plural kind of entity. More precisely, we could represent the relevant information of the expressions participating in these agreement relationships as in (40).

(40) a. $\begin{bmatrix} \langle \text{this} \rangle \\ \text{HEAD} \begin{bmatrix} \text{POS } det \\ \text{AGR} \mid \text{NUM} \quad sing \end{bmatrix} \end{bmatrix}$

 b. $\begin{bmatrix} \langle \text{team/government} \rangle \\ \text{SYN} \begin{bmatrix} \text{HEAD} \begin{bmatrix} \text{POS } noun \\ \text{AGR} \mid \text{NUM} \quad sing \end{bmatrix} \end{bmatrix} \\ \text{SEM} \mid \text{IND} \mid \text{NUM} \quad pl \end{bmatrix}$

As represented in (40a) and (40b), *this* and *government* agree each other in terms of the morphosyntactic agreement number value whereas the index value of *government* is what matters for subject-verb agreement. This in turn means that when *government* refers to the individuals in this given group, the whole NP *this government* carries a plural index value.

6.5 Partitive NPs and Agreement

6.5.1 Basic Properties

With regard to the NP-internal elements between which we may find instances of agreement, there are two main types of NP in English: simple NPs and partitive NPs, shown in (41) and

---

[8]For some speakers, a plural verb does not go with the singular subject *this team*, and the neutral determiner *the* is much better. There are also famous differences between American and British English as to agreement with collective nouns.

(42) respectively.

(41)   a.   **some** objections

   b.   **most** students

   c.   **all** students

   d.   **much** worry

   e.   **many** students

   f.   **neither** cars

(42)   a.   **some** of the objections

   b.   **most** of the students

   c.   **all** of the students

   d.   **much** of her worry

   e.   **many** of the students

   f.   **neither** of the cars

As in (42), the partitive phrases have a quantifier followed by an *of*-phrase, designating a set with respect to which certain individuals are quantified. In terms of semantics, these partitive NPs are different from simple NPs in several respects.

First, the lower NP in partitive phrases must be definite; and in the *of*-phrase, no quantificational NP is allowed, as shown in (43):

(43)   a.   Each student   vs.   each of the students   vs.   *each of students

   b.   Some problems   vs.   some of the problems   vs.   *some of many problems

Second, not all determiners with quantificational force can appear in partitive constructions. As shown in (44), determiners such as *the, every* and *no* cannot occupy the first position:

(44)   a.   *the of the students vs. the students

   b.   *every of his ideas vs. every idea

   c.   *no of your books vs. no book(s)

Third, simple NPs and partitive NPs have different restrictions relative to the semantic head. Observe the contrast between (45) and (46):

(45)   a.   She doesn't believe **much of that story**.

   b.   We listened to as **little of his speech** as possible.

   c.   How **much of the fresco** did the flood damage?

   d.   I read **some of the book**.

(46)   a.   *She doesn't believe **much story**.

   b.   *We listened to as **little speech** as possible.

   c.   *How **much fresco** did the flood damage?

   d.   *I read **some book**.

The partitive constructions in (45) allow a mass (non-count) quantifier such as *much, little* and *some* to cooccur with a lower *of*-NP containing a singular count noun. But as we can see in (46), the same elements serving as determiners cannot directly precede such nouns.

Another difference concerns lexical idiosyncrasies.

(47) a. One of the people was dying of thirst.
       b. Many of the people were dying of thirst.

(48) a. *One people was dying of thirst.
       b. Many people were dying of thirst.

The partitives can be headed by quantifiers like *one* and *many*, as shown in (47) and (48) but unlike *many*, *one* cannot serve as a determiner when the head noun is collective as in (48a).

6.5.2 Two Types of Partitive NPs

We classify partitive NPs into two types based on the agreement facts, and call them Type I and Type II. In Type I, the number value of the partitive phrase depends on the preceding head noun whereas in Type II, the number value depends on the head noun inside the *of*-NP phrase. Observe Type I examples.

(49)   Type I:
        a. **Each** of the suggestions is acceptable.
        b. **Neither** of the cars has air conditioning.
        c. **None** of these men wants to be president.

We can observe here that the verb's number value is determined by the preceding expression *each, neither* and *none*. Now see Type II:

(50)   Type II:
        a. **Most** of the fruit is rotten.
        b. **Most** of the children are here.
        c. **Some** of the soup needs more salt.
        d. **Some** of the diners need menus.
        e. **All** of the land belongs to the government.
        f. **All** of these cars belong to me.

As shown in (50), when the NP following the preposition *of* is singular or uncountable, the main verb is singular. When the NP is plural, the verb is also plural. From a semantic perspective, we see that the class of quantificational indefinite pronouns including *some, half, most* and *all* may combine either singular or plural verbs, depending upon the reference of the *of*-NP phrase. If the meaning of these phrases is about how much of something is meant, the verb is singular; but if the meaning is about how many of something is meant, the verb is plural. The expressions in (51) also exhibit similar behavior in terms of agreement.

(51)   half of, part of, the majority of, the rest of, two-thirds of, a number of (but not *the number of*)

An effective way of capturing the relations between Type I and Type II constructions involves the lexical properties of the quantifiers. First, Type I and Type II involve pronominal forms serving as the head of the constructions, which select an *of*-NP inside which the NP is definite:

(52) a. *neither of students, *some of water

    b. neither of the two linguists/some of the water

However, we know that the two types are different in terms of agreement: the pronouns in the Type I construction are lexically specified to be singular whereas the number value for Type II comes from inside the selected PP.

A slight digression is in order. It is easy to see that there are prepositions whose functions are just grammatical markers.

(53) a. John is in the room.

    b. I am fond of him.

The predicative preposition *in* here selects two arguments *John* and *the room*. Meanwhile, the preposition *of* has no predicative meaning, but just functions as a marker to the argument of *fond*. As for the PPs headed by these markers, as in the partitive construction, their semantic features are identical with the prepositional object NP. There is no semantic difference (such as definiteness effect represented as the feature DEF in the present system) between the PP *of him* and the NP *him*.

Given this analysis in which the PP in the partitive construction has the identical AGR and semantic features (e.g., DEF) with its inner NP, we can lexically encode the similarities and differences between Type I and Type II in a simple manner:

(54) a.
$$\begin{bmatrix} \langle\text{neither}\rangle \\ \text{HEAD} \begin{bmatrix} \text{POS } noun \\ \text{AGR} \mid \text{NUM } sing \end{bmatrix} \\ \text{COMPS} \left\langle \text{PP} \begin{bmatrix} \text{PFORM } of \\ \text{DEF } + \end{bmatrix} \right\rangle \end{bmatrix}$$

    b.
$$\begin{bmatrix} \langle\text{some}\rangle \\ \text{HEAD} \begin{bmatrix} \text{POS } noun \\ \text{AGR} \mid \text{NUM } \boxed{1} \end{bmatrix} \\ \text{COMPS} \left\langle \text{PP} \begin{bmatrix} \text{PFORM } of \\ \text{DEF } + \\ \text{AGR} \mid \text{NUM } \boxed{1} \end{bmatrix} \right\rangle \end{bmatrix}$$

(54) shows that both Type I *neither* and Type II *some* are lexically specified to require a PP complement whose semantic value includes the definite (DEF) feature (with the value +). This will account for the contrast in (52). However, the two types are different in terms of their AGR's NUM value. The NUM value of Type I *neither* is singular, whereas that of Type II is identified with the PP's NUM value which is actually coming from its prepositional object NP. Showing these differences in the syntactic structures, we have the alternatives in (55):

(55)   a.

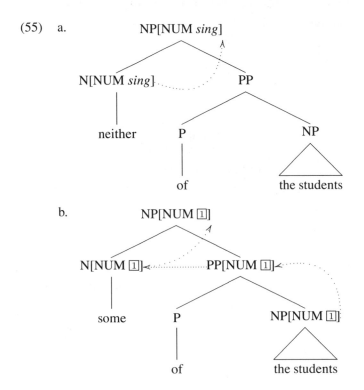

As shown in (55a), for Type I, it is *neither* which determines the NUM value of the whole NP phrase. However, for Type II, it is the NP *the students* which determines the NUM value of the whole NP.

We can check a few of the consequences of these different specifications in the two Types. Consider the contrast in (56):

(56)   a.   many of the/those/her apples

       b.   *many of some/all/no apples

(56b) is ungrammatical since *many* requires an *of*-PP phrase whose DEF value is positive.

This system also offers a simple way of dealing with the fact that quantifiers like *each* affect the NUM value as well as the countability of the *of*-NP phrase. One difference between Type I and Type II is that Type I selects a plural *of*-NP phrase whereas Type II has no such restriction. This is illustrated in (57) and (58).

(57)   Type I:

    a.   one of the suggestions/*the suggestion/*his advice

    b.   each of the suggestions/*the suggestion/*his advice

    c.   neither of the students/*the student/*his advice

(58)   Type II:

    a.   some of his advice/students

    b.   most of his advice/students

    c.   all of his advice/students

The only additional specification we need for Type I pronouns relates to the NUM value on the PP's complement as given in (59):

(59)
$$
\begin{bmatrix}
\langle each \rangle \\[4pt]
\text{HEAD} \begin{bmatrix} \text{POS } noun \\ \text{AGR} \mid \text{NUM } sing \end{bmatrix} \\[12pt]
\text{COMPS} \left\langle \text{PP} \begin{bmatrix} \text{PFORM } of \\ \text{DEF} + \\ \text{NUM } pl \end{bmatrix} \right\rangle
\end{bmatrix}
$$

We see that quantifiers like *each* select a PP complement whose NUM value is plural.

Type II pronouns do not have such a requirement on the PP complement – note that all the examples in (60) are acceptable, in contrast to those in (61) (cf. Baker, C. L. (1995)):

(60) a.   Most of John's boat has been repainted.

    b.   Some of the record contains evidence of wrongdoing.

    c.   Much of that theory is unfounded.

(61) a.   *Each of John's boat has been repainted.

    b.   *Many of the record contained evidence of wrongdoing.

    c.   *One of the story has appeared in your newspaper.

The contrast here indicates that Type II pronouns can combine with a PP whose inner NP is singular. This is simply predicted since our analysis allows the inner NP to be either plural or singular (or uncountable).

We are also in a position now to understand some differences between simple NPs and partitive NPs. Consider the following examples:

(62) a.   many dogs/*much dog/the dogs

    b.   much furniture/*many furniture/the furniture

(63) a.   few dogs/*few dog/*little dogs/*little dog

    b.   little furniture/*little furnitures/*few furniture/*few furnitures

The data here indicate that in addition to the agreement features we have seen so far, common nouns also place a restriction on the countability value of the selected specifier. Specifically, a countable noun selects a countable determiner as its specifier. To capture this agreement restriction, we introduce a new feature COUNT (COUNTABLE):

(64)

$$
\text{a.} \begin{bmatrix} \langle\text{dogs}\rangle \\ \text{HEAD} \mid \text{POS } noun \\ \text{SPR } \langle\text{DP[COUNT +]}\rangle \end{bmatrix}
\qquad
\text{b.} \begin{bmatrix} \langle\text{furniture}\rangle \\ \text{HEAD} \mid \text{POS } noun \\ \text{SPR } \langle\text{DP[COUNT –]}\rangle \end{bmatrix}
$$

The lexical specification on a countable noun like *dogs* requires its specifier to be [COUNT +], to prevent formations like **much dogs*. This in turn means that determiners must also carry the feature COUNT:

(65)

$$
\text{a.} \begin{bmatrix} \langle\text{many}\rangle \\ \text{HEAD} \begin{bmatrix} \text{POS } det \\ \text{COUNT +} \end{bmatrix} \end{bmatrix}
\qquad
\text{b.} \begin{bmatrix} \langle\text{the}\rangle \\ \text{HEAD} \begin{bmatrix} \text{POS } det \\ \text{COUNT +/–} \end{bmatrix} \end{bmatrix}
$$

$$
\text{c.} \begin{bmatrix} \langle\text{little}\rangle \\ \text{HEAD} \begin{bmatrix} \text{POS } det \\ \text{COUNT –} \end{bmatrix} \end{bmatrix}
$$

Notice here that some determiners such as *the* are not specified for a value for COUNT. Effectively, the value can be either + or −, licensing combination with either a countable or an uncountable noun (*the book* or *the furniture*).

    Now consider the following contrast:

(66)   a.   much advice vs. *many advice

          b. *much story vs. many stories

(67)   a.   much of the advice vs. *many of the advice

          b.   much of the story vs. many of the stories

Due to the feature COUNT, we understand now the contrast between *much advice* and **many advice* or the contrast between **much story* and *many stories*. The facts in partitive structures are slightly different, as (67) shows, but the patterns in the data directly follow from these lexical entries:

(68)

a.
$$\begin{bmatrix} \langle \text{many} \rangle \\ \text{HEAD} \mid \text{POS } noun \\ \text{COMPS} \left\langle \text{PP} \begin{bmatrix} \text{PFORM } of \\ \text{NUM } pl \\ \text{DEF} + \end{bmatrix} \right\rangle \end{bmatrix}$$

b.
$$\begin{bmatrix} \langle \text{much} \rangle \\ \text{HEAD} \mid \text{POS } noun \\ \text{COMPS} \left\langle \text{PP} \begin{bmatrix} \text{PFORM } of \\ \text{NUM } sing \\ \text{DEF} + \end{bmatrix} \right\rangle \end{bmatrix}$$

The pronoun *many* requires a PP complement whose inner NP is plural, whereas *much* does not.

6.5.3 Measure Noun Phrases

There are also so-called 'measure noun phrase' constructions, which are similar to partitive constructions. Consider the following contrast:

(69) a. one pound of those beans

b. three feet of that wire

c. a quart of Bob's cider

(70) a. one pound of beans

b. three feet of wire

c. a quart of cider

Notice here that (69) is a kind of partitive construction whereas (70) just measures the amount of the NP after *of*. As the examples show, measure noun phrases do not require a definite article, which is not an option for the true partitive constructions, repeated here:

(71) *many of beans, *some of wire, *much of cider, *none of yogurt, *one of strawberries

In addition, there are several more differences between partitive and measure noun phrases. For example, measure nouns cannot occur in simple noun phrases. They obligatorily require an *of*-NP phrase:

(72) a. *one pound beans vs. one pound of beans

b. *three feet wire vs. three feet of wire

c. *a quart cider vs. a quart of cider

Further, unlike partitive constructions, measure noun phrases require a numeral (or a certain determiner) as their specifier:

(73) a. *one many of the books, *several much of the beer

b. one pound of beans, three feet of wire

As noted here, *many* or *much* in the partitive constructions cannot combine with numerals like *one* or *several*; measure nouns *pound* and *feet* need to combine with a numeral like *one* or *three*.

Further complications arise due to the existence of defective measure noun phrases. Consider the following examples:

(74) a. *a can tomatoes/a can of tomatoes/one can of tomatoes

    b. a few suggestions/*a few of suggestions/*one few of suggestions

    c. *a lot suggestions/a lot of suggestions/*one lot of suggestions

Expressions like *few* and *lot* actually behave quite differently. With respect to *few*, it appears that *a few* acts like a complex word. However, *lot* acts more like a noun, but unlike *can*, it does not allow its specifier to be a numeral.

    In terms of agreement, measure noun phrases behave like Type I partitive constructions:

(75)   a. A can of tomatoes is/*are added.

        b. Two cans of tomatoes are/*is added.

We can see here that it is the head noun *can* or *cans* which determines the NUM value of the whole NP. The inner NP in the PP does not affect the NUM value at all. These observations lead us to posit the following lexical entry for a measure noun:[9]

(76)
$$
\begin{bmatrix}
\langle\text{pound}\rangle \\
\text{HEAD}\begin{bmatrix} \text{POS } noun \\ \text{NUM } sing \end{bmatrix} \\
\text{SPR } \langle\text{DP}\rangle \\
\text{COMPS } \left\langle \text{PP}\begin{bmatrix}\text{PFORM } of\end{bmatrix} \right\rangle
\end{bmatrix}
$$

That is, a measure noun like *pound* requires one obligatory SPR and a PP complement. Unlike partitive constructions, there is no definiteness restriction on the PP complement.

    Finally, there is one set of words whose behavior leaves them somewhere between quantity words and measure nouns. These are words such as *dozen*, *hundred*, and *thousand*:

(77)   a. three hundred of your friends

        b. *three hundreds of your friends

        c. *three hundreds of friends

        d. three hundred friends

        e. hundreds of friends/*hundreds friends

Consider the behavior of *hundred* and *hundreds* here. The singular *hundred*, when used as noun, obligatorily requires a PP[*of*] complement as well as a numeral specifier, as in (77a). Even if the specifier is *one*, the whole phrase triggers plural agreement: *One hundred of my friends *is/are here*. The formally plural *hundreds* requires no specifier although it also selects a PP complement. Not surprisingly, similar behavior can be observed with *thousand* and *thousands*:

(78)   a. several thousand of Bill's supporters

        b. *several thousands of Bill's supporters

---

[9]To be more specific, not all determiners are allowed here. For example, a possessive determiner will not function as a specifier of the measure noun as in *his pound of those beans*.

    c. *several thousands of supporters

    d. several thousand supporters

    e. thousands of supporters/*thousands supporters

One way to capture these properties is to assign the following lexical specifications to *hundred* and *hundreds*:

(79)
a.
$$\begin{bmatrix} \langle \text{hundred} \rangle \\ \text{HEAD} \mid \text{POS } noun \\ \text{SPR } \langle \text{DP} \rangle \\ \text{COMPS } \langle \text{PP[PFORM } of] \rangle \end{bmatrix}$$
b.
$$\begin{bmatrix} \langle \text{hundreds} \rangle \\ \text{HEAD} \mid \text{POS } noun \\ \text{SPR } \langle \ \rangle \\ \text{COMPS } \langle \text{PP[PFORM } of] \rangle \end{bmatrix}$$

Even though there may be some semantic reasons for all these different kinds of lexical specifications, for now, stating it all directly in the lexical entries will account at least for the data given here.

6.6 Modifying an NP

6.6.1 Adjectives as Prenominal Modifiers

Adjectives are expressions commonly used to modify a noun. However, not all adjectives can modify nouns. Even though most adjectives can be used either as in a modifying (attributive) function or as a predicate (as in *She is tall*), certain adjectives are restricted to their usages. Adjectives such *alive, asleep, awake, afraid, ashamed, aware*, can be used only predicatively, whereas others such as *wooden, drunken, golden, main* and *mere* are only used attributively:

(80) a. He is alive.

      b. He is afraid of foxes.

(81) a. It is a wooden desk.

      b. It is a golden hair.

      c. It is the main street.

(82) a. *It is an alive fish. (cf. living fish)

      b. *They are afraid people. (cf. nervous people)

(83) a. *This objection is main. (cf. the main objection)

      b. *This fact is key. (cf. a key fact)

The predicatively-used adjectives are specified with the feature PRD, and with a MOD value being empty as default, as shown here:[10]

---

[10] All modifiers carry the head feature MOD.

(84)
$$\begin{bmatrix} \langle alive \rangle \\ HEAD \begin{bmatrix} POS \ adj \\ PRD \ + \\ MOD \ \langle \quad \rangle \end{bmatrix} \end{bmatrix}$$

This says that *alive* is used predicatively, and does not have a specification for a MOD value (the value is empty). This lexical information will prevent predicative adjectives from also functioning as noun modifiers.[11]

In contrast to the predicative adjective, a modifying adjective will have the following lexical entry:

(85)
$$\begin{bmatrix} \langle brave \rangle \\ HEAD \begin{bmatrix} POS \ adj \\ MOD \ \langle N' \rangle \end{bmatrix} \end{bmatrix}$$

This specifies an adjective which modifies any value whose POS is *noun*. This will license a structure like the following:

(86)

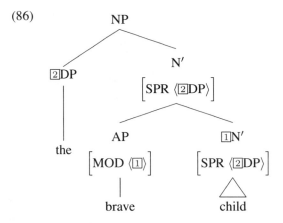

6.6.2 Postnominal Modifiers

Postnominal modifiers are basically the same as prenominal modifiers with respect to what they are modifying. The only difference is that they come after what they modify. Various phrases can function as such postnominal modifiers:[12]

(87) a. [The boy [in the doorway]] waved to his father.

---

[11] In addition, all predicative expressions select one argument, their subject (SPR). This information is not shown here.

[12] As noted in Chapter 4, the approach here assumes that the relative linear order of a head, complements, and modifiers is determined by a combination of general and language-specific ordering principles. For example, a simple AP modifier will precede its head whereas a PP or complex AP modifier will follow the head.

b. [The man [eager to start the meeting]] is John's sister.

c. [The man [holding the bottle]] disappeared.

d. [The papers [removed from the safe]] have not been found.

e. [The money [that you gave me]] disappeared last night.

All these postnominal elements bear the feature MOD. Leaving aside detailed discussion of the relative clause(-like) modifiers in b–e until Chapter 12, we can say that example (87a) will have the following structure:

(88)

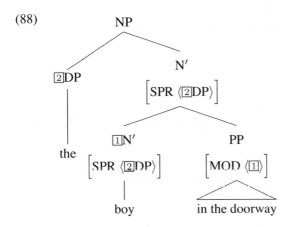

These modifiers must modify an N′, but not a complete NP. This claim is consistent with the examples above and with the (ungrammatical) examples in (89):

(89)   a. *John in the doorway waved to his father.

b. *He in the doorway waved to his father.

A proper noun or a pronoun projects directly to the NP, with no complement or specifier. If it were the case that post-nominal PPs could modify any NP, these examples ought to be acceptable.

6.7   Exercises

1. Draw tree structures for the following and mark which expression determines the agreement (AGR) and index values of the subject NP and the main verb.

    (i) a.   Neither of these men is worthy to lead Italy.
        b.   None of his customary excuses suffices Edgar now.
        c.   One of the problems was the robins.
        d.   All of the plant virus web sites have been conveniently collected in one central location.
        e.   Some of the water from melted snow also goes into the ground for plants.
        f.   Most of the milk your baby ingests during breastfeeding is produced during nursing.
        g.   All special rights of voting in the election were abolished.
        h.   One of major factors affecting the value of diamonds was their weight.
        i.   Each of these stones has to be cut and polished.
        j.   Most of her free time was spent attending concerts and plays or visiting museums and art galleries.

2. Provide a detailed analysis for the following examples, focusing on subject-verb agreement. In doing so, provide the correct AGR and IND value of the subject head noun and the main verb.

    (i) a.   The committee were/*was unanimous in their decision.
        b.   The committee have/*has all now resigned.
        c.   The crew have/*has both agreed to change sponsor.
        d.   Her family are/*is all avid skiers.
        e.   A variety of styles has/*have been in vogue for the last year.

3. Compare the following examples and assign an appropriate structure to each. What kind of lexical category can you assign to *both* and *few*? Can you provide arguments for your decisions?

    (i) a.   Both of the workers will wear carnations.
        b.   Both the workers will wear carnations.
        c.   Both workers will wear carnations.
        d.   Both will wear carnations.

    (ii) a.   Few of the doctors approve of our remedy.
         b.   Few doctors approve of our remedy.
         c.   Few approve of our remedy.

4. Provide the correct VFORM value of the underlined verb and identify the noun that semantically determines this VFORM value.

    (i) a.   An example of these substances <u>be</u> tobacco.
        b.   The effectiveness of teaching and learning <u>depend</u> on several factors.
        c.   One of the most serious problems that some students have <u>be</u> lack of motivation.

    d.   Ten years <u>be</u> a long time to spend in prison.

    e.   Everyone of us <u>be</u> given a prize.

    f.   Some of the fruit <u>be</u> going bad.

    g.   All of his wealth <u>come</u> from real estate investments.

    h.   <u>Do</u> some of your relatives live nearby?

    i.   Fifty pounds <u>seem</u> like a lot of weight to lose in one year.

    j.   News of Persephone and Demeter <u>reach</u> the great gods and goddesses of Olympus.

    k.   Half of the year <u>be</u> dark and wintry.

    l.   Some of the promoters of ostrich meat <u>compare</u> its taste to beef tenderloin.

5. Consider the following pairs of examples and explain the subject-verb and pronoun-antecedent agreement relationships, and how they affect grammaticality:

    (i) a.   The committee$_i$ hasn't yet made up its$_i$/*their$_i$ mind.

         b.   The committee$_i$ haven't yet made up their$_i$/*its$_i$ mind.

    (ii) a.   That dog is so ferocious, it even tried to bite itself.

         b. *That dog is so ferocious, it even tried to bite himself.

6. Consider the distribution of the reflexive pronouns (*myself, yourself, himself, herself*) and simple pronouns (*me, you, he, him, her*), respectively. Provide rules which can explain their distribution, in terms of what the pronoun form must, may, or must not be coreferential with. Please take the grammaticality judgements as given.

    (i) a. *I washed me.

         b.   You washed me.

         c.   He washed me.

    (ii) a.   I washed myself.

         b. *You washed myself.

         c. *He washed myself.

    (iii) a.   I washed you.

         b. *He washed him. (*He* and *him* referring to the same person.)

         c.   He kicked you.

    (iv) a. *I washed yourself.

         b.   You washed yourself.

         c. *He washed yourself.

Once you have your own hypothesis for the above data, now examine the following data, and then determine whether your previous hypothesis can account for this extra data; and if not, revise your hypothesis so that it can extend to these examples:

    (v) a.   Harry says that Sally dislikes him.

         b. *Harry says that Sally dislikes himself.

    (vi) a.   Sally wishes that everyone would praise her.

         b. *Sally wishes that everyone would praise herself.

(vii) a. Sally believes that she is brilliant.

   b. *Sally believes that herself is brilliant.

7. Read the following passages and provide detailed lexical entries for the underlined expressions. For nouns, specify their AGR and IND values.

(i) The <u>power</u> of your mind and the power of your body <u>have</u> a tight connection. If you have a strong body, your mind <u>feels</u> pumped and healthy, too. If you have a strong mind, you can <u>craft</u> your body to accomplish amazing things. I focus on constantly developing this double toughness. I train hard, play hard, and when life <u>snaps</u> at me, I live hard. This philosophy <u>gets</u> me through anything and everything.

(ii) One very important and highly productive <u>feature</u> of nouns in English is that they can be put together to form a new phrase without our having to make any structural changes to the grammar of either noun, as in *tea cup, computer screen, vacuum cleaner, chalk board, internet facility, garden fence*, etc. When two or more nouns combine like this, the first noun is said to modify the second. In a sense, the first noun is playing the role of an adjective, <u>which</u> is what most people have in mind when we think about modification, but nouns can do the job equally well. It is <u>worth</u> mentioning that not every language has this facility, but native <u>speakers</u> of English are quite happy to invent their own combinations of nouns in order to <u>describe</u> things, events or ideas that they have not come across before; this is particularly true in the workplace where we need constantly to <u>refer</u> to innovations and new concepts.[13]

---

[13] Adopted from Waylink English at `http://www.waylink.co.uk/`.

7

Raising and Control Constructions

7.1 Raising and Control Predicates

As noted in Chapter 5, certain verbs select an infinitival VP as their complement. Compare the following pairs of examples:

(1)   a.   John tries to fix the computer.

       b.   John seems to fix the computer.

(2)   a.   Mary persuaded John to fix the computer.

       b.   Mary expected John to fix the computer.

At first glance, these pairs are structurally isomorphic in terms of complements: both *try* and *tend* select an infinitival VP, and *expect* and *persuade* select an NP and an infinitival VP. However, there are several significant differences which motivate two classes, known as **control** and **raising** verbs:

(3)   a.   Control verbs and adjectives: try, hope, eager, persuade, promise, etc.

       b.   Raising verbs and adjectives: seem, appear, happen, likely, certain, believe, expect, etc.

Verbs like *try* are called 'control' or 'equi' verbs, where subject is understood to be 'equivalent' to the unexpressed subject of the infinitival VP. In linguistic terminology, the subject of the verb is said to 'control' the subject of the infinitival complement. Let us consider the 'deep structure' of (1a) representing unexpressed subject of the VP complement of *tries*:[1]

(4)   John tries [(for) John to fix the computer].

As shown here, in this sentence it is John who does the action of fixing the computer. In the original transformational grammar approach, this deep structure would be proposed and then undergo a rule of 'Equivalent NP Deletion' in which the second NP *John* would be deleted, to produce the output sentence. This is why such verbs have the label of 'equi-verbs'.

---

[1] Deep structure, linked to surface structure, is a theoretical construct and abstract level of representation that seeks to unify several related observed forms and played an important role in the transformational grammar of the 20th century. For example, the surface structures of both *The cat chased the mouse* and *The mouse was chased by the cat* are derived from the identical deep structure similar to *The cat chased the mouse.*

Meanwhile, verbs like *seem* are called 'raising' verbs. Consider the deep structure of (1b):

(5)   △ seems [John to fix the computer].

In order to derive the 'surface structure' (1b), the subject *John* needs to be raised to the matrix subject position marked by △. This is why verbs like *seem* are called 'raising' verbs.

This chapter discusses the similarities and differences of these two types of verb, and shows how we explain their respective properties in a systematic way.

7.2   Differences between Raising and Control Verbs

There are many differences between the two classes of verb, which we present here.

7.2.1   Subject Raising and Control

The semantic role of the subject: One clear difference between raising and control verbs is the semantic role assigned to the subject. Let us compare the following examples:

(6)   a.   John tries to be honest.

      b.   John seems to be honest.

These might have paraphrases as follows:

(7)   a.   John makes efforts for himself to be honest.

      b.   It seems that John is honest.

As suggested by the paraphrase, the one who does the action of trying is John in (6a). How about (6b)? Is it John who is involved in the situation of 'seeming'? As represented in its paraphrase (7b), the situation that the verb *seem* describes is not about the individual John, but is rather about the proposition that John is honest. Due to this difference, we say that a control verb like *try* assigns a semantic role to its subject (the 'agent' role), whereas a raising verb *seem* does not assign any semantic role to its subject (this is what (5) is intended to represent).

Expletive subjects: Since the raising verb does not assign a semantic role to its subject, certain expressions which do not have a semantic role or any meaning may appear in the subject position. Such items include the expletives *it* or *there*:

(8)   a.   It tends to be warm in September.

      b.   It seems to bother Kim that they resigned.

The situation is markedly different with control verbs:

(9)   a.   *It/*There tries to be warm in September.

      b.   *It/*There hopes to bother Kim that they resigned.

Since control verbs like *try* and *hope* require their subject to have an agent role, an expletive *it* or *there*, which takes no semantic role, cannot function as their subject.

We can observe the same contrast with respect to raising and control adjectives:

(10)   a.   It/*John is easy to please Maja.

b. John/*It is eager to please Maja.

Since the raising adjective *easy* do not assign any semantic role to its subject, we can have *it* as its subject. On the other hand, the control adjective *eager* assigns a role and thus does not allow the expletive *it* as its subject.

Subcategorization: If we look into what determines the subject's properties, we can see that in raising constructions, it is not the raising verb or adjective, but the infinitival complement's predicate which determines the characteristic of the subject. In raising constructions, the subject of the raising predicate is selected as the subject of the complement VP. Observe the following contrast:

(11) a. Stephen seemed [to be intelligent].

b. It seems [to be easy to fool Ben].

c. There is likely [to be a letter in the mailbox].

d. Tabs are likely [to be kept on participants].
    in the sense of: 'The participants will be spied on.'

(12) a. *There seemed [to be intelligent].

b. *John seems [to be easy to fool Ben].

c. *John is likely [to be a letter in the mailbox].

d. *John is likely [to be kept on participants].

For example, the VP *to be intelligent* requires an animate subject, and this is why (11a) is fine but (12a) is not. Meanwhile, the VP *to be easy to fool Ben* requires the expletive *it* as its subject. This is why *John* cannot be the subject in (12b). The contrast in (c) and (d) is similar. The VP [*to be a letter in the mailbox*] allows its subject to be *there* (cf. *There is a letter in the mailbox*) but not *John*. The VP [to be kept on participants] requires a subject which must be the word *tabs* in order to induce an idiomatic meaning.

In raising constructions, whatever category is required as the subject of the infinitival VP, is also required as the subject by the higher VP – hence the intuition of 'raising': the requirement for the subject passes up to the higher predicate.

However, for control verbs, there is no direct selectional relation between the subject of the main verb and that of the infinitival VP. It is the control verb or adjective itself which fully determines the properties of the subject:

(13) a. Sandy tried [to eat oysters].

b. *There tried [to be riots in Seoul].

c. *It tried [to bother me that Chris lied].

d. *Tabs try [to be kept on Bob by the FBI].

e. *That he is clever is eager [to be obvious].

Regardless of what the infinitival VP would require as its subject, a control predicate requires its subject to be able to bear the semantic role of agent. For example, in (13b) and (13c), the subject of the infinitival VP can be *there* and *it*, but these cannot function as the matrix subject – because the matrix verb *tried* requires its own subject, a 'trier'.

Selectional Restrictions: Closely related to the difference in selection for the type of subject, we can observe a related similarity with regard to what are known as 'selectional restrictions'. The subcategorization frames, which we have represented in terms of VAL (valence) features, are themselves syntactic, but verbs also impose semantic selectional restrictions on their subjects or objects. For example, the verb *thank* requires a human subject and an object that is at least animate:

(14)   a.   The king thanked the man.

b. #The king thanked the throne.

c(?)The king thanked the deer.

d. #The castle thanked the deer.

And consider as well the following examples:

(15)   a.   The color red is his favorite color.

b. #The color red understands the important issues of the day.

Unlike the verb *is*, *understands* requires its subject to be sentient. This selectional restriction then also explains the following contrast:

(16)   a.   The color red seems [to be his favorite color].

b. #The color red tried [to be his favorite color].

The occurrence of the raising verb *seems* does not change the selectional restriction on the subject. However, *tried* is different: just like *understand*, the control verb *tried* requires its subject to be sentient, at least. What we can observe here is that the subject of a raising verb carries the selectional restrictions of the infinitival VP's subject. This in turn means that the subject of the infinitival VP is the subject of the raising verb.

Meaning preservation: We have seen that the subject of a raising predicate is that of the infinitival VP complement, and it has no semantic role at all coming from the raising predicate. This implies that an idiom whose meaning is specially composed from its parts will still retain its meaning even if part of it appears as the subject of a raising verb.

(17)   a.   The cat seems to be out of the bag.

in the sense of: 'The secret is out'.

b. #The cat tries to be out of the bag.

In the raising example (17a), the meaning of the idiom *The cat is out of the bag* is retained. However, since the control verb *tries* assigns a semantic role to its subject *the cat*, 'the cat' must be the one doing the action of trying, and there is no idiomatic meaning.

This preservation of meaning also holds for examples like the following:

(18)   a.   The dentist is likely to examine Pat.

     b.   Pat is likely to be examined by the dentist.

(19)   a.   The dentist is eager to examine Pat.

     b.   Pat is eager to be examined by the dentist.

Since the raising predicate *likely* does not assign a semantic role to its subject, (18a) and (18b) have more or less identical meanings – the proposition is about the dentist examining Pat, in active or passive grammatical forms: the active subject is raised in (18a), and the passive subject in (18b).

However, the control predicate *eager* assigns a semantic role to its subject, and this forces (19a) and (19b) to differ semantically: in (19a), it is the dentist who is eager to examine Pat, whereas in (19b), it is Pat who is eager to be examined by the dentist. Intuitively, if one of the examples in (18) is true, so is the other, but this inference cannot be made in (19).

7.2.2   Object Raising and Control

Similar contrasts are found between what are know as object raising and control predicates:

(20)   a.   Stephen believed Ben to be careful.

     b.   Stephen persuaded Ben to be careful.

Once again, these two verbs look alike in terms of syntax: they both combine with an NP and an infinitival VP complement. However, the two are different with respect to the properties of the object NP in relation to the rest of the structure. Observe the differences between *believe* and *persuade* in (21):

(21)   a.   Stephen believed it to be easy to please Maja.

     b.   *Stephen persuaded it to be easy to please Maja.

(22)   a.   Stephen believed there to be a fountain in the park.

     b.   *Stephen persuaded there to be a fountain in the park.

One thing we can see here is that unlike *believe*, *persuade* does not license an expletive object (just like *try* does not license an expletive subject). And in this respect, the verb *believe* is similar to *seem* in that it does not assign a semantic role (to its object). The differences show up again in the preservation of idiomatic meaning:

(23)   a.   Stephen believed the cat to be out of the bag.

        in the sense: 'Stephen believed that the secret was out'.

     b.   *Stephen persuaded the cat to be out of the bag.

While the idiomatic reading is retained with the raising verb *believed*, it is lost with the control verb *persuaded*.

Active-passive pairs show another contrast:

(24)   a.   The dentist was believed to have examined Pat.

     b.   Pat was believed to have been examined by the dentist.

(25) a. The dentist was persuaded to examine Pat.

  b. Pat was persuaded to be examined by the dentist.

With the raising verb *believe*, there is no strong semantic difference in the examples in (24). However, in (25), there is a clear difference in who is persuaded. In (25a), it is the dentist, but in (25b), it is Pat who is persuaded. This is one more piece of evidence that *believe* is a raising verb whereas *persuade* is a control verb, with respect to the object.

7.3   A Simple Transformational Approach

How then can we account for these differences between raising and control verbs or adjectives? A simple traditional analysis, hinted at earlier, is to derive a surface structure via a derivational process, for example, from (26a) to (26b):

(26) a. Deep structure: △ seems [Stephen to be irritating]

  b. Surface structure: Stephen seems [t] to be irritating.

To derive (26b), the subject of the infinitival VP in (26a) moves to the matrix subject position, as represented in the following tree structure:

(27)

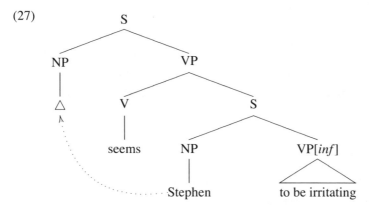

The movement of the subject *Stephen* to the higher subject position will correctly generate (26b). This kind of movement to the subject position can be triggered by the requirement that each English declarative have a surface subject (cf. Chomsky (1981)). A similar movement process can be applied to the object raising cases:

(28) a. Deep structure: Tom believes △ [Stephen to be irritating].

  b. Surface structure: Tom believes Stephen to be irritating.

Here the embedded subject *Stephen* moves not to the matrix subject but to the matrix object position:

(29)

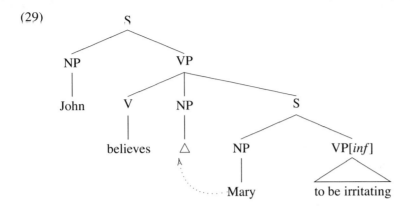

Control constructions are different: there is no movement operation involved. Instead, it is the lower subject position which has special properties. Consider the examples in (30):

(30) a. John tried to please Stephen.

  b. John persuaded Stephen to be more careful.

Since *try* and *persuade* assign a semantic roles to their subject, and objects, an unfilled position of the kind designated above by △ cannot be allowed. Instead, it is posited that there is an unexpressed subject of the infinitival VP *to please Stephen* and *to be more careful*. This is traditionally represented as the element called 'PRO' (a silent 'pro'noun), and the examples will have the following deep structures:

(31) a. John tried [PRO to please Stephen].

  b. John persuaded Stephen [PRO to be more careful].

The final tree representations of these are as follows:

(32) a.

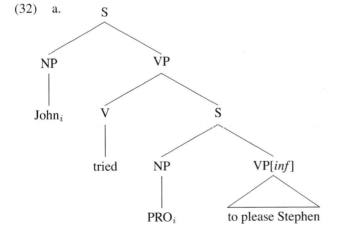

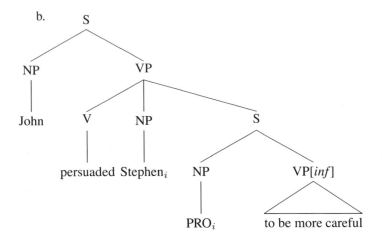

An independent part of the theory of control links PRO in each case to its antecedent, marked by coindexing. In (32a), PRO is coindexed with *John* whereas in (32b), it is coindexed with *Stephen*.

These analyses which involve derivations on tree structures are driven by the assumption that the mapping between semantics and syntax is very direct. For example, in (29), the verb *believe* semantically selects an experiencer and a proposition, and this is reflected in the initial structure. In some syntactic respects, though, *believe* acts like it has an NP object (separate from the infintival complement), and the raising operation creates this object. In contrast, *persuade* semantically selects an agent, a patient, and a proposition, and hence the structure in (32b) reflects this: the object position is there all along, so to speak.

The classical transformational approach provides a useful graphical approach to understanding the difference between raising and control. However, it requires assumptions about the nature of grammar rather different from what we have made throughout this book. In the rest of this chapter, we present a nontransformational account of control and raising.

7.4   A Nontransformational Approach

7.4.1   Identical Syntactic Structures

Instead of the movement approach in which movement operations and various kinds of empty elements or positions play crucial roles, we simply focus directly on the surface structures of raising and control constructions. Going back to *seem* and *try*, we can observe that both select an infinitival VP, as in (33), giving the structures in (34):

(33)   a. $\begin{bmatrix} \langle \text{seems} \rangle \\ \text{SPR} \quad \langle \text{NP} \rangle \\ \text{COMPS} \quad \langle \text{VP} \begin{bmatrix} \text{VFORM} & inf \end{bmatrix} \rangle \end{bmatrix}$

b.
$$\begin{bmatrix} \langle tries \rangle \\ \text{SPR} \quad \langle NP \rangle \\ \text{COMPS} \quad \langle VP\begin{bmatrix} \text{VFORM } inf \end{bmatrix} \rangle \end{bmatrix}$$

(34)   a.

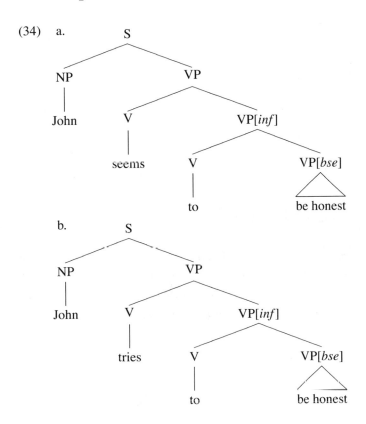

b.

As shown here, *seems* and *tries* actually have identical structures.

The object raising verb *expect* and the control verb *persuade* also have identical valence (SPR and COMPS) information:

(35)   a.
$$\begin{bmatrix} \langle expects \rangle \\ \text{SPR} \quad \langle NP \rangle \\ \text{COMPS} \quad \langle NP, VP\begin{bmatrix} \text{VFORM } inf \end{bmatrix} \rangle \end{bmatrix}$$

   b.
$$\begin{bmatrix} \langle persuaded \rangle \\ \text{SPR} \quad \langle NP \rangle \\ \text{COMPS} \quad \langle NP, VP\begin{bmatrix} \text{VFORM } inf \end{bmatrix} \rangle \end{bmatrix}$$

These two lexical entries will license the following structures:

(36) a.

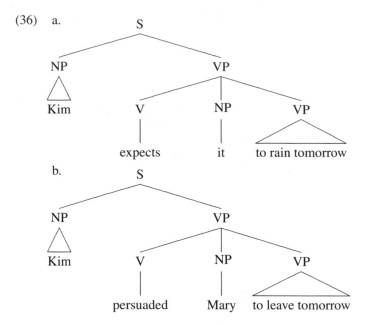

b.

As can be seen here, raising and control verbs are not different in terms of their subcategorization or valence requirements, and so they project similar structures. The question is then how we can capture the different properties of raising and control verbs. The answer is that their differences follow from the other parts of the lexical information, in particular, the mapping relations from syntax to semantics.

7.4.2 Differences in Subcategorization Information

We have observed that for raising predicates, whatever kind of category is required as subject by the infinitival VP is also required as the subject of the predicate. Some of the key examples are repeated here:

(37) a. Stephen/*It/*There seemed to be intelligent.

     b. It seemed to rain.

     c. There seemed to be a fountain in the park.

(38) a. Stephen/*It/*There tried to be intelligent.

     b. *It tried to rain.

     c. *There tried to be a fountain in the park.

While the subject of a raising predicate is identical to that of the infinitival VP complement, the subject of a control predicate has a different requirement. The subject of a control predicate is coindexed with that of the infinitival VP complement. This difference can be represented in the lexical information shown in (39). The raising verb involves shared subjects, while the control verb only shares the semantic index (of the subjects).

(39) a. $\begin{bmatrix} \langle \text{seemed} \rangle \\ \text{SPR} \qquad \langle\ \boxed{1}\ \rangle \\ \text{COMPS} \quad \left\langle \text{VP}\begin{bmatrix} \text{VFORM } \textit{inf} \\ \text{SPR } \langle\ \boxed{1}\ \rangle \end{bmatrix} \right\rangle \end{bmatrix}$

   b. $\begin{bmatrix} \langle \text{tried} \rangle \\ \text{SPR} \qquad \langle\ \text{NP}_i\ \rangle \\ \text{COMPS} \quad \left\langle \text{VP}\begin{bmatrix} \text{VFORM } \textit{inf} \\ \text{SPR } \langle\ \text{NP}_i\ \rangle \end{bmatrix} \right\rangle \end{bmatrix}$

These two lexical entries represent the difference between *seem* and *try*: for *seemed*, the subject of the VP complement is fully identical with its own subject (notated by $\boxed{1}$) whereas for *tried*, only the index value of its VP complement is identical to that of its subject, meaning that the VP complement's understood subject refers to the same individual as the subject of *tried*.[2] This index identity in control constructions is clear when we consider examples like the following:

(40)   Someone$_i$ tried NP$_i$ to leave the town.

The example here means that whoever *someone* might refer to, that same person left town. The lexical entries in (39) generate following structures for the intransitive raising and control sentences:

---

[2]This account has parallels with the treatment in Government-Binding Theory (Chomsky (1981)), in which the subject of complement of a raising verb is a trace of movement, left behind when the subject raises; in the complement of control predicates, the subject is *PRO*, a kind of pronoun, which shares only its referential index with the matrix subject.

(41) a.

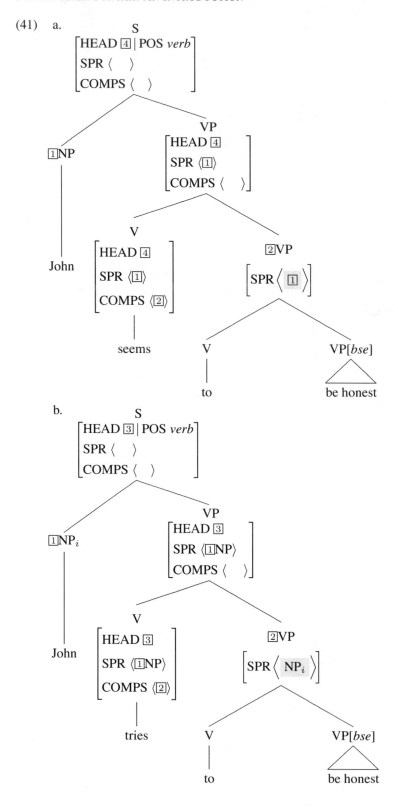

b.

It is easy to verify that these structures conform to all the grammar rules (the Head-Specifier Rule and Head-Complement Rule) and principles such as the HFP and the VALP.

Object raising and control predicates are no different. Raising verbs select a VP complement whose subject is fully identical with the object. Control verbs select a VP complement whose subject's index value is identical with that of its object. The following lexical entries show these properties:

(42)   a. $\begin{bmatrix} \langle expect \rangle \\ SPR \quad \langle \boxed{1}NP_i \rangle \\ COMPS \quad \left\langle \boxed{2}NP \, , \, VP \begin{bmatrix} VFORM \ inf \\ SPR \ \langle \boxed{2}NP \rangle \end{bmatrix} \right\rangle \end{bmatrix}$

   b. $\begin{bmatrix} \langle persuade \rangle \\ SPR \quad \langle NP \rangle \\ COMPS \quad \left\langle NP_i \, , \, VP \begin{bmatrix} VFORM \ inf \\ SPR \ \langle NP_i \rangle \end{bmatrix} \right\rangle \end{bmatrix}$

Let us look at the structures these lexical entries eventually project:

(43)

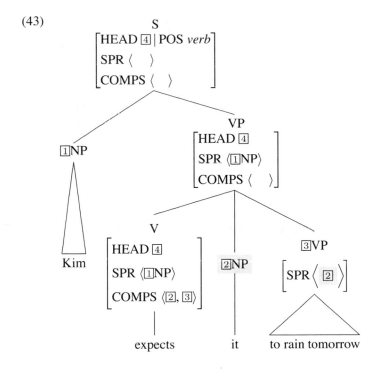

(44)

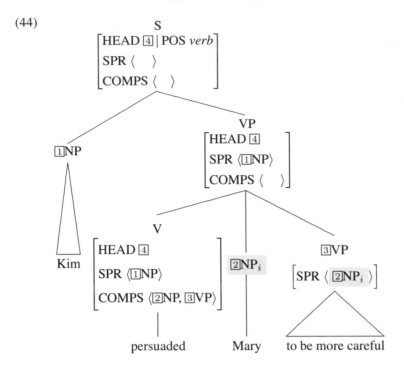

As represented here, the subject of *to rain tomorrow* in (43) is the NP object of *expects*, while the subject of *to be more careful* in (44) is coindexed with the independent object of *persuade*.

7.4.3 Mismatch between Meaning and Structure

We have not yet addressed the issue of differences in the assignment of semantic roles. We first need to introduce further semantic features, distinguished from syntactic features, for this issue is closely related to the relationship between syntax and semantics. As we have seen in Chapter 6, nouns and verbs have IND values. That is, a noun refers to an individual (e.g., i, j, k, etc) whereas a verb denotes a situation (e.g., s0, s1, s2, etc). In addition, a predicate represents a semantic property or relation. For example, the meaning of the verb *hits* in (45a) can be represented in canonical first-order predicate logic as in (45b):

(45)　a.　John hits a ball.

　　　b.　hit′(j, b)

This shows that the verb *hit* takes two arguments with the predicate relation *hit*, with the ′ notation to indicate the semantic value. The relevant semantic properties can be represented in a feature structure system as follows:

(46)
$$
\begin{bmatrix}
\langle hit \rangle \\[4pt]
SYN \mid VAL \begin{bmatrix} SPR & \langle NP_i \rangle \\ COMPS & \langle NP_j \rangle \end{bmatrix} \\[12pt]
SEM \begin{bmatrix} IND \; s0 \\ RELS \left\langle \begin{bmatrix} PRED & hit \\ AGENT & i \\ PATIENT & j \end{bmatrix} \right\rangle \end{bmatrix}
\end{bmatrix}
$$

In terms of syntax, *hit* is a verb selecting a subject and a complement, as shown in the value of the feature SYN(TAX). The semantic information of the verb is represented with the feature SEM(ANTICS). It first has the attribute IND(EX), representing what this expression refers to; as a verb, *hit* refers to a situation $s0$ in which an individual i hits an individual j. The semantic relation of hitting is represented using the feature for semantic relations (RELS). The feature RELS has as its value a list of one feature structure, here with three further features, PRED(ICATE), AGENT, and PATIENT. The predicate (PRED) relation is whatever the verb denotes: in this case, *hit* takes two arguments. The AGENT argument in the SEM value is coindexed with the SPR in the SYN value, while the the PATIENT is coindexed with COMPS. This coindexing links the subcategorization information of *hit* with the arguments in its semantic relation. Simply put, the lexical entry in (46) is the formal representation of the fact that in *X hits Y*, X is the hitter and Y is the one hit.

Now we can use these extra parts of the representation for the semantic differences in raising and control verbs. The subject of a raising verb like *seem* is not assigned any semantic role, while that of a control verb like *try* is definitely linked to a semantic role. Assuming that 's0' or 's1' stands for situations denoted by an infinitival VP, *seem* and *try* will have the following simplified meaning representations:

(47) a. seem'(s1) ('s1 seems (to be the case") = s0')

  b. try'(i, s1) ('i tries to (make) s1 (be the case) = s0')

These meaning differences are represented in terms of feature structures as follows:

(48)   a.
$$
\begin{bmatrix}
\langle\, seem\,\rangle \\[6pt]
\text{SYN} \mid \text{VAL}
\begin{bmatrix}
\text{SPR} \;\langle\, \boxed{1}\, \rangle \\[6pt]
\text{COMPS} \left\langle\, \text{VP}
\begin{bmatrix}
\text{VFORM} & inf \\
\text{SPR} & \langle\, \boxed{1}\, \rangle \\
\text{IND} & s1
\end{bmatrix}
\right\rangle
\end{bmatrix} \\[18pt]
\text{SEM}
\begin{bmatrix}
\text{IND}\; s0 \\[4pt]
\text{RELS} \left\langle\,
\begin{bmatrix}
\text{PRED} & seem \\
\text{SIT} & s1
\end{bmatrix}
\, \right\rangle
\end{bmatrix}
\end{bmatrix}
$$

   b.
$$
\begin{bmatrix}
\langle\, try\,\rangle \\[6pt]
\text{SYN} \mid \text{VAL}
\begin{bmatrix}
\text{SPR} \;\langle\, \text{NP}_i\, \rangle \\[6pt]
\text{COMPS} \left\langle\, \text{VP}
\begin{bmatrix}
\text{VFORM} & inf \\
\text{SPR} & \langle\, \text{NP}_i\, \rangle \\
\text{IND} & s1
\end{bmatrix}
\right\rangle
\end{bmatrix} \\[18pt]
\text{SEM}
\begin{bmatrix}
\text{IND}\; s0 \\[4pt]
\text{RELS} \left\langle\,
\begin{bmatrix}
\text{PRED} & try \\
\text{AGENT} & i \\
\text{SIT} & s1
\end{bmatrix}
\, \right\rangle
\end{bmatrix}
\end{bmatrix}
$$

We can see here that even though the verb *seem* selects two syntactic arguments, its meaning relation (PRED) has only one argument (SIT): note that the subject (SPR) is not coindexed with any argument in the semantic relation.[3] This means that the subject does not receive a semantic role (from *seem*). Meanwhile, *try* is different: its SPR is coindexed with the AGENT role in the semantics (RELS value) whereas its VP complement is identified with the SIT role. Thus, both the subject and complement of *try* are linked to semantic arguments whereas the subject of *seem* is not linked to any semantic argument.

    Now we look at object-related verbs like *expect* and *persuade*. Just like the contrast between *seem* and *try*, the key difference lies in whether the object (y) receives a semantic role or not:

(49)   a.   expect'(x, s1)

       b.   persuade'(x, y, s1)

What one expects, as an 'experiencer', is a proposition denoted by the VP complement, whereas what a person x persuades is not a proposition but rather, x persuades an individual y denoted

---

[3] The feature attribute SIT denotes a situation, roughly corresponding to an event or state-of-affairs.

by the object to perform the proposition denoted by the VP complement. Once again, these differences are more clearly represented in feature structures:

(50) a.
$$
\begin{bmatrix}
\langle \text{expect} \rangle \\[2pt]
\text{SYN} \mid \text{VAL}
\begin{bmatrix}
\text{SPR} \langle NP_i \rangle \\[4pt]
\text{COMPS} \left\langle \boxed{2} , \text{VP}
\begin{bmatrix}
\text{VFORM} & inf \\
\text{SPR} & \langle \boxed{2}NP \rangle \\
\text{IND} & s1
\end{bmatrix}
\right\rangle
\end{bmatrix} \\[10pt]
\text{SEM}
\begin{bmatrix}
\text{IND } s0 \\[2pt]
\text{RELS} \left\langle
\begin{bmatrix}
\text{PRED} & expect \\
\text{EXPERIENCER} & i \\
\text{SIT} & s1
\end{bmatrix}
\right\rangle
\end{bmatrix}
\end{bmatrix}
$$

b.
$$
\begin{bmatrix}
\langle \text{persuade} \rangle \\[2pt]
\text{SYN} \mid \text{VAL}
\begin{bmatrix}
\text{SPR} \langle NP_i \rangle \\[4pt]
\text{COMPS} \left\langle NP_j , \text{VP}
\begin{bmatrix}
\text{VFORM} & inf \\
\text{SPR} & \langle NP_j \rangle \\
\text{IND} & s1
\end{bmatrix}
\right\rangle
\end{bmatrix} \\[10pt]
\text{SEM}
\begin{bmatrix}
\text{IND } s0 \\[2pt]
\text{RELS} \left\langle
\begin{bmatrix}
\text{PRED} & persuade \\
\text{AGENT} & i \\
\text{THEME} & j \\
\text{SIT} & s1
\end{bmatrix}
\right\rangle
\end{bmatrix}
\end{bmatrix}
$$

As seen in the lexical entries, *expect* has two semantic arguments, EXPERIENCER and SIT: the object is not linked to a semantic argument of *expect*. In contrast, *persuade* has three semantic arguments: AGENT, THEME, and SIT. We can thus conclude that raising predicates assign one less semantic role in their argument structures than the number of syntactic dependents, while with control predicates, there is a one-to-one correlation.

7.5   Explaining the Differences

7.5.1   Expletive Subject and Object

Recall that for raising verbs, one argument is dependent for its semantic properties solely upon the type of VP complement: the subject for *seem* and the object for *believe*. This fact is borne out by the examples in (51):

(51) a. There/*It/*John seems [to be a fountain in the park].

     b. We believed there/*it/*John [to be a fountain in the park].

Control verbs are different, directly assigning a semantic role to the subject or object. Hence expletives cannot appear (illustrated here for the subject of *try*):

(52) a. *There/*It/John tries to leave the country.

     b. We believed *there/*it/John to try to leave the country.

7.5.2 Meaning Preservation

We noted above that in a raising example such as (53a), the idiomatic reading can be preserved, but not in a control example like (53b):

(53) a. The cat seems to be out of the bag.

     b. The cat tries to be out of the bag.

This is once again because the subject of *seems* does not have any semantic role: its subject is identical with the subject of its VP complement *to be out of the bag*, whereas the subject of *tries* has its own agent role.

Exactly the same explanation applies to the following contrast:

(54) a. The dentist is likely to examine Pat.

     b. Pat is likely to be examined by the dentist.

Since *likely* is a raising predicate, as long as the expressions *The dentist examines Pat* and *Pat is examined by the dentist* have roughly the same meaning, the two raising examples will also have roughly the same meaning.

However, control examples are different:

(55) a. The dentist is eager to examine Pat.

     b. Pat is eager to be examined by the dentist.

The control adjective *eager* assigns a semantic role to its subject independent of the VP complement, as given in the following lexical entry:

(56)
$$
\begin{bmatrix}
\langle eager \rangle \\
\text{SYN} \mid \text{VAL}
\begin{bmatrix}
\text{SPR } \langle NP_i \rangle \\
\text{COMPS } \left\langle VP \begin{bmatrix} \text{VFORM} & inf \\ \text{IND} & s1 \end{bmatrix} \right\rangle
\end{bmatrix} \\
\text{SEM}
\begin{bmatrix}
\text{IND } s0 \\
\text{RELS } \left\langle \begin{bmatrix} \text{PRED} & eager \\ \text{EXPERIENCER} & i \\ \text{SIT} & s1 \end{bmatrix} \right\rangle
\end{bmatrix}
\end{bmatrix}
$$

This then means that (55a) and (55b) must differ in that in the former, it is the dentist who is eager to perform the action denoted by the VP complement, whereas in the latter, it is Pat who is eager.

7.5.3 Subject vs. Object Control Verbs

Consider finally the following two examples:

(57) a. They persuaded me to leave.

   b. They promised me to leave.

Both *persuaded* and *promised* are control verbs since their object is assigned a semantic role (and so is their subject). This in turn means that their object cannot be an expletive:

(58) a. *They persuaded it to rain.

   b. *They promised it to rain.

However, the two are different with respect to the controller of the infinitival VP. Consider who is understood as the unexpressed subject of the infinitival verb here. In (57a), it is the object *me* which semantically functions as the subject of the infinitival VP. Yet, in (57b), it is the subject *they* who will do the action of leaving. Due to this fact, verbs like *promise* are known as 'subject control' verbs, whereas those like *persuade* are 'object control' verbs. This difference is straightforwardly represented in their lexical entries:

(59)
$$
\begin{bmatrix}
\langle persuade \rangle \\
\text{SPR } \langle NP_i \rangle \\
\text{COMPS } \left\langle NP_j, VP \begin{bmatrix} \text{VFORM} & inf \\ \text{SPR} & \langle NP_j \rangle \end{bmatrix} \right\rangle
\end{bmatrix}
$$

$$
\begin{bmatrix}
\langle promise \rangle \\
\text{SPR } \langle \text{ NP}_i \rangle \\
\text{COMPS} \left\langle \text{NP}_j, \text{VP} \begin{bmatrix} \text{VFORM} & inf \\ \text{SPR} & \langle \text{ NP}_i \rangle \\ \text{IND} & s1 \end{bmatrix} \right\rangle
\end{bmatrix}
$$

Based on world knowledge, we know that when one promises someone to do something, this means that the person who makes the promise will do the action. Meanwhile, when one per-suades someone to do something, the person who is persuaded will do the action. The lexical entries here reflect this knowledge of the relations in the world.

In sum, the properties of rasing and control verbs presented here can be summarized as follows:

- Unlike control predicates, raising predicates are unusual in that they do not assign a semantic role to their subject or object. The absence of a semantic role accounts for the possibility of expletives *it* or *there* or parts of idioms as subject or object with raising predicates, and not with control predicates.

- With control predicates, the VP complement's unexpressed subject is coindexed with one of the syntactic dependents. With raising predicates, the entire syntactic-semantic value of the subject of the infinitival VP is structure-shared with that of one of the dependents of the predicate. This ensures that whatever category is required by the raising predicate's VP complement is the raising predicate's subject (or object). Notice that even non-NPs can be subject in certain kinds of example (see (60)).

(60)   a.   Under the bed is a fun place to hide.

       b.   Under the bed seems to be a fun place to hide.

       c.   *Under the bed wants to be a fun place to hide. (*want* is a control verb)

7.6 Exercises

1. Draw trees for the following sentences and provide the lexical entries for the italicized verbs:

   (i) a. Kim may have *admitted* to let Mary mow the lawn.
   b. Gregory *appears* to have wanted to be loyal to the company.
   c. Jones would *prefer* for it to be *clear* to Barry that the city plans to sue him.
   d. John *continues* to avoid the conflict.
   e. The captain *ordered* the troops to proceed.
   f. He *coaxed* his brother to give him the candy.
   g. Frank *hopes* to persuade Harry to make the cook wash the dishes.
   h. John wants it to be *clear* to Ben that the city plans to honor him.

2. Explain why the following examples are ungrammatical, based on the lexical entries of the predicates:

   (i) a. *John seems to rain.
   b. *John is likely to appear that he will win the game.
   c. *Beth tried for Bill to ask a question.
   d. *He believed there to be likely that he won the game.
   e. *It is likely to seem to be arrogant.
   f. *Sandy appears that Kim is happy.
   g. *Dana would be unlikely for Pat to be called upon.
   h. *Robin is nothing in the box.
   i. *It said that Kim was happy.
   j. *There preferred for Sandy to get the job.

3. In this chapter, we have learned that predicates (verbs and adjectives) can be classified into two main groups, raising and control, as represented in the following simple table:

	Raising predicates	Control predicates
Intransitive	seem, ...	try, ...
Transitive	believe, ...	persuade, ...

   Decide in which group each of the following lexical items belongs. In doing so, consider the *it*, *there*, and idiom tests that this chapter has introduced:

   (i)   certain, anxious, lucky, sure, apt, liable, bound, careful, reluctant
   (ii)   tend, decide, manage, fail, happen, begin, hope, intend, refuse

4. As we have seen in Exercise 4 of Chapter 3, there is agreement between the copula *be* and the postcopular NP in so-called 'there' constructions, as shown again here:

   (i) a. There is/*are only one chemical substance involved in nerve transmission.
   b. There *is/are more chemical substances involved in nerve transmission.

   This kind of agreement relationship can be encoded as a property of the *be* used in this construction:

(ii)
$$
\begin{bmatrix}
\langle \text{be} \rangle \\[4pt]
\text{HEAD} \begin{bmatrix} \text{POS verb} \\ \text{AUX +} \end{bmatrix} \\[8pt]
\text{SUBJ} \left\langle \text{NP} \begin{bmatrix} \text{NFORM } \textit{there} \\ \text{AGR } \boxed{1} \end{bmatrix} \right\rangle \\[8pt]
\text{COMPS} \left\langle \text{NP[AGR } \boxed{1}\text{]}, \text{XP[PRED +]} \right\rangle
\end{bmatrix}
$$

This lexical information specifies that *be* selects *there* as its subject and two complements (NP and XP). In this case, the complement NP's agreement feature AGR is identical with that of the subject *there*. This then will ensure that the verb agrees with the postcopular NP.

Given this, how might we account for the following contrasts? Provide a structure for each example and explain the rules or principles which are violated in the ungrammatical versions:

- (ii) a. There is/*are believed to be a sheep in the park.
  - b. There *is/are believed to be sheep in the park.
  - c. There seems/*seem to be no student absent.
  - d. There is/*are likely to be no student absent.

5. Discuss the similarities and differences among the following three examples; use the *it, there* and idiom tests.

- (i) a. Pat expected Leslie to be aggressive.
  - b. Pat persuaded Leslie to be aggressive.
  - c. Pat promised Leslie to be aggressive.

Also, state see the controller is of the infinitival VP in each case.

6. Consider the following data and discuss briefly what can be the antecedent of *her* and *herself*.

- (i) a. Kevin *urged* Anne to be loyal to her.
  - b. Kevin *urged* Anne to be loyal to herself.

Now consider the following data and discuss the binding conditions of *ourselves* and *us*. In particular, determine the relevance of the ARG-ST list with respect to the possible and impossible binding relations.

- (ii) a. We$_i$ expect the dentist to examine us$_i$.
  - b. *We$_i$ expect the dentist to examine ourselves$_i$.
  - c. We expect them to examine themselves.
  - d. *We expect them$_i$ to examine them$_i$.
- (iii) a. We$_i$ persuaded the dentist to examine us$_i$.
  - b. *We$_i$ persuaded the dentist to examine ourselves$_i$.

    c.   We persuaded them$_i$ to examine themselves$_i$.

    d.   *We persuaded them$_i$ to examine them$_i$.

7. Read the following passage and provide a tree structure for each sentence, and lexical entries for the underlined words.

    (i)   If you've ever tried to persuade other people to buy your product or service, you also <u>know</u> that this can be one of the most discouraging and difficult things to try to do as a business owner. In fact, this way of <u>trying</u> to get business by trying to persuade other people is one of the <u>factors</u> that *causes* most business owners to dislike or even hate the process of marketing and selling. It's very <u>tough</u> to try to <u>convince</u> other people to buy from you, especially if it's <u>against</u> their will. After all, if you try to <u>persuade</u> someone to buy from you, you try to <u>cause</u> that person to do something. And usually there's always some kind of pressure involved in this process.

8

Auxiliary Constructions

8.1 Basic Issues

The English auxiliary system involves a relatively small number of elements interacting with each other in complex and intriguing ways. This has been one of the main reasons that the system has been one of the most extensively analyzed empirical domains in the literature on generative syntax.

Ontological Issues: One of the main issues in the study of English auxiliary system concerns ontological issues: is it necessary to posit 'auxiliary' as an independent part of speech or not? Auxiliary verbs can be generally classified as follows:

- modal auxiliary verbs such as *will, shall, may*, etc.: have only finite forms
- *have/be*: have both finite & nonfinite forms
- *do*: has a finite form only with vacuous semantic meaning
- *to*: has a nonfinite form only with apparently vacuous semantic meaning

Such auxiliary verbs behave differently from main verbs in various respects. There have been arguments for treating these auxiliary verbs as simply having the lexical category V, though being different in terms of syntactic distribution and semantic contribution. For example, in terms of similarities, both auxiliary and main verbs behave alike in carrying tense information and participating in some identical syntactic constructions such as gapping, as shown in (1):

(1)   a.   John drank water and Bill __ wine.

        b.   John may drink water, and Bill __ drink beer.

Such phenomena provide apparent stumbling blocks to assigning a totally different lexical category to English auxiliary verbs, compared to main verbs.

Distinctions between auxiliary and main verbs: One important issue that comes up in the study of the English auxiliary system is that of which words function as auxiliary verbs, and how we can differentiate them. Most reliable criteria for auxiliaryhood lie in syntactic phenomena such as negation, inversion, contraction, and ellipsis (usually known as the 'NICE' properties):

1. Negation: Only auxiliary verbs can be followed by *not* marking sentential negation (including *have* and *be*):

(2)   a. Tom will not leave.

        b. *Tom kicked not a ball.

2. Inversion: Only auxiliary verbs undergo subject-auxiliary inversion.

(3)   a. Will Tom leave the party now?

        b. *Left Tom the party already?

3. Contraction: Only auxiliary verbs have contracted forms with the suffix *n't*.

(4)   a. John couldn't leave the party.

        b. *John leftn't the party early.

4. Ellipsis: The complement of an auxiliary verb, but not of a main verb, can be elided.

(5)   a. If anybody is spoiling the children, John is __ .

        b. *If anybody keeps spoiling the children, John keeps __ .

In addition to these NICE properties, tag questions are another criterion: an auxiliary verb can appear in the tag part of a tag question, but not a main verb:

(6)   a. You should leave, shouldn't you?

        b. *You didn't leave, left you?

The position of adverbs or so-called floated quantifiers can also be adopted in differentiating auxiliary verbs from main verbs. The difference can easily be seen in the following contrasts:

(7)   a. She would never believe that story.

        b. *She believed never his story.

(8)   a. The boys will all be there.

        b. *Our team played all well.

Adverbs such as *never* and floated quantifiers such as *all* can follow an auxiliary verb, but not a main verb.

Ordering Restrictions: The third main issue in the syntax of auxiliaries centers on how to capture the ordering restrictions among them. They are subject to restrictions which limit the sequences in which they can occur, and the forms in which they can combine with other auxiliary verbs. Observe the following examples:

(9)   a. The children will have been being entertained.

        b. He must have been being interrogated by the police at that very moment.

(10)   a. *The house is been remodelling.

        b. *Margaret has had already left.

        c. *He has will seeing his children.

d. *He has been must being interrogated by the police at that very moment.

As shown here, when there are two or more auxiliary verbs, they must come in a certain order. In addition, note that each auxiliary verb requires the immediately following to be in a particular morphological form (e.g., *has eaten* vs. **has eating*).

In the study of the English auxiliary system, we thus need to address at least the following issues:

- Should we posit an auxiliary category?
- How can we distinguish main verbs from auxiliary verbs?
- How can we account for phenomena (such as the NICE group) which are sensitive to the presence of an auxiliary verb?
- How can we capture the ordering and co-occurrence restrictions among auxiliary verbs?

This chapter provides answers to these fundamental questions related to the English auxiliary system.[1]

8.2   Transformational Analyses

The seminal work on the issues above is that of Chomsky (1957). His analysis, introducing the rule in (11), directly stipulates the ordering relations among auxiliary verbs:

(11)   Aux → Tense (Modal) (have + en) (be + ing)

The PS rule in (11) would generate sentences with or without auxiliary verbs as in (12):

(12)   a.   Mary solved the problem.

b.   Mary would solve the problem.

c.   Mary was solving the problem.

d.   Mary would easily solve the problem.

For example, the following structure schematizes some examples in (12):

(13)

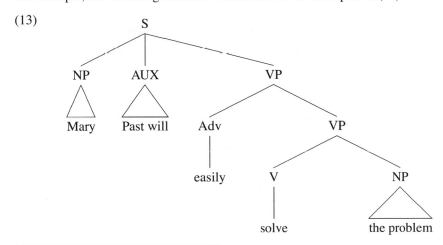

---

[1] This chapter is based on Kim (2002c).

To get to the surface structure, the famous 'Affix Hopping' rule of Chomsky (1957) ensures that the affixal tense morpheme (Past) in Tense is hopped to M (Modal) (*will*), or over onto the main verb (*solve*) if the Modal does not appear. If the modal is there, Past hops onto *will* and we get *Mary would (easily) solve the problem*. If the modal is not there, the affix Past will hop onto the main verb *solve*, giving *Mary solved the problem*.

In addition to the Affix Hopping Rule, typical transformational analyses introduce the English particular rule called '*do*-support' for dealing with the NICE properties in clauses that otherwise have no auxiliary verb:

(14)   a.   *Mary not avoided Bill.

     b.   Mary did not avoid Bill.

The presence of *not* in a position like Adv in the tree (13) has been claimed to prevent the Tense affix from hopping over to the verb (as *not* intervenes). As a last-resort option, the grammar introduces the auxiliary verb *do* onto which the affix Tense is hopped. This would then generate (14b). In other words, the position of *do* diagnoses the position of Tense in the structure.

The analysis lays bare the systematicity of the auxiliary system, but nevertheless it misses several important points. For example, the constituent structure in (13) does not provide constituent properties we find in coordinate structures, because the first auxiliary and the rest of the sentence (the VP) do not form a constituent.

(15)   a.   Fred [must have been singing songs] and [probably was drinking beer].

     b.   Fred must both [have been singing songs] and [have been drinking beer].

     c.   Fred must have both [been singing songs] and [been drinking beer].

     d.   Fred must have been both [singing songs] and [drinking beer].

As we have seen earlier, identical phrasal constituents can be conjoined. The coordination examples here indicate that a VP with one auxiliary verb or more behaves just like the one without any.

More recent analyses in this tradition (e.g., Chomsky (1986)) use X'-theory to provide IP and CP as categories for clausal syntax, which can deal with the coordination data just given.[2] Nevertheless, there are many problems which transformational analyses cannot easily overcome (for a thorough review, see Kim (2000), Kim and Sag (2002)).

8.3   A Lexicalist Analysis

In the approach we take in this book, ordering restrictions on auxiliay verbs will follow from the correct specification of their lexical properties, interacting with the regular rules of syntactic combination. The analysis requires no movement, either of whole words, or of affixes. In this section, we discuss several different subtypes of auxiliary.

---

[2]An IP (Inflectional Phrase), similar to a sentence whose verb is finite form, is a functional phrase which has of inflection such as tense and agreement. See Radford (1997).

8.3.1 Modals

One main property of modal auxiliaries such as *will, shall* and *must* is that they place no semantic restrictions on their subject, indicating their status as raising verbs (see Chapter 7).

(16)   a.   There might be a unicorn in the garden.

        b.   It will rain tomorrow.

        c.   John will leave the party earlier.

(17)   a.   *There hopes to finish the project.

        b.   *The bus hopes to be here at five.

As seen from the contrast, the type of subject in (16) depends on what kind of subject (*there* or *it* or a regular NP) is required by the verb right after the modal. This is typical of raising verbs, and different from what we see in examples with a control verb like *hope* in (17), which must have a referential subject.

Modal verbs can only occur in finite (plain or past) forms. They cannot occur neither as infinitives nor as participles.[3]

(18)   a.   I hope *to would/*to can/to study in France.

        b.   *John stopped can/canning to sign in tune.

Modals do not show 3rd person inflection in the present tense, nor a transparent past tense form.

(19)   a.   *John musts/musted leave the party early.

        b.   *John wills leave the party early.

In terms of their own selectional properties, modal verbs select a base VP as their complement:

(20)   a.   John can [kick/*kicked/*kicking/*to kick the ball].

        b.   John will [kick/*kicked/*kicking/*to kick the ball].

Reflecting these basic lexical properties, a modal auxiliary will have at least the following lexical information:

$$
(21) \quad
\begin{bmatrix}
\langle must \rangle \\[4pt]
\text{HEAD}
\begin{bmatrix}
\text{POS} & verb \\
\text{VFORM} & \textit{fin} \\
\text{AUX} & +
\end{bmatrix} \\[20pt]
\text{VAL}
\begin{bmatrix}
\text{SPR } \langle \boxed{1}\text{NP} \rangle \\[4pt]
\text{COMPS} \left\langle \text{VP}
\begin{bmatrix}
\text{VFORM} & bse \\
\text{SPR} & \langle \boxed{1}\text{NP} \rangle
\end{bmatrix}
\right\rangle
\end{bmatrix}
\end{bmatrix}
$$

---

[3] As we have seen in 5.2.1, the VFORM value *fin* includes *es*, *ed*, and *pln* whereas *nonfin* includes *ing*, *en*, *inf*, and *bse*.

In the lexical information given here, we notice at least three things: first, auxiliary verbs have the head feature AUX, which differentiates them from main verbs. In addition, the rule shows that a modal verb selects a base VP as its complement. This subcategorization information will rule out examples like the following, as well as the ungrammatical examples in (20):

(22)   a. *Kim must [VP[*fin*] bakes a cake].
       b. *Kim must [VP[*fin*] baked a cake].
       c. *Kim must [VP[*fin*] will bake a cake].

The possible and impossible structures can be more clearly represented in tree format:

(23)   a.

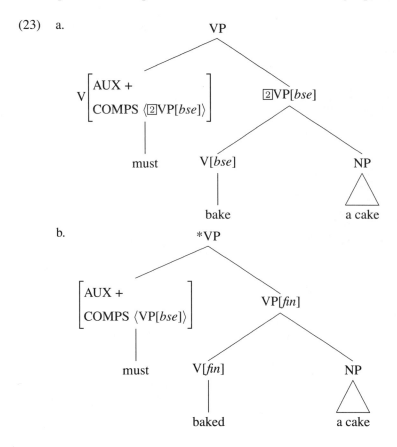

As can be easily seen here, the modal auxiliary *must* requires a VP[*bse*] as its complement: The VP[*fin*] in (23b) cannot function as the complement of *must*.

The lexical entry in (21) also specifies that the VP's subject is identical with the subject of the modal auxiliary (indicated by the box ①). This specification, a crucial property of raising verbs we have discussed in the previous chapter, rules out the ungrammatical versions of examples like the following:

(24)   a. It/*John will [VP[*bse*] rain tomorrow].
       b. There/*It may [VP[*bse*] exist a man in the park].

The VP *rain tomorrow* requires the expletive subject *it*, not any other NP, such as *John*; and the VP *exist a man in the park* requires *there* and nothing else as its subject.

In addition, since modal verbs have the specification [VFORM *fin*], they cannot occur in any environment where finite verbs are prohibited.

(25) a. *We expect there to [$_{VP[fin]}$ will rain].

   b. *It is vital that we [$_{VP[fin]}$ will study everyday].

The simple lexical information of modal verbs given in (21), which is required in almost any analysis, explains the main distributional possibilities of modal verbs.

8.3.2 *Be* **and** *Have*

The auxiliary verbs *have* and *be* are different from modal verbs. For example, unlike modals, they have nonfinite forms (*would have, would be, to have/to be*); they have a 3rd person inflection form (*has, is*); they select not a base VP as their complement, but an inflected nonfinite form. In addition, they are different from modals in that they also have uses as main verbs, though in some cases with different syntax from when they are auxiliaries.

Consider the examples in (26):

(26) a. He is a fool.

   b. He has a car.

On the assumption that every sentence has a main verb, *be* and *have* here are main verbs. However, a striking property of *be* is that it still shows the properties of an auxiliary: it exhibits all of the NICE properties, as we will see below. The usage of *be* actually provides a strong reason why the grammar should allow a verb categorized as 'V' to also have the feature specification [AUX +]; *be* in (26a) is clearly a verb, yet it also behaves exactly like an auxiliary.

The verb *be* has three main uses: as a copula selecting an predicate XP, as an aspectual auxiliary with a progressive VP following, and as an auxiliary as part of the passive construction:

(27) a. John is in the school.

   b. John is running to the car.

   c. John was found in the office.

There is no categorical or syntactic reason to distinguish these three, for they all have NICE properties: they show identical behavior with subject-auxiliary inversion, their position relative adverbs including floated quantifiers, and so forth.

(28)   Subject-Aux Inversion:

   a. Was the child in the school? (*Did the child be in the school?)

   b. Was the child running to the car?

   c. Was the child found?

(29)   Position of an adverb:

   a. The child (?never) was (never) crazy. (The child (never) became (*never) crazy.)

b. The child (?never) was (never) running to the car.

c. The child (?never) was (never) deceived.

Thus, all three uses have the lexical information given in (30) as their common denominator:[4]

(30)
$$
\begin{bmatrix}
\langle be \rangle \\[2pt]
\text{HEAD} \begin{bmatrix} \text{POS} & verb \\ \text{AUX} & + \end{bmatrix} \\[14pt]
\text{VAL} \begin{bmatrix} \text{SPR} \ \langle \boxed{1} \text{NP} \rangle \\[6pt] \text{COMPS} \left\langle \text{XP} \begin{bmatrix} \text{PRD} & + \\ \text{SPR} & \langle \boxed{1} \rangle \end{bmatrix} \right\rangle \end{bmatrix}
\end{bmatrix}
$$

All three *be*s bear the feature AUX with the + value, and select a predicative phrase whose subject is identical with *be*'s subject. Every use of *be* thus has the properties of a raising verb. The main difference between the three uses lies in the XP's VFORM value:[5]

(31) a. copula *be*: $\begin{bmatrix} \text{COMPS} \ \langle \text{XP} \rangle \end{bmatrix}$

   b. progressive *be*: $\begin{bmatrix} \text{COMPS} \ \langle \text{VP[VFORM } ing] \rangle \end{bmatrix}$

   c. passive *be*: $\begin{bmatrix} \text{COMPS} \ \langle \text{VP[VFORM } pass] \rangle \end{bmatrix}$

As given here, the copula *be* needs no further specification: any phrase that can function as a predicate can be its COMPS value. The progressive *be* requires its complement to be VP[*ing*], and the passive *be* requires its complement to be VP[*pass*]. Hence, examples like those in (32) are straightforwardly generated:

(32) a. John is [$_{AP}$ happy about the outcome].

   b. John was [$_{VP[ing]}$ seeing his children].

   c. The children are [$_{VP[pass]}$ seen in the yard].

Auxiliary *have* is rather similar in its properties to auxiliary *be*, and it selects a past participle VP complement.

(33) a. John has not sung a song.

   b. Has John sung a song?

   c. John hasn't been singing a song.

   d. John has sung a song and Mary has __ , too.

Given facts like these, we can posit the following information in the lexical entry for auxiliary *have*, part of the perfect aspect construction:

---

[4] XP here is a variable over phrasal categories such as NP, VP, AP, and PP.
[5] See Chapter 9 for the further discussion of passive constructions.

(34)

$$\begin{bmatrix} \langle have \rangle \\ HEAD \begin{bmatrix} POS & verb \\ AUX & + \end{bmatrix} \\ SPR \langle \boxed{1} \rangle \\ COMPS \left\langle VP \begin{bmatrix} VFORM & en \\ SPR & \langle \boxed{1} \rangle \end{bmatrix} \right\rangle \end{bmatrix}$$

The interaction of subcategorization and morphosyntactic information is enough to predict the ordering restrictions among modals. For example, the auxiliaries *have* and *be* can follow a modal since both have *bse* as its VFORM value:

(35) a. John can [$_{VP[bse]}$ have danced].

   b. John can [$_{VP[bse]}$ be dancing].

In addition, we can predict the following ordering too:

(36) a. He has [seen his children].

   b. He will [have [been [seeing his children]]].

   c. He must [have [been [being interrogated by the police at that very moment]]].

(37) a. *Americans have [paying income tax ever since 1913].

   b. *George has [went to America].

(37a) is ungrammatical since *have* requires a perfect participle VP. (37b) is out since the following VP is finite.

In some varieties of English, typically in British English, the main verb *have* also has the specification [AUX +], as evidenced by the (b) examples below:

(38) a. You are a student.

   b. You have not enough money.

(39) a. Are you a student?

   b. Have you enough money?

The main verbs *be* and *have* show the NICE properties; even though they are main verbs, they have the syntax of auxiliaries. This fact supports the idea that every sentence has a (main) verb in it, at least, while the surface syntax of a verb is determined by whether it has the specification [AUX +] or [AUX −].

8.3.3 Periphrastic *do*

Next we discuss the so-called "dummy" *do*, which is used as an auxiliary in the absence of other (finite) auxiliaries. This *do* also exhibits the NICE properties:

(40) a. John does not like this town.

   b. In no other circumstances does that distinction matter.

    c.   They didn't leave any food.

    d.   Jane likes these apples even more than Mary does __ .

Like the modals, *do* does not appear in nonfinite clauses.

(41)   a.   *They expected us to do/should leave him.

      b.   I found myself needing/*doing need/*should needing sleep.

There are also some properties which distinguish *do* from other auxiliaries. First, unlike other auxiliaries, *do* appears neither before nor after any other auxiliary:

(42)   a.   *He does be leaving.

      b.   *He does have been eating.

      c.   *They will do come.

    Second, the verb *do* has no obvious intrinsic meaning to speak of. Except for carrying the grammatical information about tense and agreement (in present tense), it has no semantic contribution.

    Third, if *do* is used in a positive statement, it needs to be emphatic (stressed). But in negative statements and questions, no such requirement exists.

(43)   a.   *John does leave.

      b.   John DOES leave.

(44)   a.   John did not come.

      b.   John DID not come. (more likely in this case: John did NOT come.)

(45)   a.   Did John find the solution?

      b.   How long did it last?

    The most economical way of representing these lexical properties is to give *do* the lexical entry given in (46).

(46)

$$
\begin{bmatrix}
\langle \text{do} \rangle \\[4pt]
\text{HEAD}
\begin{bmatrix}
\text{POS} & verb \\
\text{AUX} & + \\
\text{VFORM} & fin
\end{bmatrix} \\[20pt]
\text{VAL}
\begin{bmatrix}
\text{SPR} \ \langle \boxed{1}\text{NP} \rangle \\[8pt]
\text{COMPS} \ \left\langle \text{VP}
\begin{bmatrix}
\text{AUX} & - \\
\text{VFORM} & bse \\
\text{SPR} & \langle \boxed{1} \rangle
\end{bmatrix}
\right\rangle
\end{bmatrix}
\end{bmatrix}
$$

Like other auxiliaries including modals, *do* is specified to be [AUX +], which ensures that *do* is sensitive to negation, inversion, contraction, and ellipsis (NICE properties), just like the other auxiliaries. Further, *do* selects a subject NP and a VP complement whose unrealized subject is structure-shared with its subject (⊡). Treating *do* as a raising verb like other English auxiliaries is based on typical properties of raising verbs, one of which is that raising verbs allow expletives as their subject, as we have seen above:

(47) a. John may leave.

b. It may rain.

c. *John may rain.

(48) a. John did not leave.

b. It did not rain.

c. *John did not rain.

The [AUX +] specification and raising-verb treatment of *do* account for the similarities to other auxiliaries and modals.

The differences stem from the lexical specifications on the feature values for HEAD|POS and its complement VP. Unlike *have* and *be*, *do* is specified to be *fin*. This property then accounts for why no auxiliary element can precede *do*, for only the first verb in a sequence may be finite.

(49) a. He might [have left].

b. *He might [do leave].

The requirement on the complement VP of the auxiliary *do* is [VFORM *bse*]. This feature specification blocks modals from heading the VP following *do*, for modals are specified to be [*fin*], predicting the ungrammaticality of the examples in (50):

(50) a. *He does [can leave here].

b. *He does [may leave here].

These examples are also ruled out by the specification that the complement of *do* be a VP[AUX −]. This requirement will further predict the ungrammaticality of examples in (51) and (52).

(51) a. *Jim [DOES [have supported the theory]].

b. *The proposal [DID [be endorsed by Clinton]].

(52) a. *I [do [not [have sung]]].

b. *I [do [not [be happy]]].

In (51) and (52), the VPs following the auxiliary *do*, stressed or not, bear the feature [AUX +] inherited from the auxiliaries *have* and *be*. This explains their ungrammaticality.[6]

---

[6]There are special properties of *do* in imperatives, and different properties with *don't*. *Do* in imperatives can occur before another auxiliary like *be* and *have*.

(i) a. Do be honest!

b. Don't be silly!

Do and *don't* in imperatives also have one distinct property: only *don't* allows the subject *you* to follow (try inserting *you* in (ia) and (ib)). Their properties indicate that they have different lexical information from the verb forms used in non-imperatives.

8.3.4 Infinitival Clause Marker *to*

The auxiliary verbs *to* and *do*, in addition to differing by just one phonological feature, *voicing*, differ in an important syntactic property: *do* appears only in finite contexts, and *to* only in non-finite contexts. The verb *to* is, of course, the actual marker of the infinitive in English. Even though it has the form of a preposition, its syntactic behavior puts it in the class of auxiliary verbs (cf. Gazdar et al. (1985)):

(53) a. *John believed Kim to do not leave here.

     b. John believes Kim not to leave here.

These verbs share the property that they obligatorily take bare verbal complements (hence, non-base forms or modals cannot head the complement VP):

(54) a. *John believed Kim to leaving here.

     b. *John did not leaving here.

     c. *John expect to must leave.

     d. *John did not may leave.

In terms of NICE properties, *to* also falls under the VP ellipsis criterion:

(55) a. Tom wanted to go home, but Peter didn't want to __ .

     b. Lee voted for Bill because his father told him to __ .

These properties indicate that *to* should have a lexical entry like this:

(56)
$$
\begin{bmatrix}
\text{HEAD} \begin{bmatrix} \text{POS} & verb \\ \text{AUX} & + \\ \text{VFORM} & inf \end{bmatrix} \\
\text{SPR} \left\langle \boxed{1}\text{NP} \right\rangle \\
\text{COMPS} \left\langle \text{VP} \begin{bmatrix} \text{VFORM} & bse \\ \text{SPR} & \langle \boxed{1} \rangle \end{bmatrix} \right\rangle
\end{bmatrix}
$$

It is an infinitive auxiliary verb, whose complement must be headed by a V in the *bse* form.

8.4 Explaining the NICE Properties

In this section we discuss how we can account for the NICE properties, which are key diagnostics for presence of auxiliary verbs.

8.4.1 Auxiliaries with Negation

The English negative adverb *not* leads a double life: one as a nonfinite VP modifier, marking constituent negation, and the other as a complement of a finite auxiliary verb, marking sentential negation. Constituent negation is the name for a construction where negation combines with some constituent to its right, and negates exactly that constituent:

Constituent Negation: The properties of *not* as a nonfinite VP modifier can be supported from its similarities with adverbs such as *never* in nonfinite clauses as given in (57):

(57)   a.   Kim regrets [never/not [having seen the movie]].

   h   We asked him [never/not [to try to call us again]].

   c.   Duty made them [never/not [miss the weekly meetings]].

Taking *not* to modify a nonfinite VP, we can predict its various positional possibilities in nonfinite clauses, via the following lexical entry:

(58)
$$\begin{bmatrix} \langle \text{not} \rangle \\[4pt] \text{HEAD} \begin{bmatrix} \text{POS} & adv \\ \text{NEG} & + \\ \text{MOD} & \langle \text{VP[VFORM } nonfin] \rangle \end{bmatrix} \end{bmatrix}$$

The adverb *not* modifies any nonfinite VP:

(59)   Constituent Negation:

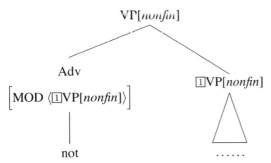

In the grammatical examples in (60) and (61), *not* modifies a nonfinite VP; in the ungrammatical examples the VP[*nonfin*] lexical constraint is violated.

(60)   a.   [Not [speaking English]] is a disadvantage.

   b.   *[Speaking not English] is a disadvantage.

   c.   *Lee likes not Kim.

(61)   a.   Lee is believed [not $_{\text{VP}[inf]}$[to like Kim]].

   b.   Lee is believed to [not $_{\text{VP}[bse]}$[like Kim].

   c.   *Lee is believed [to $_{\text{VP}[bse]}$[like not Kim]].

Sentential Negation: In contrast to constituent negation, there is sentential negation, which is the canonical expression of negation. One way to distinguish the two types of negation comes from scope possibilities in an example like (62) (cf. Warner (2000)).

(62)   The president could not approve the bill.

Negation here could have the two different scope readings paraphrased in (63).

(63) a. It would be possible for the president not to approve the bill.

     b. It would not be possible for the president to approve the bill.

The first interpretation is constituent negation; the second is sentential negation.

Sentential *not* may not modify a finite VP:

(64) a. Lee never/*not left.   (cf. Lee did not leave.)

     b. Lee will never/not leave.

This construction shows one clear difference between *never* and *not*: *not* can only modify a nonfinite VP, a property further illustrated by the following examples:

(65) a. John could [not [leave the town]].

     b. John wants [not [to leave the town]].

(66) a. *John [not [left the town]].

     b. *John [not [could leave the town]].

Another difference between *never* and *not* is found in the VP ellipsis construction. Observe the following contrast:

(67) a. Mary sang a song, but Lee never did __ .

     b. *Mary sang a song, but Lee did never__ .

     c. Mary sang a song, but Lee did not __ .

The data here indicate that *not* behaves differently from adverbs like *never* in finite contexts, even though they all behave alike in nonfinite contexts. *never* is a true diagnostic for a VP-modifier, and we use contrasts between it and *not* to reason what the properties of *not* must be.

We have seen the lexical representation for constituent negation *not* above. Sentential *not* appears linearly in the same position – following a finite auxiliary verb – but shows different syntactic properties. The most economical way to differentiate sentential negation from constituent negation is to assume that sentential negation is actually a syntactic complement of a finite auxiliary verb (cf. Kim and Sag (1995, 2002)). That is, we can assume that when *not* is used as a marker of sentential negation, it is selected by the preceding finite auxiliary verb via a lexical rule:

(68) Negative Auxiliary Verb Lexical Rule:

$$\begin{bmatrix} \text{HEAD} \begin{bmatrix} \text{AUX} & + \\ \text{VFORM} & \textit{fin} \end{bmatrix} \\ \text{COMPS} \ \langle \boxed{1}\text{XP} \rangle \end{bmatrix} \Rightarrow \begin{bmatrix} \text{HEAD} \begin{bmatrix} \text{AUX} & + \\ \text{VFORM} & \textit{fin} \\ \text{NEG} & + \end{bmatrix} \\ \text{COMPS} \ \langle \text{Adv[NEG +]}, \boxed{1}\text{XP} \rangle \end{bmatrix}$$

This lexical rule allows a finite auxiliary verb with a complement (☐) to select an extra complement, marked [NEG +]. This rule gives a lexical entry which licenses the following structure for sentential negation:

(69)

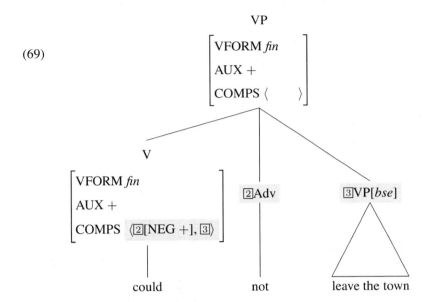

As shown here, the negative finite auxiliary verb *could* selects two complements, the adverb *not* and the VP *leave the town*, and all together these produce a well-formed finite VP.

By treating *not* as an modifier meaning constituent negation and as a complement marking sentential negation, we can account for the scope differences in (62) and various other phenomena including VP Ellipsis (see 8.4.4). For example, the present analysis will assign two different structures for the string (62):

(70)   a.

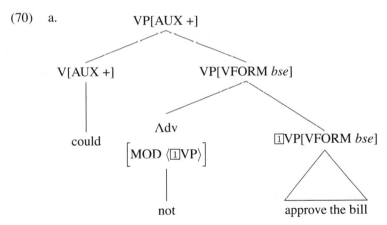

b.

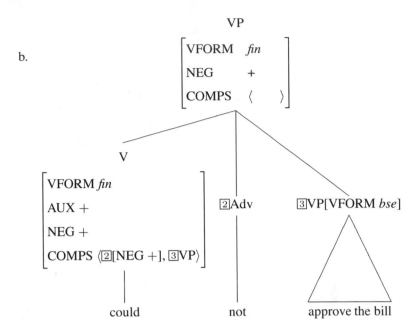

In the structure (70a), *not* modifies just a nonfinite VP, with scope narrower than *could*. Meanwhile, in (70b), *not* is at the same level in the syntax as *could*, and semantically *not* scopes over *could*. In this case, the feature [NEG +] percolates up to the VP and then to the whole sentence. The semantic consequence of this structural difference can be seen in the different tag questions appropriate for each interpretation:

(71)   a.   The president [could [not [approve the bill]]], couldn't/*could he?

   b.   The president [[could] [not] [approve the bill]], could/*couldn't he?

The tag question forms show that (71a) is actually a positive statement, even though some part of it is negative. On the other hand, (71b) is a negative statement.

8.4.2   Auxiliaries with Inversion

Questions in English are formed by structures which invert the subject and the auxiliary:[7]

(72)   a.   Are you studying English syntax?

   b.   What are you studying nowadays?

The long-standing transformational approach assumes that the auxiliary verb is moved from a medial position to the clause-initial position (the node labels would typically differ in current analyses, but the structure of the movement is what is relevant here):

---

[7]For the analysis of *wh*-questions like (72b), see chapter 10.

(73)

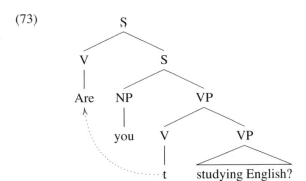

However, there are certain exceptions that present problems for the analysis of inverted auxiliaries involving a movement transformation. Observe the following contrast:

(74) a. I shall go downtown.

    b. Shall I go downtown?

Here there is a semantic difference between the auxiliary verb *shall* in (74a) and the one in (74b): the former conveys a sense of simple futurity – in the near future, I will go downtown – whereas the latter example has a deontic sense, asking whether it is appropriate for me to go downtown. If the inverted verb is simply moved from an initial medial position in (74b), it is not clear how the grammar can represent this meaning difference.

English also has various interpretations for the subject-auxiliary inversion construction:[8]

(75) a. Wish: May she live forever!

    b. Matrix Polar Interrogative: Was I that stupid?

    c. Negative Imperative: Don't you even touch that!

    d. Subjunctive: Had they been here now, we wouldn't have this problem.

    e. Exclamative: Boy, am I tired!

Each of these constructions has its own constraints which cannot fully be predicted from other constructions. For example, in 'wish' constructions, only the modal auxiliary *may* is possible. In negative imperatives, only *don't* allows the subject to follow. These idiosyncratic properties support a non-movement approach, in which auxiliaries can be specified to have particular uses or meanings when inserted into particular positions in the syntax.

This in turn means that our grammar adds the following SAI grammar rule as a well-formed condition:

---

[8] See Fillmore (1999) for detailed discussion.

(76)   Subject-Aux Inversion (SAI) Rule:

$$S\left[SPR \ \langle \ \rangle\right] \rightarrow \mathbf{H}\begin{bmatrix} HEAD \begin{bmatrix} INV & + \\ AUX & + \end{bmatrix} \\ SPR \ \boxed{A} \\ COMPS \ \boxed{B} \end{bmatrix}, \ \boxed{A}, \ \boxed{B}$$

This rule thus licenses an an inverted, finite, auxiliary verb to combine with its subject (the SPR value $\boxed{A}$) and complements (the COMPS value $\boxed{B}$), forming a well-formed subject-auxiliary inverted phrase like the following:

(77)

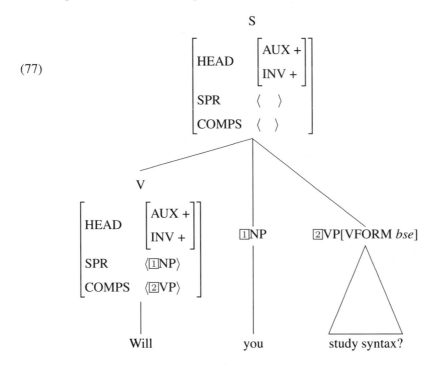

As shown in the structure, the inverted *will* combines with the subject NP *you* and the VP complement at the same level.

Even though most of the auxiliary verbs will be classified as [INV +/−], some are lexically defined just as [INV −]. For example, consider *better*.

(78)   a.   You better not drink.

        b.   You can do it, but you better not __ .

        c. *Better you not drink.

Even though the word *better* functions at least in spoken English as an auxiliary verb, it always carries [INV −], as attested by the above contrast: it cannot be inverted.

8.4.3 Contracted Auxiliaries

Auxiliary verbs actually show two kinds of contraction: either with a preceding subject or with a negation (but not both):

(79) a. They'll be leaving.

     b. They'd leave soon.

(80) a. They wouldn't leave soon.

     b. They shouldn't leave soon.

Contracted negation forms show several lexical idiosyncrasies as in *willn't*, *amn't*, and *mayn't*. It is common to analyze *n't* as a kind of inflectional affix (cf. Zwicky and Pullum (1983)). In the approach we adopt here, we would posit an inflectional rule applying to a specific set of verbs, as in (81):

(81)   *N't* Inflection Lexical Rule:

$$
\begin{bmatrix} \text{PHON} \; \langle \boxed{1} \rangle \\ \text{HEAD} \begin{bmatrix} \text{POS} & \textit{verb} \\ \text{VFORM} & \textit{fin} \\ \text{AUX} & + \end{bmatrix} \end{bmatrix}
\Rightarrow
\begin{bmatrix} \text{PHON} \; \langle \boxed{1} + \text{n't} \rangle \\ \text{HEAD} \begin{bmatrix} \text{VFORM} & \textit{fin} \\ \text{AUX} & + \\ \text{NEG} & + \end{bmatrix} \end{bmatrix}
$$

This means that a word like *can* will be mapped to *can't*, gaining the NEG feature:

(82)
$$
\begin{bmatrix} \langle \text{can} \rangle \\ \text{HEAD} \begin{bmatrix} \text{POS} & \textit{verb} \\ \text{VFORM} & \textit{fin} \\ \text{AUX} & + \end{bmatrix} \end{bmatrix}
\Rightarrow
\begin{bmatrix} \langle \text{can't} \rangle \\ \text{HEAD} \begin{bmatrix} \text{VFORM} & \textit{fin} \\ \text{AUX} & + \\ \text{NEG} & + \end{bmatrix} \end{bmatrix}
$$

As we have seen earlier, the head feature NEG will play an important role in forming tag questions:

(83) a. They can do it, can't they?

     b. They can't do it, can they?

     c. *They can't do it, can't they?

     d. *They can't do it, can he?

The tag part of such a question has the opposite value for NEG compared to that in the main part of the clause, and its subject needs to have the same index value as the matrix subject. For this, we can introduce the feature XARG (external argument) for each predicate and link the subject to this value.[9] This means that English has independently the following Tag Question

---

[9]Traditionally, arguments are classified into external and internal ones in which the former usually refers to the subject. The introduction of such a semantic feature is necessary if we want to make the subject value visible on the S node (see Bender and Flickinger (1999) and Sag (2007)). That is to say, although a VP has a SPR value for its subject,

Rule:[10]

(84)   Tag-Question Rule:

$$S \rightarrow S \begin{bmatrix} NEG \ \boxed{1} \\ XARG \ i \end{bmatrix}, \quad S \begin{bmatrix} NEG \ \neg\boxed{1} \\ INV \ + \\ XARG \ i \end{bmatrix}$$

This rule means that a tag part can be added when it has the opposite NEG value whose subject index is identical with that of the matrix subject. This will then project the following structure for (83a):

(85)

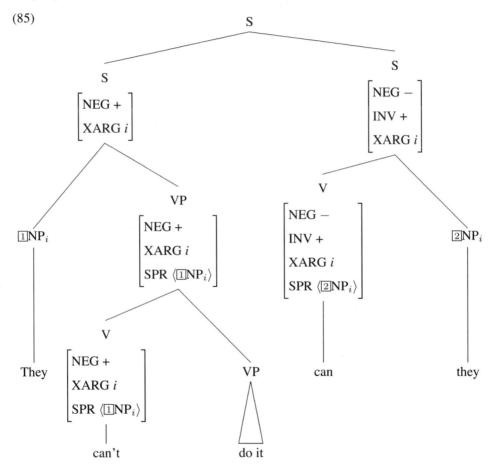

As represented here, the NEG feature of the matrix verb is passed up to the first S. The tag question then needs to have the opposite NEG value in accordance with the rule in (84). The

once the VP and subject combine, the resulting S no longer has any information about any features of the subject – including its semantic index. XARG is a mechanism for making this information visible at the S level, which is where the tag question adjoins.

[10]This rule is simplified. To be more precise, we need to ensure that the second S, corresponding to the tag part, must have only the auxiliary and the subject. See Bender and Flickinger (1999) and Sag (2007).

semantic feature XARG identified with the subject starts from the auxiliary verb and then is semantically composed into the meaning of S. The XARG value in a sense makes the subject's index value visible at the top level of the sentence in question so that the tag subject can also refer to this.

8.4.4 Auxiliaries with Ellipsis

The standard generalization of Verb Phrase Ellipsis (VPE) is that it is possible only after an auxiliary verb, as shown in the contrast (86) and (87).

(86) a. Kim can dance, and Sandy can __ , too.

b. Kim has danced, and Sandy has __ , too.

c. Kim was dancing, and Sandy was __ , too.

(87) a. *Kim considered joining the navy, but I never considered __ .

b. *Kim got arrested by the CIA, and Sandy got __ , also.

c. *Kim wanted to go and Sandy wanted __ , too.

The VP complement of an auxiliary verb, but not a main verb, can undergo VP ellipsis as long as the context provides enough information for its interpretation.

The syntactic part of this generalization can be succinctly stated in the form of lexical rule:

(88)   VP Ellipsis Rule:

$$\begin{bmatrix} \text{HEAD} \,|\, \text{AUX} & + \\ \text{COMPS} & \langle \text{XP} \rangle \end{bmatrix} \Rightarrow \begin{bmatrix} \text{HEAD} \,|\, \text{AUX} & + \\ \text{COMPS} & \langle \ \rangle \end{bmatrix}$$

As the rule is stated to apply to any XP after a verb with the [AUX +] specification, it can apply to more than just VPs, and to more than just the canonical auxiliary verbs, but also *be* and *have* in their main verb uses. With *be*, non-VP complements can be elided:

(89) a. Kim is happy and Sandy is __ too.

b. When Kim was in China, I was __ too.

The main verb *have* is somewhat restricted, but the contrast in (90) is clear. Even though *have* is a main verb in (90a), it can allow an elided complement, unlike the main verb *bring* in (90b):

(90) a. A: Have you anything to share with the group?

B: No. Have you __ ?

b. A: Have you brought anything to share with the group?

B: No. *Have you bought __ ?

Given the lexical rule (88) which specifies no change in the ARG-ST, a canonical auxiliary verb like *can* will have a counterpart minus its phrasal complement on the COMPS list:

(91)

$$
\begin{bmatrix}
\langle can \rangle \\
\text{SPR} \quad \langle \boxed{1}\text{NP} \rangle \\
\text{COMPS} \quad \langle \boxed{2}\text{VP}[bse] \rangle \\
\text{ARG-ST} \quad \langle \boxed{1}, \boxed{2} \rangle
\end{bmatrix}
\Rightarrow
\begin{bmatrix}
\langle can \rangle \\
\text{SPR} \quad \langle \boxed{1} \rangle \\
\text{COMPS} \quad \langle \ \rangle \\
\text{ARG-ST} \quad \langle \boxed{1}, \boxed{2} \rangle
\end{bmatrix}
$$

Notice here that even though the VP complement is elided in the output, the ARG-ST is intact.

In the first part of the example in (92), there are three auxiliary verbs:

(92)   Kim must have been dancing and $\begin{cases} \text{a. Sandy must have been \_\_ , too.} \\ \text{b. Sandy must have \_\_ , too.} \\ \text{c. Sandy must \_\_ , too.} \end{cases}$

There are therefore various options for an elided VP: the complement of *been*, or *have*, or *must*.

The analysis also immediately predicts that ellipsis is possible with the infinitival marker *to*, for this is an auxiliary verb, too:

(93)   a.   Tom wanted to go home, but Peter didn't want to __ .

   b.   Lee voted for Bill because his father told him to __ .

(94)   a.   Because John persuaded Sally to __ , he didn't have to talk to the reporters.

   b.   Mary likes to tour art galleries, but Bill hates to __ .

Finally, the analysis given here will also account for the contrast shown above in (67); a similar contrast is found in the following examples:

(95)   a.   *Mary sang a song, but Lee could never__ .

   b.   Mary sang a song, but Lee could not __ .

The negator *not* in (95b) is a marker of sentential negation and can be the complement of the finite auxiliary verb *could*. This means we can apply the VPE lexical rule to the auxiliary verb *could* after the negation lexical rule (68), as shown (96):

(96)

$$
\begin{bmatrix}
\langle could \rangle \\
\text{SPR} \quad \langle \boxed{1}\text{NP} \rangle \\
\text{COMPS} \quad \langle \boxed{2}\text{Adv[NEG +]}, \boxed{3}\text{VP}[bse] \rangle \\
\text{ARG-ST} \quad \langle \boxed{1}, \boxed{2}, \boxed{3} \rangle
\end{bmatrix}
\Rightarrow
\begin{bmatrix}
\langle could \rangle \\
\text{SPR} \quad \langle \boxed{1} \rangle \\
\text{COMPS} \quad \langle \boxed{2} \rangle \\
\text{ARG-ST} \quad \langle \boxed{1}, \boxed{2}, \boxed{3} \rangle
\end{bmatrix}
$$

As shown here in the right-hand form, the VP complement of the auxiliary verb *could* is not realized as a COMP element, though the negative adverb is. This form would then project a syntactic structure in (97):

(97)

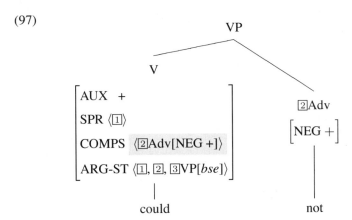

As represented here, the auxiliary verb *could* forms a well-formed head-complement structure with *not*.

Why is there a contrast in the examples in (95)? The reason is that *not* can 'survive' VPE because it can be licensed in the syntax as a complement of an auxiliary, independent of the following VP. However, an adverb like *never* is only licensed as a modifier of VP (it is adjoined to VP to give another VP), and hence if the VP were elided, we would have a hypothetical structure like this:

(98)

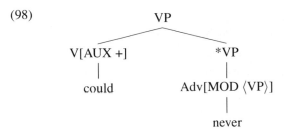

Here, the adverb *never* modifies a VP through the feature MOD, which guarantees that the adverb selects the head VP that it modifies. In an ellipsis structure, the absence of such a VP means that there is no VP for the adverb to modify. In other words, there is no well-formed phrasal structure – predicting the ungrammaticality of *has never* as opposed to *has not*.[11]

---

[11] As we have seen in 6.6.1, all modifiers carry the head feature MOD whose value is the expression they modify.

8.5 Exercises

1. Each of the following sentences contains an item (in the parentheses) which we might want to call an auxiliary. In each case, construct relevant examples that will clarify whether it actually is an auxiliary:

   (i) a. John got sent to prison. (got)
      b. He ought to leave his luggage here. (ought)
      c. They needn't take this exam. (need)
      d. You better not leave it here. (better)
      e. He dared not argue against his parents. (dared)
      f. He used to go there very often. (used).

   Explain your reasoning from the examples you provide.

2. Draw trees for the following sentences:

   (i) a. The gardener must trim the rose bushes today.
      b. This should be the beginning of a beautiful friendship.
      c. I am removing the shovel from the shed.
      d. The travelers have returned from their vacation.
      e. Springfield would have built a police station with the federal grant.
      f. Stringrays could have been cruising near the beach.
      g. She seem to have given financial assistance to an important French art dealer.

3. Provide an analysis of the grammaticality or ungrammaticality of the following examples together, with a tree structure for each, and lexical entries for the words playing the crucial roles in the determination of grammaticality.

   (i) a. Ann may spend/*spending/*spends/*spent her vacation in Italy.
      b. It has rained/*raining/*rains/*rain every day for the last week.
      c. Tagalog is spoken/*speak/*speaks/*spoke in the Philippines.
      d. The roof is leaking/*leaked/*leaks/*leak.

   (ii) a. *Americans have musted pay income tax ever since 1913.
      b. *George is having lived in Toledo for thirty years.
      c. *The house is been remodeling.
      d. *Margaret has had already left.
      e. *A medal was been given to the mayor by the sewer commissioner.
      f. *Does John have gone to the library?
      g. *John seems fond of ice cream, and Bill seems, too.

   (iii) a. Sam may have been being interrogated by the FBI.
      b. *Sam may have been being interrogating by the FBI.
      c. *Sam may be had been interrogating by the FBI.

4. Analyze the following sentences providing tree structures and lexical entries for the verbs:

   (i) a. Have social problems made police work difficult?

b.   The senator should not have forgotten the concerns of her constituents.

c.   Tokyo has not loosened trade restrictions.

d.   They love to play golf, but I do not.

e.   Did the doctor prescribe aspirin?

f.   George has spent a lot of money, hasn't he?

g.   Sandy will read your reports, but Harold will not.

What grammar rules are needed for your structures? Are any lexical rules involved in getting to the correct forms of the verbs?

5.   English allows what is called 'negative inversion' as illustrated in (ii):

(i) a.   He can hardly believe that it's already over.

b.   I could have little known that more trouble was just around the corner.

c.   I have never been spoken to so rudely!

(ii) a.   [Hardly] was there any rain falling.

b.   [Little] did I know that more trouble was just around the corner.

c.   [Never] have I been spoken to so rudely!

(iii) a.   He had hardly collected the papers on his desk, had he/*hadn't he?

b.   He never achieved anything, did he/*didn't he?

Draw tree structures for the sentences (ii) and provide the lexical entries for *hardly*, *little* and *never*. The examples in (iii) indicate that these adverbs all involve some kind of negation in the sentence in which they appear. In addition, think of how your analysis can account for the unacceptable examples in (iv):

(iv) a.   As a statesman, he scarcely could do anything worth mentioning.

b.   As a statesman, scarcely could he do anything worth mentioning.

c.   *As a statesman, scarcely he could do anything worth mentioning.

6.   Observe the following contrast and state a rule that can describe the usage of words like *any*. Does your rule involve negative words like *not* or *hardly* – if so, how? In addition, construct examples replacing *any* with *some* and determine if there are any differences between these two types of word.

(i) a.   *Anyone isn't sleeping in my bed.

b.   *Any zebras can't fly.

c.   *Anything hasn't happened to his optimism.

d.   *Any of the citizens hardly ever say anything.

(ii) a.   I didn't find any bugs in my bed.

b.   Nobody told them anything.

c.   We never found any of the unicorns.

(iii) a.   Never have I stolen from any members of your family.

b.   Why haven't any books been returned?

c.   Hardly any of the citizens ever say anything.

7. After reading the following passage, provide lexical entries for the underlined words and draw trees for the sentences which include them.

    (i)   This expanded role for auxiliaries in English has <u>resulted</u> in some curious rules. One is that when a sentence is to be negated, the word *not* must <u>follow</u> not the main verb (as used to be the case), but the auxiliary. This rule creates an awkward dilemma in the occasional instance when the sentence to be negated actually doesn't have an auxiliary verb. Thus, if I <u>wish</u> to deny the sentence, *I walked home*, I must add an entirely meaningless auxiliary from the verb *do* just to <u>stand</u> as the prop for the word *not*. The result is the sentence, *I didn't walk home*. Now, *do* and *did* are often added to show emphasis, but in those cases they <u>are</u> spoken with emphasis. Thus, there is a difference between saying *I didn't walk home* and saying *I DIDN'T walk home*. The latter sentence expresses emphasis, but in the former sentence the verb *did* expresses nothing at all; it is merely there to <u>hang</u> the *not* on. If we tried to say, *I walked not home*, this would have an unacceptably odd sound to it. It would, indeed, sound archaic. English <u>literature</u> is <u>full</u> of such archaisms, since putting *not* after the main verb was still good usage in the time of Shakespeare and a century or more later.[12]

---

[12] Adopted from 'Creationism & Darwinism, Politics & Economics' by Kelley L. Ross.

9

Passive Constructions

9.1 Introduction

One important aspect of syntax is how to capture systematic relations between related constructions. For example, the following two sentences are similar in meaning:

(1) a. One of Korea's most famous poets wrote these lines.

   b. These lines were written by one of Korea's most famous poets.

We recognize (1b) as the passive counterpart of the active sentence (1a). These two sentences are truth-conditionally similar: they both describe the event of writing the lines by one Korean poet. The only difference involves grammatical functions: in the active voice (1a), *one of Korea's most famous poets* is the subject, whereas in the passive voice (1b), *these lines* is the subject.

Observing these differences, the question that arises is: Why do we use different voices for expressing or describing the same situation or proposition? It is generally accepted that the passive construction is used for certain discourse-motivated reasons. For example, when it is more important to draw our attention to the person or thing acted upon, we use passive. Compare the following:

(2) a. Somebody apparently struck the unidentified victim during the early morning hours.

   b. The unidentified victim was apparently struck during the early morning hours.

We can easily see here that the passive in (2b) assigns more attention to the victim than the active in (2a) does. In addition, when the actor in the situation is not important or specific, there is often a preference to use the passive voice:

(3) a. Targets can be observed at any angle.

   b. During the early evening, Saturn can be found in the north, while Jupiter rises in the east.

Similarly, we use the passive voice in formal, scientific, or technical writing or reports to place an emphasis or an objective presentation on the process or principle being described. For example, compare the following pair:

(4) a. I poured 20cc of acid into the beaker.

    b.   About 20cc of acid was poured into the beaker.

It is clear that unlike the active sentence (4a), the passive sentence (4b) assigns a more objective perspective to the process described.

    In this chapter, leaving aside these discourse- or genre-motivated features of the use of passive constructions, we will look into the syntactic and semantic relationships between active and passive as well as the properties of different passive constructions.

9.2   Relationships between Active and Passive

Consider the two canonical active and passive counterpart sentences:

(5)   a.   The executive committee approved the new policy.

        b.   The new policy was approved by the executive committee.

How do these construction types differ?

Grammatical Functions and Subcategorization: As briefly noted earlier, one of the main differences we can observe between (5a) and (5b) is that the passive sentence has a 'promoted' object: *the new policy* is the passive sentence subject, while the notional subject *the executive committee* is realized, optionally, in a PP (headed by *by*). By definition, a transitive verb form such as *taken* or *chosen* must have an object:

(6)   a.   John has taken <u>Bill</u> to the library.

        b.   John has chosen <u>Bill</u> for the position.

(7)   a.   *John has taken __ to the library.

        b.   *John has chosen __ for the position.

Yet, with the passive construction of such verbs, the object NP is not present in post-verbal position, and must not be:

(8)   a.   *The guide has been taken <u>John</u> to the library.

        b.   *The department has been chosen <u>John</u> for the position.

(9)   a.   John has been taken __ to the library.

        b.   John has been chosen __ for the position.

The absence of the object in the passive is due to the fact that the argument that would have been the object of the active verb has been promoted to be the subject in the passive.

    Apart from the direct object, other subcategorization requirement stays unchanged in a passive form. For example, the active form *handed* in (10) requires an NP and a PP[*to*] as its complements, and the passive *handed* in (11) still requires the PP complement:

(10)   a.   Pat handed a book to Chris.

       b.   *Pat handed to Chris.

       c.   *Pat handed a book.

(11)   a.   A book was handed to Chris (by Pat).

b. *A book was handed (by Pat).

Other Selectional Properties: The third important property, following from the fact that the active verb's object is promoted to the passive construction's subject, is that other selectional properties of the verb are preserved. For example, if the usual postverbal constituent should be an expletive form like *it*, this requirement is on the subject in the passive. Compare the following:

(12)　a.　They believe it/*Stephen to be easy to annoy Ben.

　　　b.　They believe there to be a dragon in the wood.

(13)　a.　It/*Stephen is believed to be easy to annoy Ben.

　　　b.　There is believed to be a dragon in the wood.

If the active complement is itself a clause, so must the subject of the passive verb be a clause:

(14)　a.　No one believes/suspects [that he is a fool].

　　　b.　[That he is a fool] is believed/suspected by no one.

Finally, if the postverbal constituent can be understood as part of an idiom, so can the subject in the passive:

(15)　a.　They believe the cat to be out of the bag.

　　　b.　The cat is believed to be out of the bag.

We thus can conclude that the subject of the passive form is the argument which corresponds to the object of the active.

Morpho-syntactic changes: In addition to changes in argument realization, the passive construction requires the auxiliary verb *be* in conjunction with the the *passive* form of the verb (a subtype of the *en* form, see 5.2.1). In addition to 'passive *be*' italicized in the examples below, there can be other auxiliary verbs, with the passive auxiliary last in the sequence:

(16)　a.　John drove the car. → The car *was* driven.

　　　b.　John was driving the car. → The car was *being* driven.

　　　c.　John will drive the car. → The car will *be* driven.

　　　d.　John has driven the car. → The car has *been* driven.

　　　e.　John has been driving the car. → The car has been *being* driven.

　　　f.　John will have been driving the car. → The car will have been *being* driven.

Semantics: In terms of meaning, as noted above, there is no change in the semantic role assigned to the argument which is the subject in the passive. The agent argument of active verb is expressed as an optional oblique argument of the PP headed by the preposition *by* in the passive, or not at all:

(17)　a.　Pat handed Chris a note.

 b. Chris was handed a note (by Pat).

(18) a. TV puts ideas into children's heads.

 b. Ideas are put into children's heads (by TV).

The observations above mean that any grammar needs to capture the following basic properties of passive:

- Passive turns the active object into the passive subject;
- Passive leaves other aspects of the COMPS value of the active verb unchanged;
- Passive optionally allows the active subject to be the object in a PP headed by the preposition *by*;
- Passive makes the appropriate morphological change in the form of the main verb, and requires the auxiliary *be*;
- Passive leaves the semantics unchanged.

9.3 Approaches to Passive

There could be several ways to capture the systematic syntactic and semantic relationships between active and passive forms. Given our discussion so far, one might think of relying on grammatical categories in phrase structure (NP, VP, S, etc.), or on surface valence properties (SPR and COMPS), often informally characterized as grammatical functions, or semantic roles (agent, patient etc.). In what follows, we will see that we need to refer to all of these aspects of the representation in a proper treatment of English passive constructions.

9.3.1 From Structural Description to Structural Change

Before we look into syntactic analyses for the formation of passive sentences, it is worth reviewing Chomsky's (1957) Passive Formation Rule formulated in terms of structural descriptions (SD) and structural change (SC):

(19)   Passive Formation Rule:

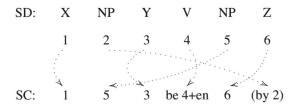

SD: X   NP   Y   V   NP   Z
            1   2   3   4   5   6

SC: 1   5   3   be 4+en   6   (by 2)

This rule means that if there is anything that fits the SD in (19), it will be changed into the given SC: that is, if we have any string in the order of "X – NP – Y – V – NP – Z" (in which X, Y, and Z are variables), the order can be changed into "X – NP – Y – be – V+en – Z – by NP". For example, consider one example:

(20)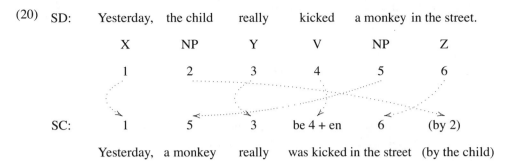

As noted here, the main change that occurs in the SC is that the first NP became an optional PP whereas the second NP became the first NP. The rule also accompanies the addition of *be* and the change of the main verb's VFORM into the passive form. Even though this old SD-SC style rule does not reflect constituenthood of the expressions in the given sentence and is not satisfactory enough to account for all different types of passivization that we will see in the following, this seminal work has influenced the development of subsequent transformational analyses for English passive constructions.

9.3.2 A Transformational Approach

A typical transformational approach assuming movement for passive involves the operation shown in (21) (Chomsky (1982)):

(21)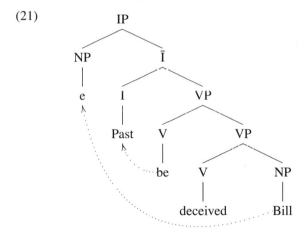

The operation moves the object *Bill* to the subject position and the verb *be* to I (Infl) position, generating the output sentence *Bill was deceived*. This kind of movement analysis is based on the following three basic assumptions:

- Move α: Move a category.
- Case Theory: NP needs Case. The subject receives NOM (nominative) case from tense, and the object receives ACC (accusative) from an active transitive verb.[1]

---

[1] In English, case is morphologically visible only on pronouns: *he* is nominative, whereas *him* is accusative, for example.

- A passive participle does not license ACC case.

In the lower position inside VP, the NP *Bill* in (21) cannot receive ACC case, since by assumption the passive participle form *deceived* cannot assign any case. Hence, *was deceived Bill* would violate Case Theory, for every NP must be assigned case. If the NP is moved to the subject position, where case is assigned by the tensed verb *was*, then Case Theory is satisfied.

Even though this kind of movement or derivational analysis can be appealing in capturing the relationships between canonical active and passive examples, it leaves many facts unexplained. In what follows, we will see more complicated types of passive construction in English, and the need to refer to not only grammatical categories but also grammatical functions, as well as semantic/pragmatic constraints on passive.

9.3.3 A Lexicalist Approach

If we look into more passive examples, we can see that we need to refer to lexical and semantic properties of the transitive verbs. First, there are many exceptions to passive. For example, transitive verbs like *resemble* or *fit* do not have any passive in some senses (see section 9.5 also):

(22) a. The model resembles Kim in nearly every detail.

     b. *Kim is resembled by the model in nearly every detail.

(23) a. The coat does not fit you.

     b. *You are not fitted by the coat.

Such a transitive verb presumably fits the tree structure in (21), but cannot be passivized.

In contrast, there are also verbs like *rumor, say* and *repute* which are used only in the passive, as seen in the following contrast:

(24) a. I was born in 1970.

     b. It is rumored that he is on his way out.

     c. John is said to be rich.

     d. He is reputed to be a good scholar.

(25) a. *My mother bore me in 1970.

     b. *Everyone rumored that he was on his way out.

     c. *They said him to be rich.

     d. *They reputed him to be a good scholar.

Unlike verbs like *resemble*, these verbs are not used as active forms.

Such non-passive examples are hard to explain if we rely only on the assumption that passives are derived from actives from configurational transformation rules. It seems that such lexical idiosyncrasies can be better treated in terms of a lexical process which allows us to refer to the lexical and semantic properties of the verb in question. One way to capture these observed lexical properties of passive is to posit a simplified lexical rule like the following:

(26)   Passive Lexical Rule (to be revised):

$$
\begin{bmatrix} trans\text{-}v \\ \text{SPR } \langle \boxed{1}\text{NP} \rangle \\ \text{COMPS } \langle \boxed{2}\text{NP}, \dots \rangle \end{bmatrix}
\Rightarrow
\begin{bmatrix} pass\text{-}trans\text{-}v \\ \text{HEAD } | \text{ VFORM } pass \\ \text{SPR } \langle \boxed{2}\text{NP} \rangle \\ \text{COMPS } \langle \dots, \left(\text{PP}\left[by + \boxed{1}\text{NP} \right] \right) \rangle \end{bmatrix}
$$

This simple rule says that if there is a transitive verb (*trans(itive)-v*) lexeme selecting one SPR ($\boxed{1}$) and at least one COMPS element ($\boxed{2}$ and others), then there is a related passive verb (*pass-trans-v*). This output verb selects the first element on the original COMPS list as its SPR ($\boxed{2}$NP) and the SPR in the input as an optional PP(consisting of *by* and $\boxed{1}$NP) with the remaining COMPS value unchanged (...). The lexical process also accompanies the change in the VFORM value into *pass*.[2]

As it stands, this lexical rule is not precise enough. For example, consider the following:

(27) a. He kicked the ball.   vs. b. The ball was kicked by him.

      c. John kicked him.   vs. d. He was kicked by John.

We can observe that the case on the first argument of the predicate has changed from *he* in the active to *him* in the passive. However, this difference is entirely predictable: all subjects of finite clauses in English are nominative, and all objects of verbs and prepositions are accusative. However, the passive rule as stated above literally switches the specifier and complement elements, and it would preserve the case specifications on these elements – an accusative object like *her* would become an accusative subject under the rule given above.

Now, rather than stating the case changes directly in the rule, we can change it to refer only to the index value of the subject and object:[3]

---

[2] As we noted in Chapter 5, in terms of the morphological form, the VFORM *pass* is a subtype of *en*.

[3] Notice that the lexical rule given here can also be represented in terms of the ARG-ST (Sag et al. (2002)):

(i) $$\begin{bmatrix} trans\text{-}v \\ \text{ARG-ST } \langle \text{XP}_i, \text{XP}_j \dots \rangle \end{bmatrix} \Rightarrow \begin{bmatrix} pass\text{-}trans\text{-}v \\ \text{ARG-ST } \langle \text{XP}_j, \dots \left(\text{PP}_i[\text{PFORM } by] \right) \rangle \end{bmatrix}$$

This rule rearranges the elements of the input ARG-ST, also accompanying the change in the VFORM value into *pass*. That is, the second element in the input ARG-ST becomes the first element in the ARG-ST of the output passive verb. Whatever follows the second argument in the input is intact, but the first element in the ARG-ST becomes the object of the optional PP. The Argument Realization Constraint in (4.4.3) will ensure that the first element in the ARG-ST is realized as the SPR and the remaining elements as the COMPS value as given in (28). Given that there is no discrepancy between the ARG-ST values and the VAL (SPR and COMPS) values, we can formulate the passive rule as in (28) too.

(28)   Passive Lexical Rule (Final):

$$
\begin{bmatrix}
trans\text{-}v \\
\text{SPR } \langle XP_i \rangle \\
\text{COMPS } \langle XP_j, \dots \rangle
\end{bmatrix}
\Rightarrow
\begin{bmatrix}
pass\text{-}v \\
\text{HEAD } | \text{ VFORM } pass \\
\text{SPR } \langle XP_j \rangle \\
\text{COMPS } \langle \dots, (PP_i[\text{PFORM } by]) \rangle
\end{bmatrix}
$$

With this revised lexical rule, the case of the various NPs will be predicted by general principles of case marking in English clauses – a SPR of a finite verb is nominative, and the first element on the COMPS list of V or P is accusative. The passive rule now refers only to the index values of the SPR and COMPS expressions.

Let us see how all this works, concentrating on a simple example:

(29)   a.   John sent her to Seoul.

       b.   She was sent to Seoul (by John).

The active verb *send* is turned into the passive verb *sent* by the Passive Lexical Rule in (28):

(30)
$$
\begin{bmatrix}
\langle send \rangle \\
\text{HEAD|POS } verb \\
\text{SPR } \langle NP_i \rangle \\
\text{COMPS } \langle NP_j, \boxed{2}PP[to] \rangle
\end{bmatrix}
\Rightarrow
\begin{bmatrix}
\langle sent \rangle \\
\text{HEAD} \begin{bmatrix} \text{POS } verb \\ \text{VFORM } pass \end{bmatrix} \\
\text{SPR } \langle NP_j \rangle \\
\text{COMPS } \langle \boxed{2}PP, (PP_i[by]) \rangle
\end{bmatrix}
$$

As seen here in the output form, the passive *sent* takes a SPR whose index value is identical to that of the first element of the COMPS list in the input. The passive *sent* also inherits the PP[*to*] complement, tagged $\boxed{2}$, and selects an optional PP whose index value is identical to the SPR (subject) of the input.[4] This output lexical entry will then license the following structure for (29b):

---

[4] As noted in Chapter 6.5.2, a preposition functioning as a marker rather than as a predicator with semantic content does not contribute to the meaning of the head PP. This means that its index value is identical to that of its object NP.

(31)

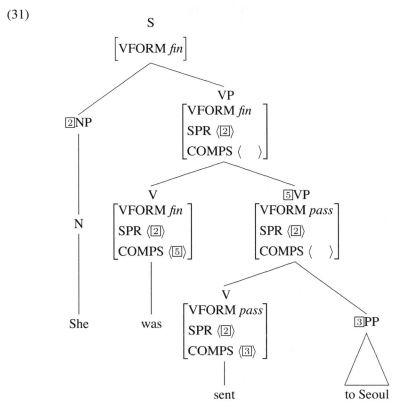

As given in the structure, the passive *sent* combines with its PP[*to*] complement, forming a VP that still requires a SPR. This VP functions as the complement of the auxiliary *be (was)*. As we saw in Chapter 8, *be* is a raising verb, with the repeated lexical entry in (32), whose subject (SPR value) is identical to its VP complement's subject *She*:

(32)

$$\begin{bmatrix} \langle \text{be} \rangle \\ \text{HEAD} \mid \text{POS } \textit{verb} \\ \text{SPR } \langle \boxed{2} \rangle \\ \text{COMPS} \left\langle \text{VP} \begin{bmatrix} \text{VFORM} & \textit{pass} \\ \text{SPR} & \langle \boxed{2} \rangle \end{bmatrix} \right\rangle \end{bmatrix}$$

The SPR requirement on *be* is passed up to the highest VP in accordance with the VALP that regulates the value of SPR and COMPS (see Chapter 5.1). When this VP combines with the subject *she* in accordance with the Head-Specifier Rule, the well-formed passive sentence is complete.

The Passive Lexical Rule in (28) can be also applied to verbs which select for a CP complement. Consider the following examples:

(33) a. They widely believed that John was ill.

b. That John was ill was widely believed.

The application of the Passive Lexical Rule to the active *believe* will generate the passive output shown in the following:

(34)

$$\begin{bmatrix} \langle \text{believe} \rangle \\ \text{HEAD|POS } verb \\ \text{SPR } \langle \text{NP}_i \rangle \\ \text{COMPS } \langle \text{CP}_j \rangle \end{bmatrix} \Rightarrow \begin{bmatrix} \langle \text{believed} \rangle \\ \text{HEAD} \begin{bmatrix} \text{POS } verb \\ \text{VFORM } pass \end{bmatrix} \\ \text{SPR } \langle \text{CP}_j \rangle \\ \text{COMPS } \langle (\text{PP}_i) \rangle \end{bmatrix}$$

The output passive verb *believed* then can license a structure like the following:

(35)

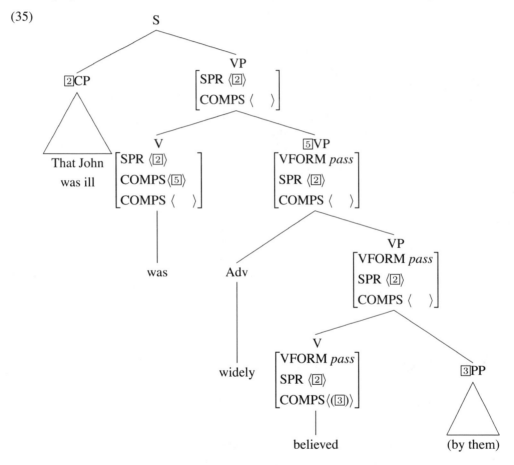

The passive verb *believed* first combines with its optional complement *by them*, and then with the modifier *widely*. The resulting VP then combines with the raising verb *be* in accordance with the Head-Complement Rule. This system, licensing each local structure by the defined grammar rules and principles, thus links the CP subject of *be* to that of *believed*.

The same account also holds when the complement is an indirect question:

(36)   a.   They haven't decided [which attorney will give the closing argument].

b. [Which attorney will give the closing argument] hasn't been decided (by them).

The active *decided* selects an interrogative sentence as its complement, and the Passive Lexical Rule (28) can apply to this verb:[5]

(37)

$$\begin{bmatrix} \langle \text{decide} \rangle \\ \text{HEAD|POS } verb \\ \text{SPR } \langle \text{NP}_i \rangle \\ \text{COMPS } \langle \text{S}_j[\text{QUE} +] \rangle \end{bmatrix} \Rightarrow \begin{bmatrix} \langle \text{decided} \rangle \\ \text{HEAD} \begin{bmatrix} \text{POS } verb \\ \text{VFORM } pass \end{bmatrix} \\ \text{SPR } \langle \text{S}_j[\text{QUE} +] \rangle \\ \text{COMPS } \langle (\text{PP}_i[by]) \rangle \end{bmatrix}$$

The output passive *decided* then will generate the following structure (for simplicity, we do not show COMPS with empty < > values):

(38)

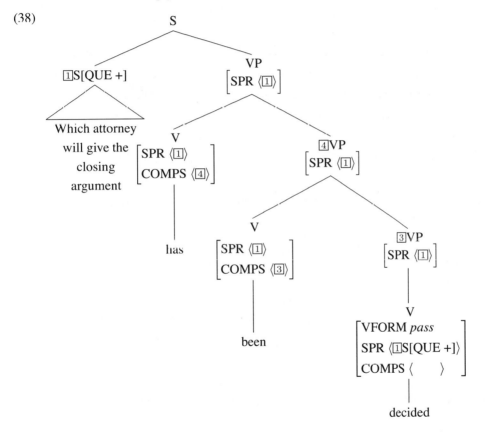

The passive verb *decided* selects an optional PP complement as its complement and an indirect question as its subject, as in the lexical entry in (37). To keep the structure in (38) simple, we have assumed the option without the PP. The raising verb first combines with the first VP, the result of which again combines with the auxiliary raising verb *has*. Notice that since *be*

---

[5]We assume that indirect or direct questions are marked by the feature QUE(STION); see Chapter 10.

and *have* are raising verbs, their VP complement has the same subject as their own. By these identifications, the subject of *has* is identical to that of the passive verb *decided*.

9.4 Prepositional Passives

In addition to the passivization of an active transitive verb, English also allows the so-called 'prepositional verb' to undergo passivization as illustrated in the following:

(39) a. You can *rely on* Ben.

     b. Ben can be *relied on*.

(40) a. They *talked about* the scandal for days.

     b. The scandal was *talked about* for days.

As we noted here, the object of the preposition in the active can function as the subject of the passive sentence. Notice that such prepositional passives are possible with the verbs selecting a PP with a specified preposition:

(41) a. The plan was *approved of* by my mother. (My mother approved of the plan.)

     b. The issue was *dealt with* promptly. (They dealt with the issue promptly.)

     c. That's not what's *asked for*. (That's not what they asked for.)

     d. This should be *attended to* immediately. (We should attend to this immediately.)

(42) a. *Boston was *flown to*. (They flew to/near/by Boston.)

     b. *The capital was *gathered near* by a crowd of people. (A crowd of people gathered near/at the capital.)

     c. *The hot sun was *played under* by the children. (The children played under/near the hot sun.)

The propositions in (41) are all selected by the main verbs (no other prepositions can replace them). Meanwhile, each preposition in (42) is not selected by the main verb, since it can be replaced by another one as noted in their active sentences.

One thing to observe is that there is a contrast between active and passive prepositional verbs with respect to the appearance of an adverb (see Chomsky (1972), Bresnan (1982)). Observe the following:

(43) a. That's something I would have paid *twice* for.

     b. These are the books that we have gone *most thoroughly* over.

     c. They look *generally* on John as selfish.

(44) a. *Everything was paid *twice* for.

     b. *Your books were gone most *thoroughly* over.

     c. *He is looked *generally* on as selfish.

The contrast here shows us that unlike the active, the passive does not allow any adverb to intervene between the verb and the preposition.

There can be two possible structures that can capture these properties: ternary and reanalysis structures. The ternary structure generates a flat structure like the following:

(45)

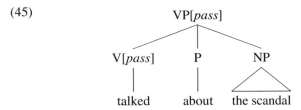

Unlike such a flat or ternary structure, there has been another possible structure assumed in the literature as given in (46):

(46)

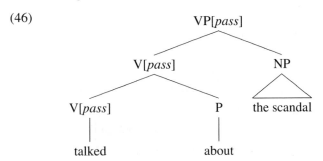

This structure is different from (45) in the sense that the passive verb and the preposition is 'reanalyzed' as a verb again (in this sense this is often called 'reanalysis'). Both (45) and (46) can capture the coherence between the prepositional verb and the preposition itself. Even though both have their own merits, we choose the structure (46), in which the passive verb and the preposition form a unit. We can observe that there are environments where the passive verb (but not active verb) forms a coherent lexical unit with the following preposition:

(47) a. Pavarotti relied on Loren and Bond __ on Hepburn.

  b. *Pavarotti relied on Loren and Bond __ Hepburn.

  c. Loren was relied on by Pavarotti and Hepburn __ by Bond.

  d. *Loren was relied on by Pavarotti and Hepburn __ on by Bond.

What we can observe here is that unlike in the active verb, in the passive *relied on* acts like a lexical unit in the gapping process: the passive *relied* alone cannot be gapped.

This contrast supports the reanalysis structure for the passive. In order for the grammar to allow the passive V to be combined with the following P (which is defined to be 'LIGHT' in the sense that it is not a prosodically heavy element), we introduce the following grammar rule:[6]

(48)   Head-Light Rule:

    V → V, X[LIGHT +]

---

[6] See Abeillé and Godard (2000) for the motivation of introducing the feature LIGHT, with regard to French data.

The rule allows a head V to combine with a LIGHT element such as a preposition in the prepositional passive verb construction.[7]

Given this structural assumption, how then can we generate prepositional passives? We first need to ensure that the object of the prepositional verb is promoted to the subject in the passive, as represented in the following:

(49)   Prepositional Passive Lexical Rule:

$$
\begin{bmatrix} prep\text{-}v \\ \text{SPR } \langle NP_i \rangle \\ \text{COMPS } \langle PP_j[\text{PFORM } \boxed{4}] \rangle \end{bmatrix} \Rightarrow \begin{bmatrix} pass\text{-}prep\text{-}v \\ \text{VFORM } pass \\ \text{SPR } \langle NP_j \rangle \\ \text{COMPS } \left\langle P\begin{bmatrix} \text{LIGHT } + \\ \text{PFORM } \boxed{4} \end{bmatrix}, (PP_i[\text{PFORM } by]) \right\rangle \end{bmatrix}
$$

This rule ensures that a prepositional verb (*prepositional-v*) can have a counterpart passive verb. This passive verb selects a SPR whose index value is identical to that of the input verb's PP complement (in other words, the object of the preposition). The output passive verb also has two complements: a preposition with the same PFORM as the input and an optional PP complement expressing the agent argument (see below for the function of the feature LIGHT).

Let's see how the Prepositional Passive Rule and the Head-Light Rule combined together can account for a prepositional passive:

(50)   a.   The lawyer looked into the document.

       b.   The document was looked into by the lawyer.

The active prepositional verb *look* can undergo the Prepositional Passive Lexical Rule as represented in the following:

(51)

$$
\begin{bmatrix} \langle look \rangle \\ \text{SPR } \langle NP_i \rangle \\ \text{COMPS } \langle PP_j[into] \rangle \end{bmatrix} \Rightarrow \begin{bmatrix} \langle looked \rangle \\ \text{VFORM } pass \\ \text{SPR } \langle NP_j \rangle \\ \text{COMPS } \left\langle P\begin{bmatrix} \text{LIGHT } + \\ \text{PFORM } into \end{bmatrix}, (PP_i[by]) \right\rangle \end{bmatrix}
$$

The output passive verb selects one subject whose index value is identical to that of the input's PP complement. It also selects two complements: a preposition whose PFORM is identical with that of the input PP and an optional PP[*by*] linked to the input subject. This output will then license a structure like the following:

---

[7]In languages like Korean, German, and even French, such a syntactic combination is prevalent for the formation of complex predicates (see Kim (2004b)). In English, particles can also be taken to carry a positive value for LIGHT.

(52)

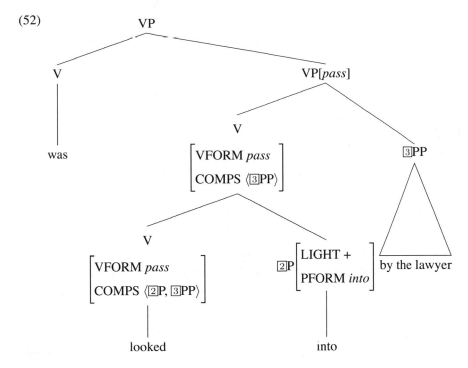

The Head-Light Rule in (48) allows the passive verb to combine with the preposition *into* first, forming still a lexical element. This resulting lexical element then combines with its PP complement *by the lawyer* in accordance with the Head-Complement Rule.[8]

---

[8]This means that in the Head-Complement Rule the complement that the head combines with is phrasal.

9.5   Exercises

1. Draw tree structures for each of the following sentences and then provide the lexical entry for the italicized passive verb.

    (i) a. Peter has been *asked* to resign.
        b. I assume the matter to have been *filed* in the appropriate records.
        c. Smith wants the picture to be *removed* from the office.
        d. The events have been *described* well.
        e. Over 120 different contaminants have been *dumped* into the river.
        f. Heart disease is *considered* the leading cause of death in the United States.
        g. The balloon is *positioned* in an area of blockage and is *inflated*.
        h. There was *believed* to have been a riot in the kitchen.
        i. Cancer is now *thought* to be unlikely to be caused by hot dogs.

2. Provide the active counterpart of the following examples and explain how we can generate each of them, together with tree structures, lexical entries, and grammar rules.

    (i) a. That we should call the police was suggested by her son.
        b. Whether this is feasible hasn't yet been determined.
        c. Paying taxes can't be avoided.

    Also see if there are any relationships between the above examples and the following passives:

    (ii) a. It was suggested by her son that we should call the police.
         b. It hasn't yet been determined whether this is feasible.

3. verbs like *get* and *have* can be used in so-called 'pseudo-passives':

    (i) a. Frances has had the drapes *cleaned*.
        b. Shirley seems to have Fred *promoted*.
    (ii) a. Nina got Bill *elected* to the committee.
         b. We got our car radio *stolen* twice on holiday.

    In addition to these, *have* and *get* also allow constructions like the following:

    (iii) a. Frances has had her *clean* the drapes.
          b. Nina got them *to elect* Bill.

    After drawing tree structures for the above examples, discuss the lexical properties of *have* and *get* – for example, what are their ARG-STs like?

4. Consider the following prepositional passive examples and then analyze them as far as you can with tree structures.

    (i) a. Ricky can be relied on.
        b. The news was dealt with carefully.
        c. The plaza was come into by many people.
        d. The tree was looked after by Kim.

    In addition, consider the passive examples in (ii):

    (i) a. We cannot put up with the noise anymore.

         b. He will keep up with their expectations.

    (ii) a. This noise cannot be put up with.

         b. Their expectations will be kept up with.

Can our analysis given in this chapter account for such examples? Also observe the following examples (in (iv)), which illustrate two different kinds of passive:

    (iii) a. They paid a lot of attention to the matter.

         b. The son took care of his parents.

    (iv) a. The matter was paid a lot of attention to.

         b. A lot of attention was paid to the matter.

Can you think of any way to account for such examples?

5. We have seen that when the verb does not select a specified preposition, it usually does not undergo passivization. However, observe the following contrast:

    (i) a. *New York was slept in.

         b. The bed was slept in.

    (ii) a. *The lake was camped beside by my sister.

         b. The lake is not to be camped beside by anybody.

Why do we have such a contrast with the same type of prepositional verb? In answering this, think about the following contrast too, with respect to semantic or pragmatic facotrs:

    (iii) a. *Six inches were grown by the boy.

         b. *A pound was weighed by the book.

         c. *A mile to work was run by him.

    (iv) a. The beans were grown by the gardener.

         b. The plums were weighed by the greengrocer.

In addition, can your semantic or pragmatic constraints explain the following contrast too? If not, what kind of generalization can you think of to account the contrast here?

    (v) a. *San Francisco has been lived in by my brother.

         b. The house has been lived in by several famous personages.

    (vi) a. *Seoul was slept in by the businessman last night.

         b. This bed was surely slept in by a huge guy last night.

6. In certain environments, passives allow the auxiliary verb part to be *get* instead of *be*:

    (i) a. Rosie got struck by lightning.

         b. I got phoned by a woman friend.

         c. He got hit in the face with the tip of a surfboard.

         d. John's bike got fixed or got stolen.

Get passives usually convey the speaker's personal involvement or reflect the speaker's opinion as to whether the event described is perceived as having favorable or unfavorable consequences. This is why it is rather unacceptable to use the *get* passive when the predicate is stative or the subject-referent has no control over the process in question:

(ii) a. *The king got feared by everyone.

b. *The lesson got read by a choirboy.

c. *The letter got written by a poet.

d. *Tom got understood to have asked for a refund.

e. *Mary got heard to insult her parents.

Based on these observations, provide the lexical entries for *get* in passive and tree structures for (ia) and (ib).

7. Read the following passages and identify all the grammatical errors in the verbs' VFORM values. In addition, provide the lexical information for the correct form.

(ii) Syntax is the discipline that examining the rules of a language that dictate how the various parts of sentences gone together. While morphology looks at how individual sounds formed into complete words, syntax looks at how those words are put together for complete sentences. One part of syntax, calling inflection, deals with how the end of a word might changed to tell a listener or reader something about the role that word is playing. Regular verbs in English, for example, change their ending based for the tense the verb is representing in a sentence, so that when we see *Robert danced*, we know the sentence is in the past tense, and when we see *Robert is dancing*, we know it is not. As another example, regular nouns in English become plural simply by adding an *s* to the end. Cues like these play a large role for helping hearers understanding sentences.[9]

---

[9] From http://www.wisegeek.com/what-is-syntax.htm

10

Wh-Questions

10.1 Clausal Types and Interrogatives

Like other languages, English also distinguishes a set of clause types that are characteristically used to perform different kinds of speech acts:

(1)   a.   Declarative: John is clever.

          b.   Interrogative: Is John clever? Who is clever?

          c.   Exclamative: How clever you are!

          d.   Imperative: Be very clever.

Each clause type in general has its own functions to represent a speech act. For example, a declarative makes a statement, an interrogative asks a question, an exclamative represents an exclamatory statement, and an imperative issues a directive. However, these correspondences are not always one to one. For example, the declarative in (2a) represents not a statement but a question, while the interrogative in (2b) actually indicates a directive:

(2)   a.   I ask you if this is what you want.

          b.   Would you mind taking out the garbage?

In this chapter, we will focus on the syntactic structure of interrogatives, putting aside the mapping relationships between form and function.

There are basically two types of interrogative: yes-no questions and *wh*-questions:

(3)   a.   Yes-No questions: Can the child read the book?

          b.   *Wh*-questions: What can the child read?

Yes-no questions are different from their declarative counterparts by having subject and auxiliary verb in an inverted order. As we have seen in Chapter 8, such yes-no questions are generated through the combination of an inverted finite auxiliary verb with its subject as well as with its complement in accordance with the SAI Rule:

(4)

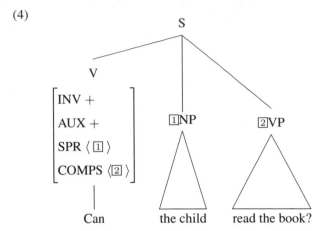

In addition to the subject-auxiliary inversion, *wh*-questions are introduced by one of the interrogative words such as *who, what, which* or *where*. The *wh*-phrases formed from these *wh*-words have a variety of functions in the clause. For example, they can be the subject, object, oblique complement, or even an adjunct:

(5)   a.   [Who] called the police?

       b.   [Which version] did they recommend?

       c.   [With what] did the baby eat the food?

       d.   [How] did he eat the food?

The *wh*-phrase need not be an NP – it can be a PP, AP, or AdvP:

(6)   a.   [$_{NP}$ Which man] [did you talk to __]?

       b.   [$_{PP}$ To which man] [did you talk __]?

       c.   [$_{AP}$ How ill] [has Hobbs been __]?

       d.   [$_{AdvP}$ How frequently] [did Hobbs see Rhodes __]?

As seen in these examples, in terms of structure, each *wh*-question consists of two parts: a *wh*-phrase and an inverted sentence with a missing phrase (indicated by the underline). The *wh*-phrase (filler) and the missing phrase (gap) must have an identical syntactic category as a way of ensuring their linkage:

(7)   a.   *[$_{NP}$ Which man] [did you talk [$_{PP}$ __]]?

       b.   *[$_{PP}$ To which man] [did you talk to [$_{NP}$ __]]?

Another important property is that the distance between the filler and the gap is not bound within one sentence, and it can be 'long-distance' or 'unbounded':

(8)   a.   [[Who] do you think [Tom saw __]]?

       b.   [[Who] do you think [Mary said [Tom saw __]]]?

       c.   [[Who] do you think [[Hobbs imagined [Mary said [Tom saw __]]]]]?

As can be seen here, as long as the link between the filler and the gap is appropriate, the distance between the two can be unbounded. We can observe similar phenomena in the so-called topicalization construction:

(9)   a.   Most dogs, Tom didn't see __ .

        b.   Most dogs, Mary thought Tom didn't see __ .

        c.   Most dogs, Hobbs said Mary thought Tom didn't see __

This long-distance relationship means that we put *wh*-questions and other similar constructions like topicalization into the same family, with the name 'long-distance dependencies'.

10.2   Movement vs. Feature Percolation

Traditionally, there have been two different ways to link the filler *wh*-phrase with its missing gap. One traditional way of linking the two is to assume that the filler *wh*-phrase is moved to the sentence-initial position by movement operations as represented in (10) (cf. Chomsky (1981a)):

(10)

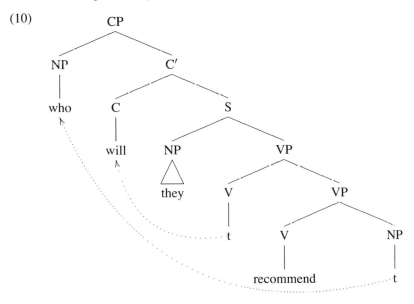

The *wh*-phrase *who* is originally in the object position of *recommend* and then moved to the specifier position of the intermediate phrase C'. The auxiliary verb *will* is also moved from the V position to the C.

This kind of movement operation can be appealing at first glance in capturing the linkage between the filler and gap. However, the notion of moving an overt element to form a *wh*-question immediately runs into a problem with examples like the following:

(11)   a.   Who did Kim work for __ and Sandy rely on __ ?

        b. *Who did Kim work for __ and Sandy rely __ ?

        c. *Who did Kim work for __ and Sandy rely on Mary?

If we adopt a movement process for (11a), there must be an operation in which the two NP gaps (marked by the underlines) are collapsed into one NP and become *who*. We cannot simply move one NP, because it will generate an ill-formed example like (11b).

There is also a class of so-called 'movement paradox' examples, provided by Bresnan (1991, 2001). First, consider the following topicalization example, which also displays the relevant type of 'long distance' relationship:

(12) a. You can rely on [Edward's help].

      b. [Edward's help], you can rely on __

(13) a. We talked about [the fact that he was sick for days].

      b. [The fact that he was sick for days], we talked about __ .

In a movement approach, both of the (b) examples are derived from the (a) examples by moving the NPs to the sentence initial position. However, not every putatively 'derived' example has a well-formed source:

(14) a. *You can rely on that he will help you.

      b. [That he will help you], you can rely on __ .

(15) a. *We talked about [that he was sick for days].

      b. [That he was sick], we talked about __ for days.

(16) a. *This theory captures that arrows don't stop in midair.

      b. [That arrows don't stop in midair] is captured __ by this theory.

If we take the same rationale as for (13), it is difficult to explain how the putative source example is ungrammatical while a derived form is grammatical. This inconsistency between the fronted phrase and the putative missing phrase casts doubt on the existence of movement operations in such examples.

Instead of postulating movement as an operation, we can assume that there is no movement process at all, but instead a mechanism of communication through the tree, known as feature percolation, to generate such *wh*-questions. For example, the information that an NP is missing or gapped can be passed up in the tree until the gap meets its corresponding filler:

(17)

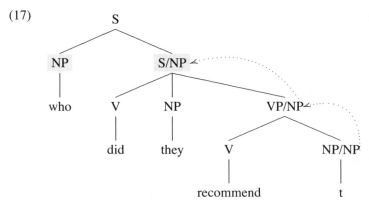

The notations such as NP/NP (read as 'NP slash NP') or S/NP ('S slash NP') here mean that the category to the left of the slash is incomplete and missing one NP. This missing information is percolated up to the point where it meets its filler *who*. There is thus no notion of movement here, but just a feature percolation up to the point where the missing gap meets its filler.

This kind of feature percolation system can account for the contrast given in (11a) and (11b). Let us look at partial structures of these two examples:

(18)   a.

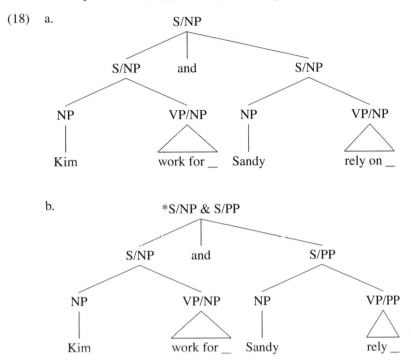

b.

In (18a), the missing gaps are both NPs whereas in (18b), an NP and a PP are missing. Since the mechanism of feature unification allows two nonconflicting phrases to be unified into one, two S/NP phrases in (18a) are merged into one S/NP. Simply, the whole coordinate structure is 'missing an NP' and this description is true of each internal conjunct. However, in (18b) we cannot unify the two different phrases S/NP and S/PP into one since they have conflicting slash values (see section 3.2 for the analysis of these 'paradox' examples). This observation, known in the literature as the 'Coordinate Structure Constraint', goes back to Ross (1967).

10.3   Feature Percolation with No Abstract Elements

10.3.1   Basic Systems

As a more formal way of stating the feature percolation system, we can introduce the feature attribute GAP for an empty phrase and pass this up to the point where the gap value is discharged by its filler. However, even within such an approach, an issue remains of positing an empty element. An empty element is an abstract entity introduced for a theoretical reason (for example, the GAP feature may 'start off' at the bottom of the tree in virtue of an invisible element t (trace) of category NP/NP, as in Gazdar et al. (1985)). Though the introduction of an empty element with no phonological value might be reasonable, examples like the following raise issues that are not easily solved (Sag and Fodor (1994), Sag (2000)):

(19)   a. *Who did you see [$_{NP}$[$_{NP}$ __] and [$_{NP}$ a picture of [$_{NP}$ __]]]?

       b. *Who did you compare [$_{NP}$ [$_{NP}$ __] and [$_{NP}$ __]]?

On the assumption that empty elements are identical to canonical phrases except for the fact that they have no phonological values at all, nothing would block us from coordinating two empty phrases, leading to incorrect predictions. If we can avoid positing empty elements that we cannot see or hear, it would be better in theoretical as well as empirical terms (cf. Pullum (1991)).

One way to do without an abstract element is to encode the missing information in the lexical head (Sag et al. 2003). For example, the verb *recommend* can be realized with different overt complements:

(20)   a.   These qualities recommended him to Oliver.

       b.   The UN recommended an enlarged peacekeeping force.

(21)   a.   This is the book which the teacher recommended __ .

       b.   Who will they recommend __ ?

In (20), the verb *recommend* is realized in canonical uses whereas the one in (21) is not. That is, in (20), the object of the verb is present as its sister, whereas in (21) the object is in a nonlocal position. This difference can be represented as a difference in possibilities allowed by the following revised ARC:

(22)   Argument Realization Constraint (ARC, second approximation):
            The first element on the ARG-ST list is realized as SPR, the rest as COMPS or GAP in syntax.

This revised ARC will then allow the following realizations for *recommend*:

(23)

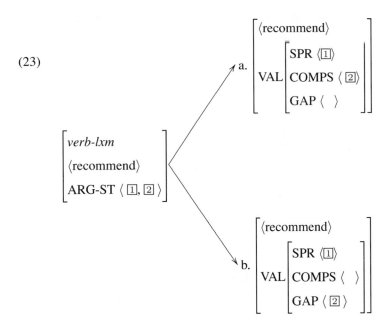

In (23a), the two arguments of the verb *recommend* are realized as the SPR and COMPS value respectively, whereas in (23b) the second argument is realized not as a COMPS value but as a GAP value. Each of these two different realizations will project the following structures for examples like (20b) and (21b), respectively:

(24) a.

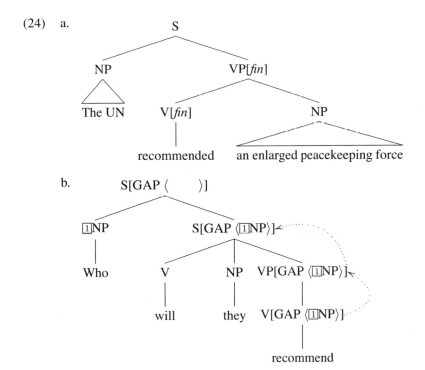

b.

The main difference between the two is that in (24a), the object of *recommend* is its sister whereas in (24b) it is not. That is, in the former the object is local to the verb whereas in the latter it is nonlocal. In (24b), the verb contains a GAP value which is identified with the object. This GAP value is passed up to the VP and then to the lower S. At this level, this GAP value is discharged by the filler *who*, more specifically, by the following Head-Filler Rule:

(25)   Head-Filler Rule:

$$S\left[GAP \; \langle \quad \rangle\right] \to \boxed{1}XP, \quad S\left[GAP \; \langle\boxed{1}XP\rangle\right]$$

This grammar rule says that when a head expression S containing a nonempty GAP value combines with its filler value, the resulting phrase will form a grammatical head-filler phrase with the GAP value discharged. This completes the 'top' of the long-distance or unbounded dependency.

10.3.2   Non-subject Wh-questions

Let us see how the present system generates a non-subject *wh*-question, using the verb *put* for illustration. This verb will select three arguments as given here:

(26)
$$\begin{bmatrix} \langle \text{put} \rangle \\ \text{ARG-ST} \; \langle \text{NP, NP, PP} \rangle \end{bmatrix}$$

The ARC will ensure that of these three arguments the first one must be realized as a SPR element, and the rest either as COMPS or as GAP elements. We thus will have at least the following three realizations for the verb *put*:[1]

(27)
a.
$$\begin{bmatrix} \langle \text{put} \rangle \\ \text{VAL} \begin{bmatrix} \text{SPR} \; \langle \boxed{1} \rangle \\ \text{COMPS} \; \langle \boxed{2}, \boxed{3} \rangle \\ \text{GAP} \; \langle \quad \rangle \end{bmatrix} \\ \text{ARG-ST} \; \langle \boxed{1}, \boxed{2}, \boxed{3} \rangle \end{bmatrix}$$
b.
$$\begin{bmatrix} \langle \text{put} \rangle \\ \text{VAL} \begin{bmatrix} \text{SPR} \; \langle \boxed{1} \rangle \\ \text{COMPS} \; \langle \boxed{3} \rangle \\ \text{GAP} \; \langle \boxed{2} \rangle \end{bmatrix} \\ \text{ARG-ST} \; \langle \boxed{1}, \boxed{2}, \boxed{3} \rangle \end{bmatrix}$$
c.
$$\begin{bmatrix} \langle \text{put} \rangle \\ \text{VAL} \begin{bmatrix} \text{SPR} \; \langle \boxed{1} \rangle \\ \text{COMPS} \; \langle \boxed{2} \rangle \\ \text{GAP} \; \langle \boxed{3} \rangle \end{bmatrix} \\ \text{ARG-ST} \; \langle \boxed{1}, \boxed{2}, \boxed{3} \rangle \end{bmatrix}$$

Each of these three lexical entries will then generate sentences like the following:

(28)   a.   John put the books in a box.

b.   Which books did John put in the box?

c.   Where did John put the books?

As we see here, the complements of the verb *put* are realized in three different ways. The verb *put* in (27a) has the canonical realization of the verb's arguments, generating an example like (28a). Meanwhile, in (27b), the object NP argument is realized as a GAP as reflected in (28b) whereas in (27c), the PP is realized as a GAP as shown in (28c). The following structure represents how the lexical realization (27b) provides for examples like (28b) in more detail:

---

[1] The SPR value can be gapped too. See the next section.

(29)

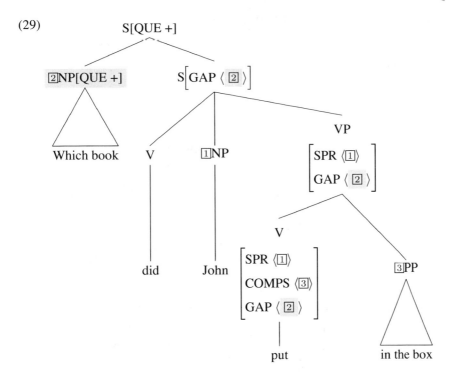

Let us look at the structure working from bottom to top. At the bottom, the verb *put* has one PP complement with its NP complement as a GAP value. This GAP information is passed all the way up to the lower S where it is discharged by the filler NP *which book*. Each phrase is licensed by the grammar rules: the verb *put* with this GAP information first combines with just the necessary PP complement *in the box*, in accordance with the Head-Complement Rule. The inverted auxiliary verb *did* combines with the subject NP *John* and the just-described VP in accordance with the SAI rule. The resulting S is still incomplete because of the nonempty GAP value (every sentence needs to have an empty GAP value). This GAP value is discharged when the Head-Filler Rule in (25) combines the filler NP *which book* with the incomplete S.[2]

This kind of feature percolation system, involving no empty elements, works well even for long-distance dependency examples. Consider the following structure:

---

[2]Every *wh*-element in questions carries the feature [QUE +].

(30)

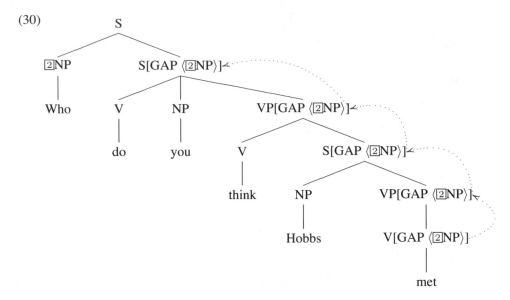

The GAP value starts from the lexical head *met* whose second argument is realized as a GAP value. Since the complement of the verb *met* is realized as a GAP value, the verb *met* will not look for its complement in the local domain (as its sister node). The GAP information will be passed up to the embedded S, which is a nonhead daughter. It is the following NIP that ensures that the GAP value in the head daughter or nonhead daughter is passed up through the structure until it is discharged by the filler *who* by the Head-Filler Rule:[3]

(31)   Nonlocal Feature Inheritance Principle (NIP):
         A phrase's nonlocal feature such as GAP and QUE is the union of its daughters' nonlocal feature values minus any bound nonlocal features.

The role of this principle is clear from the embedded S in (30): The principle allows the GAP in this nonhead S to pass up to the VP.

   With this principle together, we can observe that the treatment of long distance dependency within the feature percolation system involves three parts: top, middle, and bottom. The bottom part introduces the GAP value according to the ARC. The middle part ensures the GAP value is inherited 'up' to the mother in accordance with the NIP. Finally, the top level terminates the GAP value by the filler in accordance with the Head-Filler Rule.

   It is also easy to verify how this system accounts for examples like (32) in which the gap is a non-NP:

(32) a. [In which box] did John put the book __ ?
      b. [How happy] has John been __ ?

The Head-Filler Rule in (25) ensures that the categorial status of the filler is identical with that of the gap. The structure of (32a) can be represented as following:

---

[3]The nonlocal features will be 'bound' either by a grammar rule like the Head-Filler Rule (see (25)) or a lexical constraint (see the discussion of 'easy' constructions in Chapter 12.2).

(33)

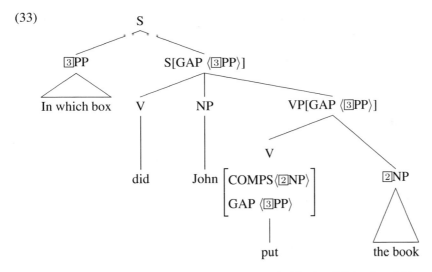

In this structure, the missing phrase is a PP encoded in the GAP value. This value is percolated up to the lower S and discharged by the filler *in which box*.

In addition, notice that in this approach we have a more clear account for the examples we have seen in (11), which we repeat here:

(34)   a.   Who did Kim work for __ and Sandy rely on __ ?
       b.   *Who did Kim work for __ and Sandy rely on Mary?

As we have seen earlier in Chapter 2, English allows two identical phrases to be conjoined. This then means that the GAP value in each conjunct also need to be identified:

(35)   Coordination Rule:

          XP → XP[GAP $\boxed{A}$] conj XP[GAP $\boxed{A}$]

This grammar rule then explains the contrast in (34), as represented in the simplified structures:

(36)   a.

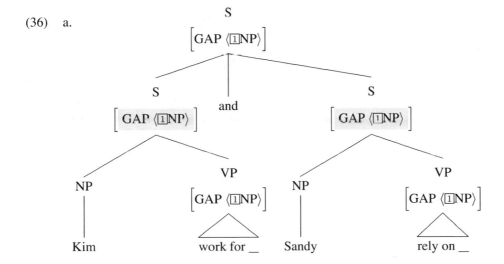

b.

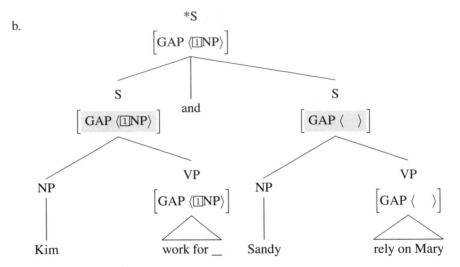

In (36a), the GAP value in the first conjunct is identical with that in the second conjunct, satisfying the Coordination Rule. The feature unification will allow these two identical GAP values to be unified into one. However in (36b), the GAP values in the two conjuncts are different, violating the Coordination Rule and thus cannot be unified.

Notice that this feature-based analysis can also offer a way of dealing with the movement paradox examples we observed in (14), repeated here:

(37) a. You can rely on his help/*that he will help you.

b. His help, you can rely on __ .

c. That he will help you, you can rely on __ .

The introduction of a GAP value is a lexical realization process in the present system, implying that we can assume that the complement of the preposition *on* in such a usage can be realized either as an NP in (38b), or as a *nominal* GAP element as in (38c):

(38)
a.
$$\begin{bmatrix} prep\text{-}v\text{-}p \\ \langle \text{on} \rangle \\ \text{ARG-ST } \langle \boxed{1}\text{XP} \rangle \end{bmatrix}$$
b.
$$\begin{bmatrix} \langle \text{on} \rangle \\ \text{COMPS } \langle \text{NP} \rangle \\ \text{GAP } \langle \quad \rangle \end{bmatrix}$$
c.
$$\begin{bmatrix} \langle \text{on} \rangle \\ \text{COMPS } \langle \quad \rangle \\ \text{GAP } \langle \text{XP}[nominal] \rangle \end{bmatrix}$$

This realization means that when the preposition *on* is serving as the part of a prepositional verb (*prep-v-p*) like *rely on*, its prepositional complement can be either realized as an NP or as a *nominal* GAP element. This has the consequence that if the argument of *on* is realized as a COMPS element, it must be an NP as in (37a). However, when its argument is realized as a GAP, the GAP value can either be an NP as in (37b) or a CP as in (37c). This is possible since, as we have seen in Chapter 5, the POS type *nominal* subsumes both *comp* and *noun*. This lexical realization in (38c) will then project a structure like the following:

(39)

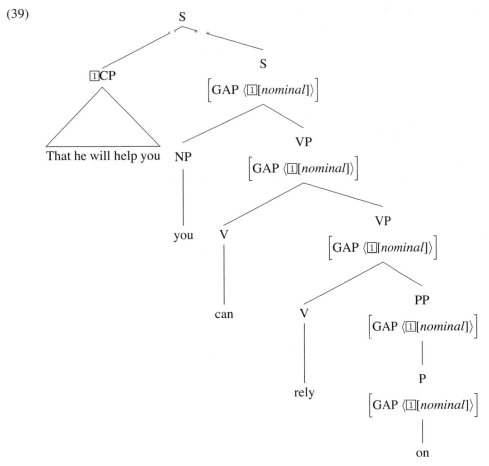

The present system, allowing some flexibility in argument realization, can capture these move-ment paradox examples, and its applicability suggests that movement is not the best mechanism to account for apparent displacement in syntax.

10.3.3 Subject Wh-Questions

Now consider examples in which the subject is the focus of the *wh*-question:

(40) a. Who put the book in the box?

  b. Who DID put the book in the box?

  c. Who can put the book in the box?

We can notice that when the subject *who* is questioned, the presence of an auxiliary verb is optional. That is, the question in (40a) is well-formed, even though no auxiliary is present. The related example (40b) is also well-formed, but is used only when there is emphasis on the auxiliary.

  As a first step to account for such examples, we can, adopting a similar structure like non-subject *wh*-questions, posit a structure like (41) in which the subject is gapped:

(41) a. Who __ put the book in the box?

      b. Who __ can put the book in the box?

In the current context, our grammar requires no additional mechanism other than slightly revising the ARC:

(42)   Argument Realization Constraint (ARC, final):
          The first element on the ARG-ST list is realized as SPR or GAP, the rest as COMPS or GAP in syntax.

This revised ARC eventually guarantees that the values of the ARG-ST is the sum of that of SPR, COMPS, and GAP. The system then allows the following lexical realization for *put*, in addition to those in (27):

(43) $\begin{bmatrix} \langle \text{put} \rangle \\ \text{VAL} \begin{bmatrix} \text{SPR} \langle \ \rangle \\ \text{COMPS} \langle \boxed{2}, \boxed{3} \rangle \\ \text{GAP} \langle \boxed{1} \rangle \end{bmatrix} \\ \text{ARG-ST} \langle \boxed{1}, \boxed{2}, \boxed{3} \rangle \end{bmatrix}$

This realization in which the subject is gapped then projects the following structure for (41a):

(44)

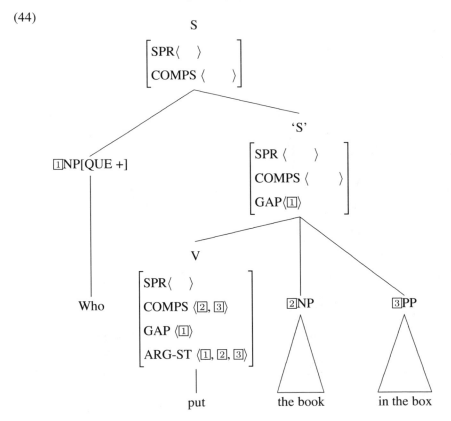

As shown in the structure, the subject of *put* is realized as the GAP value, passing up to the mother node. This node looks like a VP, but in fact it is a projection of V with an empty SPR list, and hence is effectively a kind of S (by definition, S is a projection of V which has an empty SPR and COMPS list). This incomplete sentence 'S' with the subject missing then can combine with the filler *who* according to the Head-Filler Rule.

Even though the 'S' with the subject gapped cannot function as an independent sentence as in **Visited him*, it can function as the complement of a verb like *think* as in sentences like the following:

(45) a. Who do you think [visited Seoul last year]?

  b. That's the UN delegate that the government thinks [visits Seoul last year].

The verb *think* can select either a finite S or a CP as in *I think (that) she knows chorus*. This means that the verb can also combine with an 'S' with the subject being gapped:

(46)

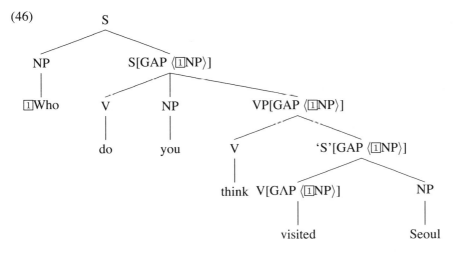

This kind of analysis can provide a way of explaining the so-called '*that*-trace effect' in (47) as well as the 'adverbial amelioration effect' in (48):

(47) a. Who do you believe that Sara invited __ ?

  b. Who do you believe __ invited Sara?

  c. *Who do you believe that __ invited Sara?

(48) a. *Who do you think that __ would be nominated for the position?

  b. Who do you think that [under these exceptional circumstances] __ would have anything to do with such a scheme?

What we can notice in (47) is that when the complementizer *that* is present, we cannot have the seemingly subject gap. However, the subject gap can be salvaged by the presence of an intervening phrase, such as an adverbial, as shown in (48). We can attribute this observed idiosyncratic behavior to the lexical peculiarities of the complementizer *that*. Consider the possible and impossible structures:[4]

(49)   a.

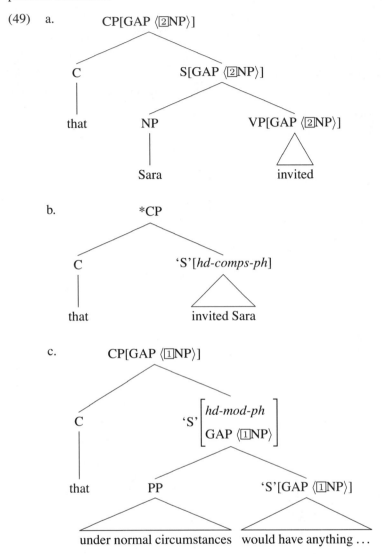

b.

c.

(49a) is a well-formed structure in which the embedded clause has an object gap. (49b) is out in which the complementizer combines with the subject missing 'S'. (49c) is fine even though it also has the subject missing 'S'. As we have noted throughout the chapters, English grammar rules license well-formed phrases identified by the phrasal types such as *hd-spr-ph*, *hd-comps-ph*, *hd-mod-ph* and so forth. As represented in the structures here, the complementizer *that* can select either an S or 'S', but cannot combine with a *head-comps-ph* 'S' (a finite VP with its subject gapped). This kind of negative constraint assigns a special status to the complementizer usage of *that*.

---

[4]The italicized *hd-comps-ph* and *hd-mod-ph* here indicates the type name of the phrase 'S'.

10.4 Indirect Questions

10.4.1 Basic Structure

Among the verbs selecting a sentential or clausal complement (S or CP), there are also verbs selecting an indirect question:

(50) a. John asks [whose book his son likes __].

  b. John has forgotten [which player his son shouted at __].

  c. He told me [how many employees Karen introduced __ to the visitors].

It is not the case that all verbs allow an indirect question as their complement:

(51) a. Tom denied [(that) he had been reading the article].

  b. *Tom denied [which book he had been reading].

(52) a. Tom claimed [(that) he had spent five thousand dollars].

  b. *Tom claimed [how much money she had spent].

Factive verbs like *deny* or *claim* cannot combine with an indirect question: only a finite declarative clause can function as their complement. Verbs selecting an indirect question as their complement can be in general classified by their meaning:

(53) a. interrogative verbs: *ask, wonder, inquire, ...*

  b. verbs of knowledge: *know, learn, forget, ...*

  c. verbs of increased knowledge: *teach, tell, inform, ...*

  d. decision verbs/verbs of concern: *decide, care, ...*

We can easily see that the clausal complement of these verbs cannot be a canonical CP, and must be an indirect question:

(54) a. *John inquired [that he should read it].

  b. *Peter will decide [that we should review the book].

(55) a. John inquired [which book he should read].

  b. Peter will decide [which book we should review].

A caution here is that there are some verbs, such as *forget, tell* and *know*, that select either a [QUE +] or a [QUE −] complement.

(56) a. John told us that we should review the book.

  b. John told us which book we should review.

There are thus at least three different types of verb which take clausal complements, in terms of their semantic functions (e.g., whether the complement is interpreted as declarative or question), reflected in the following lexical entries:

(57)

$$
\text{a. } \begin{bmatrix} \langle wonder \rangle \\ \text{HEAD} \mid \text{POS } verb \\ \text{SPR } \langle \boxed{1} \rangle \\ \text{COMPS } \langle [\text{QUE} +] \rangle \end{bmatrix} \quad
\text{b. } \begin{bmatrix} \langle deny \rangle \\ \text{HEAD} \mid \text{POS } verb \\ \text{SPR } \langle \boxed{1} \rangle \\ \text{COMPS } \langle [\text{QUE} -] \rangle \end{bmatrix} \quad
\text{c. } \begin{bmatrix} \langle tell \rangle \\ \text{HEAD} \mid \text{POS } verb \\ \text{SPR } \langle \boxed{1} \rangle \\ \text{COMPS } \langle [\text{QUE} \pm] \rangle \end{bmatrix}
$$

The feature QUE originates from a *wh*-word like *who* or *which* and is used to distinguish between indirect questions and declarative clauses. The difference in the QUE value of the verb's complement will ensure that each verb combines with an appropriate clausal complement. For example, the verb *wonder*, requiring a [QUE +] clausal complement, will be licensed in a structure like the following:

(58)

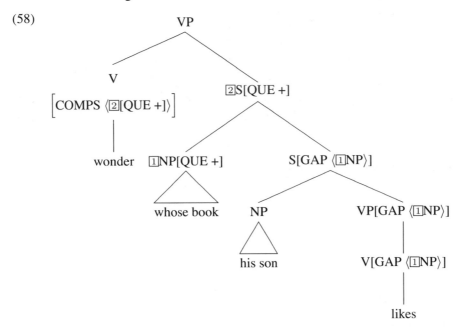

The GAP value of *likes* is passed up to the lower S and discharged by the filler *whose book*. The *wh*-word *whose* carries the feature [QUE +] which, similar to the feature GAP, will pass up to the point where it is required by a verb or to the highest position to indicate that the given sentence is a question. For example, in (59), the feature QUE marks that the whole sentence is a question, whereas in (60) it allows the embedded clause to be an indirect question:

(59) a. $[_{\text{S[QUE +]}}$ In which box did he put the book __]?
      b. $[_{\text{S[QUE +]}}$ Which book by his father did he read __]?

(60) a. John asks $[_{\text{S[QUE +]}}$ in which box he put the book].
      b. John asks $[_{\text{S[QUE +]}}$ which book by his father he read].

The percolation of the feature QUE upward from a *wh*-word can be ensured by the NIP that guarantees nonlocal features like QUE to be passed up until they are bound off or selected by a sister (like a filler phrase, or a selecting V). This principled constraint allows the QUE value to pass up to the mother from a deeply embedded nonhead as illustrated in the following:

(61) a. Kim has wondered [[in which room] Gary stayed __].

 b. Lee asked me [[how fond of chocolates] the monkeys are __]].

Let us consider the structure of (61a):

(62)

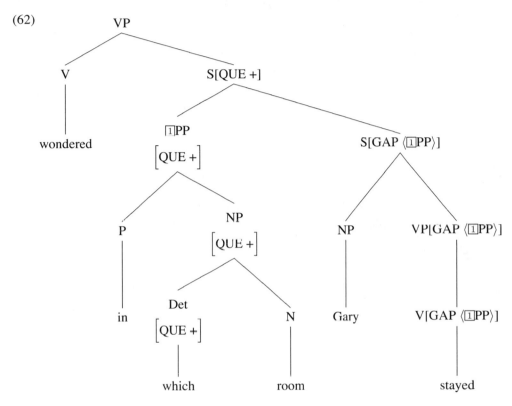

Even though *which* is embedded in the PP and functions as the Det of the inner NP, its QUE value will pass up to the S, granting it the status of an indirect question. The verb *wonder* then combines with this S, satisfying its subcategorization requirement. If the verb combines with a [QUE −] clausal complement, we would then have an ungrammatical structure:

(63) a. *Kim has wondered [$_{[QUE\ -]}$ that Gary stayed in the room].

 b. *Kim asked me [$_{[QUE\ -]}$ that the monkeys are very fond of chocolates].

As we have seen above, the category of the missing phrase within the S must correspond to that of the *wh*-phrase in the initial position. For example, the following structure is not licensed simply because there is no Head-Filler Rule that allows the combination of the filler NP with an S missing a PP:

(64)

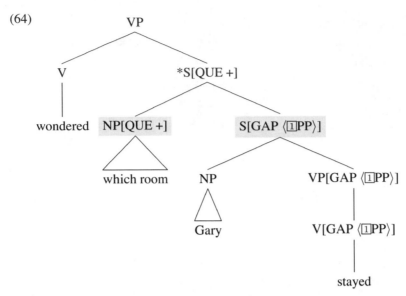

In a similar fashion, the present system also predicts the following contrast:

(65) a. John knows [whose book [Mary bought __] and [Tom borrowed __ from her]].
      b. *John knows [whose book [Mary bought __] and [Tom talked __]].

The partial structure of these can be represented as following:

(66) a.

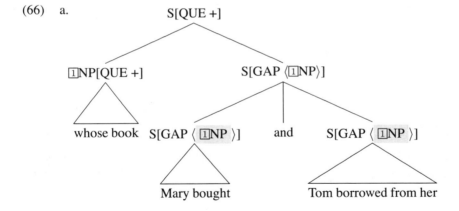

b.

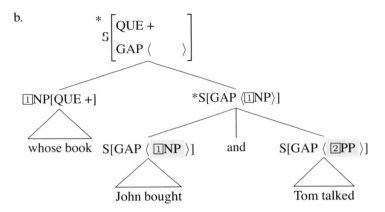

As long as the two GAP values are identical, we can unify the two into one as in (66a). However, if the GAP values are different as in (66b), there is no way to unify them in the coordination structure.

10.4.2 Non-Wh Indirect Questions

English also has indirect questions headed by the complementizer *whether* or *if*:

(67) a. I don't know [whether/if I should agree].

  b. She gets upset [whether/if I exclude her from anything].

  c. I wonder [whether/if you'd be kind enough to give us information].

These indirect questions are all internally complete in the sense that there is no missing element. This means that the complementizers *whether* and *if* will have at least the following lexical information:

(68)
$$
\begin{bmatrix}
\langle \text{whether} \rangle \\
\text{SYN} \begin{bmatrix} \text{HEAD | POS } comp \\ \text{VAL | COMPS } \langle S \rangle \\ \text{QUE +} \end{bmatrix}
\end{bmatrix}
$$

According to this lexical information, *whether* selects a finite S and provides a [QUE +] value, licensing a structure like the following:

(69)

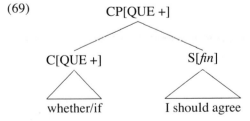

One thing to note here is that *if* and *whether* are slightly different even though they both carry a positive QUE feature.[5] Just like indirect questions, the clauses headed by *whether* can

---

[5]See Exercise 4 of Chapter 2.

serve as a prepositional object.

(70) a. I am not certain about [when he will come].

      b. I am not certain about [whether he will go or not].

However, an *if*-clause cannot function as prepositional object:

(71) a. *I am not certain about [if he will come].

      b. *I am not certain about [if he will go or not].

There is also a difference between *if* and *whether* in infinitival constructions:

(72) a. I don't know [where to go].

      b. I don't know [what to do].

      c. I don't know [how to do it].

      d. I don't know [whether to agree with him or not].

(73) a. *I don't know [if to agree with him].

      b. *I don't know [that to agree with him or not].

This means that *whether* and *if* can both bear the feature QUE (projecting an indirect question), but different with respect to the fact that only *whether* behaves like a true *wh*-element.[6]

10.4.3 Infinitival Indirect Questions

In addition to the finite indirect questions, English also has infinitival indirect questions:

(74) a. Fred knows [which politician to support].

      b. Karen asked [where to put the chairs].

Just like the finite indirect questions, these constructions have the familiar bipartite structures: a *wh*-phrase and an infinitival clause missing one element.

Notice at this point that in English there exist at least four different ways for the subject to be realized: as a canonical NP, gap, and PRO, or *pro*:

(75) a. The student protected him. (a canonical NP)

      b. Who __ protected him? (a gap NP)

      c. To protect him is not an easy task. (PRO)

      d. Protect him! (*pro*)

In (75a), the subject is a 'canonical' NP whereas those in the others are 'non-canonical'. In the *wh*-question (75b), the subject is a GAP value; in (75c), the infinitival VP has an understood, unexpressed subject PRO whereas the imperative in (75d) the subject is an unexpressed one, though understood as the second person subject *you*. Traditionally, the unexpressed pronoun subject of a finite clause is called 'small *pro*' whereas that of an nonfinite clause is called 'big PRO' (Chomsky (1982)), as they have slightly different referential properties. In the terms we

---

[6]One way to distinguish the *wh*-elements including *whether* from *if* is to have an extra feature WH to distinguish them.

are using in this book, this means, we have 'canonical' pronouns like *he* and *him* as well as 'non-canonical' realizations of the pronouns. To allow a VP with a non-canonical subject to be projected into a complete S, we can assume the following Head-Only Rule:

(76)   Head-Only Rule:

S[SPR ⟨   ⟩] → VP[SPR ⟨NP[*noncan-pro*]⟩]

The rule says a VP whose subject is either a *pro* or a PRO can be directly projected into a complete sentence with the subject being discharged. A finite VP will, however, not be projected into an S, since it selects a canonical subject. The rule as given will license the following structures:

(77)

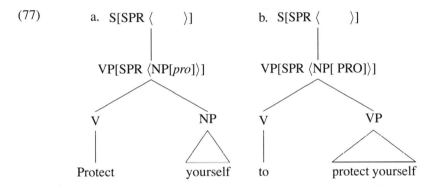

The subject of the VP here is *pro* or PRO: either can be licensed, and this rule in (76) allows a VP to form a complete sentence with no pronounced subject. With this new rule, we then can have the following structure:[7]

---

[7]Following Sag et al. (2003) and Huddleston and Pullum (2002), we also take the imperative form of the verb here is *finite*.

(78)

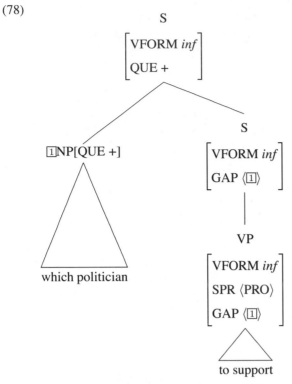

Consider the structure from the bottom up. The verb *support* selects two arguments whose second argument can be realized as a GAP:

(79)

$$\begin{bmatrix} \langle support \rangle \\ VAL \begin{bmatrix} SPR \ \langle \boxed{1}NP[PRO] \rangle \\ COMPS \ \langle \ \rangle \\ GAP \ \langle \boxed{2}NP \rangle \end{bmatrix} \\ ARG\text{-}ST \ \langle \boxed{1}NP, \boxed{2}NP \rangle \end{bmatrix}$$

The verb will then form a VP with the infinitival marker *to*. Since this VP's subject is PRO, the VP can be projected into an S with the accusative NP GAP value in accordance with the Head-Only Rule in (76). The 'S' then forms a well-formed head-filler phrase with the filler *which politician*. The QUE value on the phrase ensures the whole infinitival clause to function as an indirect question which can be combined with the verb *knows*.

One constraint we observe in the infinitival *wh*-questions is that the subject of the infinitival part cannot be overtly realized:

(80) a. *Fred knows [which politician <u>for Karen/her</u> to vote for].

b. *Karen asked [where <u>for Jerry/him</u> to put the chairs].

The data indicate that in infinitival indirect questions, the subject of the infinitival VP cannot appear. If we look at the structure, we can easily see why this is not a legitimate structure:[8]

(81)

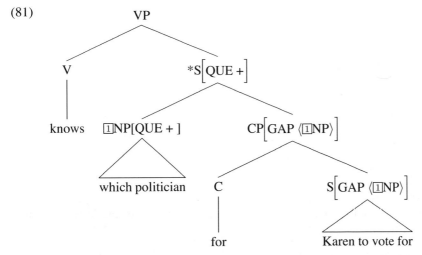

The structure indicates that the Head-Filler Rule licenses the combination of an S with its filler, not a CP with its filler.

10.4.4 Adjunct Wh-questions

The main-clause *wh*-questions and indirect questions we have seen so far have a GAP value originating from an argument position of a verb or preposition. How can the present system account for examples like the following, in which *wh*-phrases are intuitively not arguments but adjuncts?

(82) a. How carefully have you considered your future career?

b. When can we register for graduation?

c. Where do we go to register for graduation?

d. Why have you borrowed my pencil?

One way to deal with such examples is to take the adverbial *wh*-phrase to modify an inverted question:

---

[8]The grammar needs to block examples like (i) in which the infinitival VP combines with its subject:

(i) a. *Fed knows [$_S$ which politician [$_S$ her [to vote for]]].

b. *Karen asked [$_S$ whom [$_S$ him [to vote for]]].

As in (78), the Head-Filler Rule allows an S (directly projected from an infinitival VP) to combine with its filler. As a way of blocking such examples, we may assume an independent constraint that the infinitival subject can appear only together with the complementizer *for* because the subject needs to get the accusative case from it (cf. Chomsky (1982)).

(83)

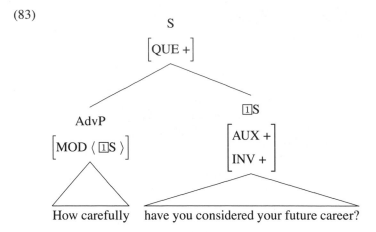

The structure indicates that the AdvP modifies the inverted S.

Matters become more complicated when we consider questions with the interpretation of *wh*-words (cf. Huang (1982)).

(84) a. When did he say that he was fired?
　　　b. Where did he tell you that he met Mary?
　　　c. How did you guess that he fixed the computer?

These sentences are ambiguous with respect to the local interpretation of the *wh*-words. (84a) can question either the time he made the statement or the time he was fired; (84b) can question the place he told you the fact or the place he met Mary. The same is true in (84c): the *wh*-word can question the proposition of the main clause or that of the embedded clause.

These data indicate that in addition to a structure like (83) in which the adverbial *wh*-word modifies the whole sentence, we need a structure where the adverbial *wh*-phrase linked to the embedded clause. As a way of doing it, following Sag (2005) and others, we can assume that English allows the extension of the ARG-ST to include a limited set of adverbial elements as an argument. For example, we can extend the regular verb *fix* to include an adverbial as its argument.

(85)　　Extended ARG-ST:

$$\begin{bmatrix} \langle \text{fix} \rangle \\ \text{ARG-ST } \langle \boxed{1}\text{NP}, \boxed{2}\text{NP} \rangle \end{bmatrix} \rightarrow \begin{bmatrix} \langle \text{fix} \rangle \\ \text{ARG-ST } \langle \boxed{1}\text{NP}, \boxed{2}\text{NP}, \text{AdvP} \rangle \end{bmatrix}$$

This extended ARG-ST then can allow us its adverbial argument to be realized as a GAP value according to the ARC:

(86)
$$\begin{bmatrix} \langle \text{fix} \rangle \\ \text{SPR } \langle \boxed{1}\text{NP} \rangle \\ \text{COMPS } \langle \boxed{2}\text{NP} \rangle \\ \text{GAP } \langle \boxed{3}\text{AdvP} \rangle \\ \text{ARG-ST } \langle \boxed{1}\text{NP}, \boxed{2}\text{NP}, \boxed{3}\text{AdvP} \rangle \end{bmatrix}$$

This lexical realization will then be able to project a structure like the following for the sentence ((84)c).

(87)

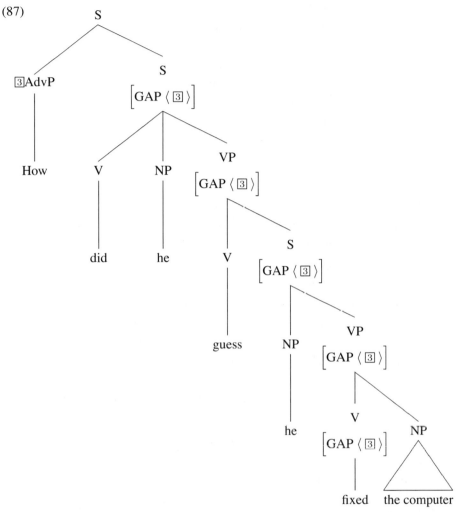

This structure indicates that the *wh*-word *how* originates from the subordinate clause VP. We have seen that the GAP value originates from the verb *fixed* whose arguments can include an adverbial element. Note this does not mean that we can extend the ARG-ST randomly. For example, the argument extension cannot be applied to examples like the following:

(88)   a.   Why do you wonder whether she will invite me?
       b.   How often did he ask when she will meet at the party?

In these examples we have only one interpretation where the *wh*-phrase modifies the matrix verb *wonder* or *ask*. This means that the argument extension is limited, depending on context.

10.5 Exercises

1. Draw tree structures for the following sentences and indicate which grammar rules license the combination of each phrase.

   (i) a. What causes students to select particular majors?
        b. Who will John ask for information about summer courses?
        c. Which textbook did the teacher use in the class last summer?
        d. Whose car is blocking the entrance to the store?

   (ii) a. When can we register for graduation?
        b. Why do you think he left?
        c. Where do we go to register for graduation?

   (iii) a. Who do you guess will be here?
         b. Who do you think borrowed my book?
         c. Which city does Fred think that you believe that John lives in?

2. Draw tree structures for the following sentences involving indirect questions and provide the lexical entries for the underlined words.

   (i) a. I wonder on which shelf John will *put* the book?
        b. What proof that he has implicated have you *found*?
        c. Joseph has *forgotten* how many matches he has won.
        d. Fred will *warn* Martha that she should claim that her brother is patriotic.
        e. That Bill tried to *discover* which drawer Alice put the money in made us realize that we should have left him in Seoul.
        f. Jasper *wonders* which book he should attempt to persuade his students to buy.
        g. The committee *knows* whose efforts to achieve peace the world should honor.

3. Explain why the following examples are ungrammatical.

   (i) a. *I wonder if on which shelve John will put the book.
        b. *Which house does your friend live?
        c. *I wonder what city that Romans destroyed.
        d. *John was wondering to whom he was referring to.
        e. *Who do you think that has given the tickets to Bill?
        f. *What city will Fred say that Mary thinks that John lives?
        g. *On whom does Dana believe Chris knows Sandy trusts?
        h. *The politician denied how the opponent was poisoned.
        i. *Fred knows which book for the children to read during the summer vacation.

4. Look at the following data set and state the constraints on the usage of the *ing* verbs (*mending, investigating, restoring*). In addition, draw trees for the a-examples together with the lexical entries for the main and participle verbs.

   (i) a. This needs mending.
        b. *This needs mending the shoe.
        c. *He mended.

    d. He mended the shoe.

(ii) a. This needs investigating.

    b. *This needs investigating the problem.

    c. *They investigated.

    d. They investigated the problem.

5. Provide the lexical entries for each of the underlined words and then draw structures for those sentence that include the underlined word.

(i)   Within grammar <u>lies</u> the power of expression. Understand grammar, and you will understand just how amazing a language is. You <u>uncover</u> the magician's tricks, you find the inner workings of not only your own language, but you can also see how it is different from the language you're studying. You will find that different languages are better for expressing different ideas, and you will be <u>able</u> to make conscious decisions about how you <u>communicate</u>. Once you <u>know</u> how to use each part of speech, you will be able to expand outside of the box and express yourself in ways that no one has ever expressed themselves before. A solid understanding of the grammar of a language gives you the skeleton, and your words bring it to life. That is why we study grammar.[9]

---

[9] From 'GRAMMAR (no, don't run, I want to be your friend!)' by Colin Suess

11

Relative Clause Constructions

11.1 Introduction

English relative clauses, modifying a preceding NP, are also another type of long distance dependency constructions in the sense that the distance between the filler and the gap can be unbounded:

(1)   a.   The video [which [you recommended __]] was really terrific.

    b.   The video [which [I thought [you recommended __]]] was really terrific.

    c.   The video [which [I thought [John told us [you recommended __]]]] was really terrific.

Such English relative clauses can be classified according to several criteria. We can first classify them by the type of missing element in the relative clause:

(2)   a.   the student who __ won the prize

    b.   the student who everyone likes __

    c.   the baker from whom I bought these bagels __

    d.   the person whom John gave the book to __

    e.   the day when I met her __

    f.   the place where we can relax __

As seen here, the missing phrase can be subject, object, or oblique argument, prepositional object, or even a temporal or locative adjunct.

Relative clauses can also be classified by the type of relative pronoun: in English we find *wh*-relatives, *that*-relatives, and bare relatives.[1]

(3)   a.   The president [who [Fred voted for]] has resigned.

    b.   The president [that [Fred voted for]] dislikes his opponents.

    c.   The president [__ [Fred voted for]] has resigned.

---

[1] We consider *that* in relative clauses to be a form of a relative pronoun.

Wh-relatives like (3a) have a *wh*-type relative pronoun, (3b) has the relative pronoun *that*, while (3c) has no relative pronoun at all.

Relative clauses can also be classified according to the finiteness of the clause. Unlike the finite relative clauses in (1)–(3), the following examples illustrate infinitival relatives:

(4) a. He is the kind of person [with whom to consult __].

  b. These are the things [for which to be thankful __].

  c. We will invite volunteers [on whom to work __].

In addition, English allows so-called 'reduced' relative clauses. The examples in (5) are 'reduced' in the sense that the string '*wh*-phrase + be' appears to be omitted, as indicated by the parentheses:

(5) a. the person (who is) standing on my foot

  b. the prophet (who was) descended from heaven

  c. the bills (which were) passed by the House yesterday

  d. the people (who are) in Rome

  e. the people (who are) happy with the proposal

This chapter first reviews the basic properties these various types of English relative clauses, and then provides analyses of their syntactic structures.

11.2 Non-subject *Wh*-Relative Clauses

Let us consider some canonical relative clauses, first:

(6) a. the senators [who [Fred met __]]

  b. the apple [that [John ate __]]

  c. the problem [__ [you told us about __]]

Just like *wh*-questions, we can notice that relative clauses have bipartite structures: a *wh*-element and a sentence with a missing element (S/XP):

(7) a. *wh*-element S/XP

  b. that   S/XP

  c. [__]   S/XP

Assuming that relative *wh*-words carry the REL feature whose index value is identical with the noun that the relative clause modifies, we can represent the structure of (6a) as following:

(8)

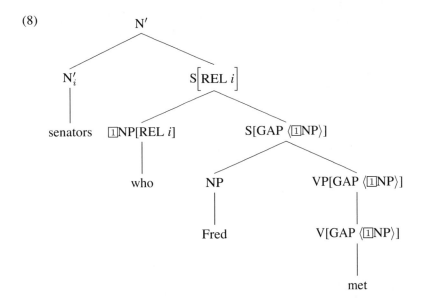

As shown in the structure, the object of the verb *met* is realized as a GAP value, and the filler *who* functions as its filler. The combination of the filler *who* and the gapped sentence *Fred met* thus forms a well-formed head-filler phrase. This filler *who* has the nonlocal REL feature whose value is an index. The REL value, identical with the antecedent noun, then percolates up to the mother in accordance with the NIP (Nonlocal Inheritance Principle).

One question that arises here is what mechanism ensures that the relative clause functions as a modifier of a noun or noun phrase, carrying the MOD feature? In Chapter 6, we saw that phrases such AP, nonfinite VP, and PP can modify an NP (these examples can be taken as 'reduced' relatives):

(9) a. the people [happy with the proposal]

    b. the person [standing on my foot]

    c. the bills [passed by the House yesterday]

    d. the paper [to finish by tomorrow]

    e. the student [in the classroom]

All these postnominal elements bear the feature MOD, originating from the head *happy, standing, passed* and *to*:

(10)

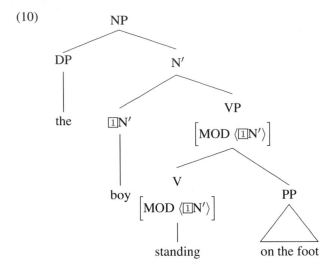

Notice that not all phrases can function as postmodifiers. In particular, a base VP or finite VP cannot be found in this environment:

(11)   a. *the person [stand on my foot]

        b. *the person [stood on my foot]

        c. *the person [stands on my foot]

Also, a complete sentence cannot function as a postnominal modifier, either:

(12)   a. *The student met the senator [John met Bill].

        b. *The student met the senator [that John met Bill].

        c. *The student met the senator [for John to meet Bill].

Only relative clauses with one missing element may serve as postnominal modifiers, indicating that they also have the MOD feature. Since all the relative clauses (except bare relatives) are introduced by a relative pronoun, it is reasonable to assume that a clause with the [REL i] feature also bears the MOD feature as a constructional constraint, according to the following rule:[2]

(13)   Head-Rel Modifier Rule:

$$N' \rightarrow \boxed{1}N'_i, \quad S\begin{bmatrix} REL & i \\ MOD & \langle\boxed{1}\rangle \\ GAP & \langle \ \rangle \end{bmatrix}$$

The rule, as a subtype of the Head-Modifier Rule, basically ensures that a clause marked with the REL feature modifies a preceding noun with the identical index value. This grammar rule now then ensures the presence of the MOD feature in the relative clause (8):

---

[2]Following Sag (1997), one can develop an analysis in which the MOD value is introduced from a verb whose argument contains a GAP value.

(14)

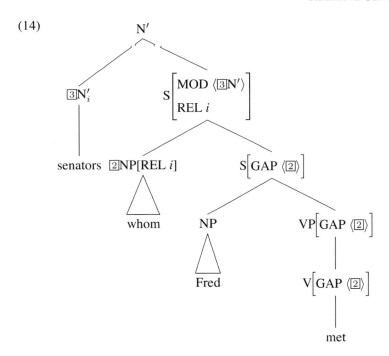

As shown here, the verb *met* realizes its object as a GAP value, which percolates up to the S, where it is discharged by the relative pronoun *whom*. In addition, in accordance with the Head-Rel Modifier Rule in (13), the relative clause, forming a head-filler phrase, now carries the MOD feature as well.

Since the relative clause is a type of head-filler phrase, there must be a total syntactic identity between the gap and the filler with a REL value:

(15) a. Jack is the person [[$_{NP}$ whom] [Jenny fell in love with [$_{NP}$ —]]].

b. Jack is the person [[$_{PP}$ with whom] [Jenny fell in love [$_{PP}$ —]]].

(16) a. *Jack is the person [[$_{NP}$ whom] [Jenny fell in love [$_{PP}$ —]]] .

b. *Jack is the person [[$_{PP}$ with whom] [Jenny fell in love with [$_{NP}$ —]]].

In (15a) and (15b), the gap and the filler are the same category, whereas those in (16) are not. The putative gap in (16a) is a PP and the one in (16b) an NP, but the fillers are the non-matching categories NP and PP, respectively.

In addition, the gap can be embedded in a deeper position as long as it finds the appropriate filler:

(17)

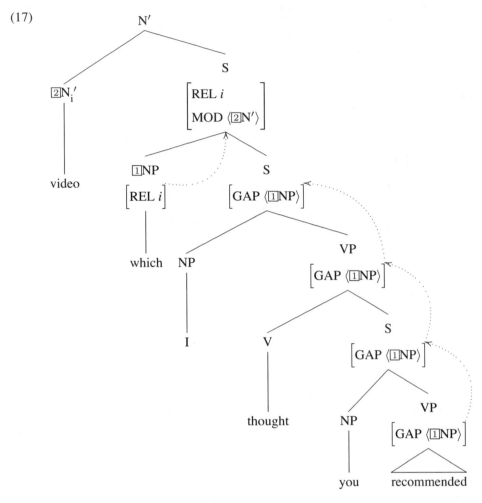

The GAP value starts from the verb of the embedded clause and passes up to the top S in accordance with the NIP. The value is discharged by the filler *wh*-phrase *which* carrying the REL feature. This nonlocal REL feature, in accordance with the NIP, is also passed up to the top S to ensure that the clause functions as a modifier.

Just like the QUE feature, the nonlocal REL feature can also come from a deeper position within the nonhead daughter of the relative clause:

(18)   a.   I met the critic [whose remarks [I wanted to object to __]].

   b.   This is the friend [for whose mother [Kim gave a party __]].

   c.   The teacher set us a problem [the answer to which [we can find __ in the textbook]].

The simplified structure of (18b) can easily illustrate this point:

(19)

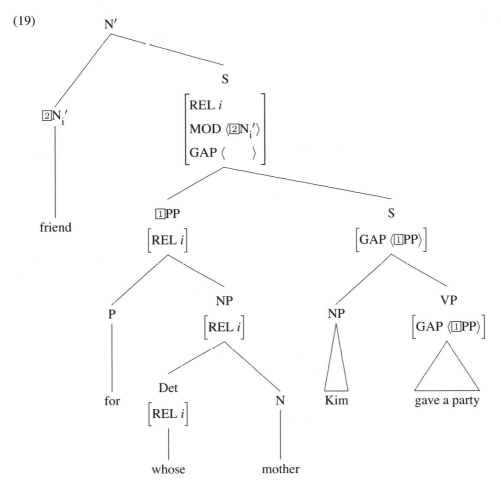

The REL feature is embedded in the specifier of the inner NP, but the NIP guarantees that this value is passed up to the top S so that it can function as a modifier to the antecedent *friend*.

11.3 Subject Relative Clauses

Subject relative clauses are not very much different from non-subject relatives clauses in terms of modifying a nominal expression. One main difference is that the presence of a *wh*-relative pronoun including *that* is obligatory, and bare relative clauses are ungrammatical:

(20) a. We called the senators [who] met Fred.

b. The kid picked up the apple [that] fell down on the ground.

(21) a. *[The student [__ met John]] came.

b. *[The problem [__ intrigued us]] bothered me.]

Subject relative clauses involve a missing subject – a [REL *i*] subject is gapped, represented like this:

(22)

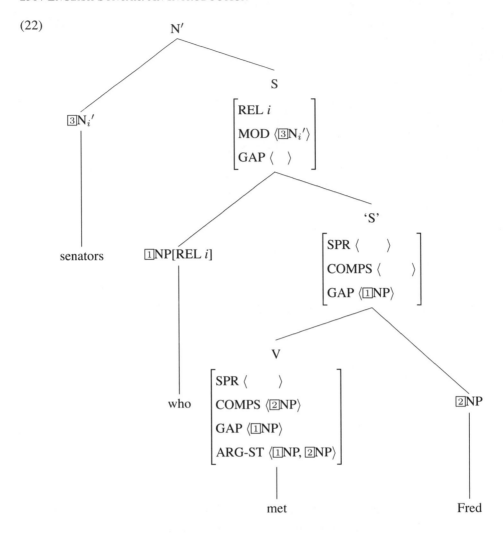

As shown in the structure, the subject of *met* is realized as the GAP value which passes up to the mother node. As noted in the previous chapter, this mother node is an 'S' with the empty COMPS and SPR value though it looks like a VP. It is an S with a gap in it, and this combines with the filler *who* by the Head-Filler Rule. The resulting S is a complete one carrying the REL and MOD specifications that allows the resulting clause to modify *senators* in accordance with the Head-Rel Modifier Rule.

Notice that this analysis then does not license bare subject relatives given like (21). The VP with the missing subject *met John* cannot carry the MOD feature at all even if it can function as an 'S' that can combine either with a *wh*-question phrase or a *wh*-relative phrase. However, the analysis also predicts that the subject of an embedded clause can be gapped in sentences like the following:

(23) a. He made a statement [which [$_S$ everyone thought [$_S$ __ was really interesting and important]]].

b. They all agreed to include those matters [[$_S$ which [everyone believed [$_S$ __ had been excluded from the Treaty]]]].

As we saw in Chapter 10, verbs like *think* and *believe* combine with a CP, an S, or even a 'S' with the subject being gapped:

(24)

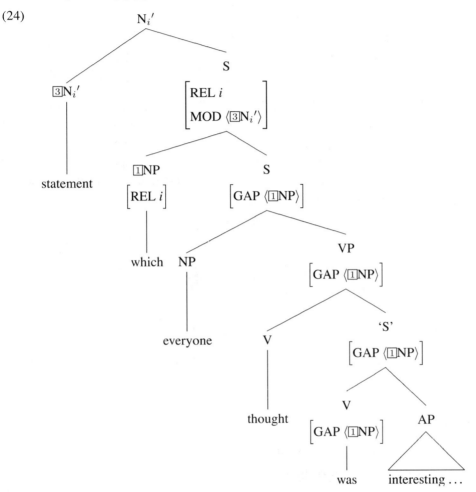

The VP *was interesting* here forms an 'S' with the subject being gapped. This 'S' combines with the verb *thought*, forming an incomplete VP with the GAP information. This GAP value percolates up to the lower S and then is discharged by the relative pronoun *which* which induces the MOD value to the relative clause so that it can modify the antecedent *statement*.

11.4 That-relative clauses

As noted earlier, *that* can be used either as a complementizer or as a relative pronoun:

(25)   Complementizer *that*:

a. Mary knows that John was elected.

b. That John was elected surprised Frank.

   c. Mary told Bill that John was elected.

(26)   Relative Pronoun *that*:

   a. This is the book [that we had read].

   b. The president abandoned the people [that voted for him].

   c. It is an argument [that people think will never end in Egypt].

Coordination data indicate that *that* can also be used a relative pronoun:

(27) a. *Every essay [she's written] and [that/which I've read] is on that pile.

    b. Every essay [which she's written] and [that I've read] is on that pile.

    c. Every essay [that she's written] and [which I've read] is on that pile.

The contrast here can easily be accounted for if we assign the REL feature to *that*. As we have seen earlier, the Coordination Rule requires two identical phrases to be conjoined. In (27b) and (27c), two [REL *i*] Ss are conjoined, whereas in the unacceptable example (27a), two different phrases, S with a gap element and S with no gap, are conjoined. This means that *that* will appear in the following two different environments:

(28)   *a.*   CP   *b.* S[REL *i*]

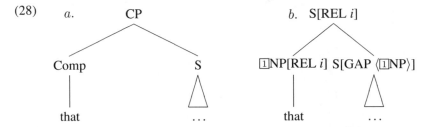

The relative pronoun *that* is different from *wh*-relative pronoun in several respects. For example, the relative pronoun *that* disallows genitive and piped piping (Sag (1997)):

(29) a. the student whose turn it was

    b. *the student that's turn it was

(30) a. the pencil with which he is writing

    b. *the pencil with that he is writing

In addition, *that* is used only in finite relative clauses:

(31) a. a pencil with which to write

    b. *a pencil with that to write

One way to account for these differences from the other *wh*-relative pronouns is to assume that the relative pronoun *that* has no accusative case, hence cannot be the complement of a preposition that assigns accusative to it. The relative *who*, unlike relative pronouns like *whose, whom* and *which*, has the same property in this respect:

(32) a. *The people [in who we placed our trust] . . . .

    b. *The person [with who we were talking] . . . .

(33) a. The company [in which they have invested] . . .

  b. The people [in whose house we stayed] . . .

  c. The person [with whom he felt most comfortable] . . .

11.5 Infinitival and Bare Relative Clauses

An infinitival clause can also function as a modifier to the preceding noun. Infinitival relative clauses in principle may contain a relative pronoun but need not:

(34) a. He bought a bench [on which to sit __].

  b. He bought a refrigerator [in which to put the beer __].

(35) a. There is a book [(for you) to give to Alice].

  b. There is a bench [(for you) to sit on].

Let us consider infinitival *wh*-relatives first. As we have seen in the previous chapter, an infinitival VP can be projected into an S when its subject is realized as the unrealized subject PRO. This will then allow the following structure for (34a):

(36)

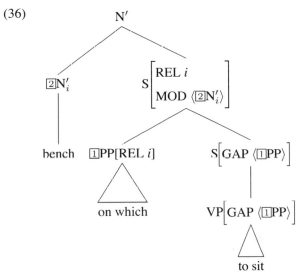

As shown here, the VP *to sit* has a GAP value which functions as the complement of *sit*. The infinitival VP, missing its PP complement, realizes its SPR as a PRO and thus can be projected into an S in accordance with the Head-Only Rule. This S forms a head-filler phrase with the PP *on which*. The resulting S also inherits the REL value from the relative pronoun *which* and thus bears the MOD feature. Once again, we observe that every projection observes the grammar rules as well as other general principles such as the HFP, the VALP, and the NIP.

  Infinitival *wh*-relatives have an additional constraint on the realization of the subject.

(37) a. a bench on which (*for Jerry) to sit __

  b. a refrigerator in which (*for you) to put the beer __

The examples indicate that *wh*-infinitival relatives cannot have an overt subject (such as *(for)*
Jerry) realized. We saw before that the same is true for infinitival *wh*-questions; the data are
repeated here:

(38) a. Fred knows [which politician (*for Karen) to vote for].

  b. Karen asked [where (*for Washington) to put the chairs].

This tells us that both infinitival *wh*-relatives and infinitival *wh*-questions are subject to the same
constraint. The reason for the ungammaticality of an example like (37a) can be understood if
we look at its structure:

(39)

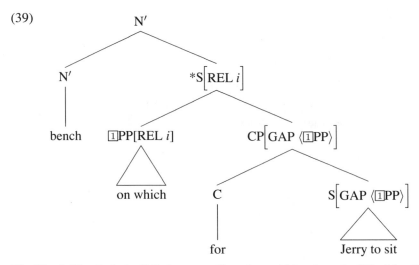

The Head-filler Rule in (25) does not allow the combination of a CP with a PP. The S here is ill-
formed: there is no rule that allows the combination of a CP/PP with a PP to form a head-filler
phrase.

  How then can we deal with infinitival bare relative clauses like (40)?

(40) a. the paper [(for us) to read __ by tomorrow]

  b. the paper [(for us) to finish __ by tomorrow]

Notice here that unlike infinitival *wh*-relative clauses, there is no relative pronoun. Given that
the infinitival VP can be projected into an S, we can assign the following structure to (40b)
when the subject is not overt:

(41)

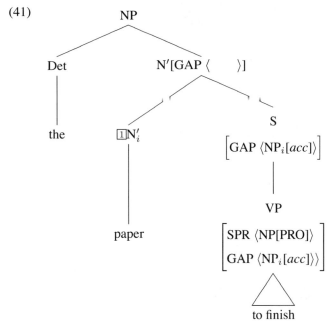

The VP *to finish* has a GAP value for its object, and its subject is PRO. According to the Head-only Rule in (76), this VP then will be projected into an incomplete 'S'. There are two analytic issues now: how to introduce the MOD feature and how to discharge the GAP value when there is no filler. As we noted above, English also allows finite bare relatives with the gapped element being accusative:

(42)   a.   the person [I met __]

       b.   the box [we put the books in __]

Note that unlike the traditional view, we can have bare relatives with the nominative subject being gapped:

(43)   a.   He made a statement [everyone thought [__ was interesting and important]].

       b.   They all agreed to include those matters [everyone believed [__ had been excluded from the Treaty]].

The subject gapped bare relative is only possible when it is combined by a matrix verb like *thought* and *believed*, but not when it directly modifies its antecedent as in (21). This in turn means that we have the following constructional differences for bare relatives:

(44)   a.

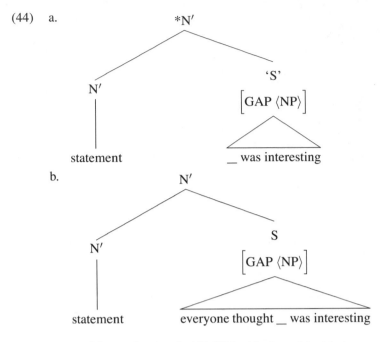

b.

As represented here, the simple 'S' (VP with the subject being gapped) cannot function as a bare relative modifier, but the S whose embedded subject is gapped can well serve as a bare relative clause. To reflect this observation and allow us to discharge the GAP value in such bare relative clauses, we can assume the following rule for English:

(45)   Bare Head-Rel Modifier Rule:

$$N'\begin{bmatrix} GAP \langle \quad \rangle \end{bmatrix} \rightarrow \boxed{1}N'_i, \quad S\,|\,CP\begin{bmatrix} MOD \langle \boxed{1} \rangle \\ GAP \langle NP_i \rangle \end{bmatrix}$$

This rule allows a finite or infinitival clause (S or CP, but not an 'S' or VP) bearing an NP GAP value to function as a modifier of the preceding noun (the MOD value is added as a constructional constraint). One specification in the rule is that the GAP value be discharged even if there is no filler: the index of the head noun is identified with that of the discharged gap. This rule will then allow examples like (43) as well as authentic examples like the following:

(46)   I just know that the Big 12 South teams [everyone knew [__ would win actually] won the game].

11.6   Restrictive vs. Nonrestrictive Relative Clauses

In addition to the types of relative clause we seen before, there is an interpretive distinction between 'restrictive' and 'nonrestrictive'. Consider these examples:

(47)   a.   The person who John asked for help thinks he is foolish.

b.   Mary, who John asked for help, thinks he is foolish.

The relative clause in (47a) semantically restricts the denotation of *person* whereas the one in (47b) just adds extra information about *Mary*. Let us consider one more pair of examples:

(48) a. John has two sisters who became lawyers. ('restrictive')

   b. John has two sisters, who became lawyers. ('non-restrictive')

The second example suggests that John has only two sisters, while the first means that two of his sisters are lawyers, but leaves open the possibility that he has other sisters. The denotation of the restrictive relative phrase (RRC) *two sisters who became lawyers* is thus the intersection the set of two sisters and the set of lawyers. There can be more than two sisters, but there are only two who became lawyers. Meanwhile, the nonrestrictive phrase (NRC) *two sisters, who became lawyers* means that there are two sisters and they all became lawyers: there is no intersection meaning here.

   This meaning difference has given rise to the idea that the RRC modifies the meaning of N′ – a noun phrase without a determiner – whereas the NRC modifies a fully determined NP (cf. McCawley (1988):

(49)   Restrictive Relative Clause:

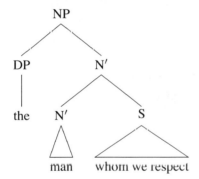

(50)   Non-restrictive Relative Clause:

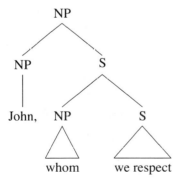

These two structural differences are intended to reflect the fact that the RRC is interpreted as restricting the set of man under consideration to a particular subset (those who we respect) whereas the NRC just add information about the antecedent 'John'.

Though this structural difference is fragile in some cases,[3], it can provide us with a way of explaining why the RRC cannot modify a pronoun or proper noun:[4]

(51) a. I met the man who grows peaches.

b. I met the lady from France who grows peaches.

(52) a. *I met John who grows peaches.

b. *I met her who grows peaches.

Given that the meanings of 'John' and 'her' refer to only single individuals, we expect that no further modification or restriction is possible. Nonrestrictive relative clauses as (53) can modify proper nouns or pronouns, simply because they just add information about the referent into the discourse:

(53) a. In the classroom, the teacher praised John, whom I also respect.

b. Reagan, whom the Republicans nominated in 1980, lived most of his life in California.

The relative clause *whom I also respect* modifies the proper noun *John* without restricting it, and has the same interpretation as a conjoined clause like *The teacher praised John, and I also respect him.*

Such a meaning difference also causes another difference: only a restrictive clause can modify a quantified NP like *every N* or *no N*:

(54) a. Every student who attended the party had a good time.

b. *Every student, who attended the party, had a good time.

(55) a. No student who scored 80 or more in the exam was ever failed.

b. *No student, who scored 80 or more in the exam, was ever failed.

Strictly speaking, phrases with *no* or *every* as determiners do not refer to an individual or given set of individuals, and therefore cannot have their reference further elaborated by a nonrestrictive modifier (see Huddleston and Pullum (2002)).

Whether the syntax involves N' or NP has also been used to explain why a restrictive clause must precede a nonrestrictive clause:

(56) a. The contestant who won the first prize, who is the judge's brother-in-law, sang dreadfully.

b. *The contestant, who is the judge's brother-in-law, who won the first prize sang dreadfully.

((56b) is interpretable as involving a sequence of two nonrestrictive clauses.) Partial structures of these two can be represented as follows:

---

[3]See Arnold (2004) and the references cited therein

[4]In certain expressions of English, *who* relative clause can modify the pronoun *he*:

(i) a. He who laughs last laughs best.

b. He who is without sin among you, let him cast the first stone.

(57)   a.

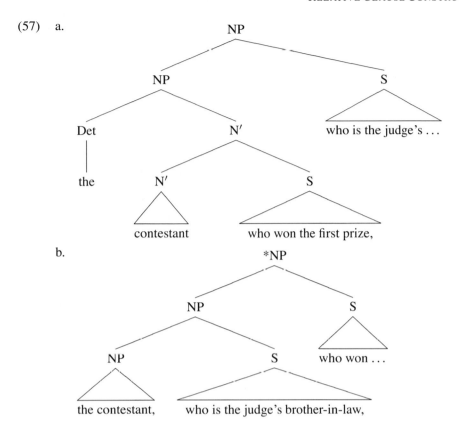

b.

Only in (57a) can the first relative clause be interpreted restrictively, as it is attached at the N′ level. Strictly speaking, as noted above, (57b) is not ill-formed, but can only have an interpretation in which both relative clauses are nonrestrictive.[5]

   Though several issues remain unsettled of describing the differences between RRCs and NRCs in terms of structures,[6] it seems to be clear that the two relative clause types display interesting differences not found in other languages like Korean and Japanese.

---

[5] One additional difference between restrictive and nonrestrictive clauses is that *that* is used mainly in restrictive clauses.

(i)   a.   The knife [which/that] he threw into the sea had a gold handle.
       b.   The knife, [which/??that] he threw into the sea had a gold handle.

[6] The structural difference of attaching nonrestrictive clauses to NP and restrictive clauses to N′ fails to account for certain facts. For example, a restrictive clause appears to attach to NP in cases where the relative clause modifies an indefinite pronoun as in *everyone who smiled must have been happy* or examples where the clauses modifies two conjoined full NPs as in *the man and the woman who are neighbors are getting to know each other*. In order to account for such examples, we need to develop a more elaborated syntactic and semantic analysis. See Fabb (1990), Sag (1997), Arnold (2004), Chaves (2007) and the references there for further discussion.

11.7   Constraints on the GAP

We have observed that in *wh*-interrogatives and relative clauses, the filler and the gap can be in a long-distance relationship. Yet, there are constructions where this dependency seems to be restricted in certain ways. Consider the following examples:

(58)   a.   [Who] did he believe [that he would one day meet __]?

       b.   [Which celebrity] did he mention [that he had run into __]?

(59)   a. *[Who] did he believe [the claim that he had never met __]?

       b. *[Which celebrity] did he mention [the fact that he had run into __]?

Why do we have the contrast here? Let us compare the partial structures of (58a) with (59a):

(60)   a.

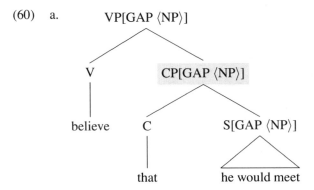

       b.

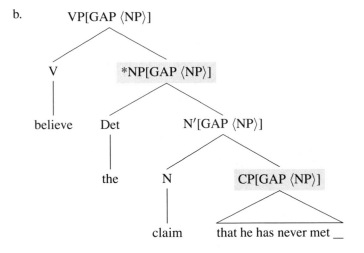

As we can see in (60a), the syntax allows a CP with GAP value. However, the combination in (60b) of an NP containing a CP cannot have a GAP value. This is traditionally known as a 'Complex NP' (Ross (1967)) and is considered an 'island' in the sense that it is effectively isolated from the rest of the structure. That is, an element within this island cannot be extracted from it, or linked to an expression outside. It is also usually assumed that English has island constraints as follows:

• Coordinate Structure Constraint (CSC): In a coordinate structure, no element in one conjunct alone can be *wh*-questioned or relativized.

(61)   a.   Bill cooked supper and washed the dishes.

        b.   *What did Bill cook __ and wash the dishes?

        c.   *What did Bill cook supper and wash __ ?

• Complex Noun Phrase Constraint (CNPC): No element within a CP or S dominated by an NP can be *wh*-questioned or relativized.

(62)   a.   He refuted the proof that you cannot square it.

        b.   *What did he refute the proof that you cannot square __ ?

(63)   a.   They met someone [who knows the professor].

        b.   *[Which professor] did they meet someone who knows __ ?

• Sentential Subject Constraint (SSC): An element within a clausal subject cannot be *wh*-questioned or relativized.

(64)   a.   [That he has met the professor] is extremely unlikely.

        b.   *Who is [that he has met __] extremely unlikely?

• Left-Branching Constraint (LBC): No NP that is the leftmost constituent of a larger NP can be *wh*-questioned or relativized:

(65)   a.   She bought [John's] book.

        b.   *[Whose] did she buy __ book?

• Adjunct Clause Constraint: An element within an adjunct cannot be questioned or relativized.

(66)   a.   Which topic did you choose __ without getting his approval?

        b.   *Which topic did you get bored [because Mary talked about __]?

• Indirect *Wh*-question Constraint: An NP that is within an indirect question cannot be questioned or relativized.

(67)   a.   Did John wonder who would win the game?

        b.   *What did John wonder who would win __ ?

Various attempts have been made to account for such island constraints. Among these, we sketch an analysis within the present system that relies on licensing constraints on subtree structures. As we have seen in the previous chapters, the present analysis provides a straightforward account for the CSC:

(68)

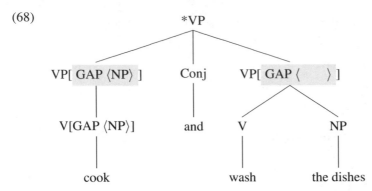

Even though two VPs are coordinated, they are not identical in terms of the GAP values. This violates the Coordination Rule which requires that only identical categories can be coordinated.

Except for this clear constraint, the existence of the other island constraints has been questioned through acceptable examples which actually violate the island constraints. For example, the following examples are all acceptable even though they violate a claimed island constraint (Sag et al. to appear):

(69)   a.   What did he get the impression that the problem really was __ ? (CNPC)

      b.   This is the paper that we really need to find the linguist who
           understands __ . (CNPC)

In addition, observe the following examples (cf. Ross (1987), Kluender (2004)):

(70)   a.   *Which rebel leader did you hear [Cheney's rumor [that the CIA
           assassinated __]]?

      b.??Which rebel leader did you hear [the rumor [that the CIA assassinated __]]?

      c.   ?Which rebel leader did you hear [a rumor [that the CIA assassinated __]]?

      d.   Which rebel leader did you hear [rumors [that the CIA assassinated __]]?

All these examples have identical syntactic structures but are different in the degree of acceptability. The data indicate that it is not the syntactic structure, but the properties of the head of the complex NP influence the acceptability grade of the sentences, implying that processing factors closely interact with the grammar of filler-gap constructions (Sag et al. (2006)).

11.8 Exercises

1. Find a grammatical error in each of the following sentences and then explain the nature of the error.

    (i) a. Students enter high-level educational institutions might face many problems relating to study habits.

    b. A fellow student saw this felt sorry for Miss Kim and offered her his own book.

    c. Experts all agree that dreams cause great anxiety and stress are called nightmares.

    d. The victims of the earthquake their property was destroyed in the disaster were given temporary housing by the government.

2. Draw tree structures for the following examples and discuss which grammar rules license each phrase.

    (i) a. This is the book which I need to read.

    b. This is the very book that we need to talk about.

    c. The person whom they intended to speak with agreed to reimburse us.

    d. The motor that Martha thinks that Joe replaced costs thirty dollars.

    (ii) a. The official to whom Smith loaned the money has been indicted.

    b. The man on whose lap the puppet is sitting is ventriloquist.

    c. The teacher set us a problem the answer to which we can find in the textbook.

    d. We just finished the final exam the result of which we can find out next week.

3. Draw structures for the following ungrammatical examples and identify which island constraints are violated.

    (i) a. *What did Herb start to play only after he drank __ ?

    b. *Who did Herb believe the claim that cheated?

    c. *What did Herb like fruit punch and?

    d. *What was that the Vikings ate a real surprise to you?

    e. *What did you meet someone who understands?

4. Compare the following pairs of examples by considering the structure of each. In particular, consider whether the structure involves a relative clause or a CP complement.

    (i) a. The fact that scientists have now established all the genes in the human body is still not widely known.

    b. The fact that the scientists used the latest technology to verify was reported at the recent conference.

    (ii) a. They ignored the suggestion that Lee made.

    b. They ignored the suggestion that Lee lied.

    (iii) a. They denied the claim that we had advanced by ourselves.

    b. They denied the claim that they should report only to us.

5. English also allows adverbial relative clauses like those in (i). Can the analysis in this chapter explain such examples? If it can, how? If it cannot, can you think of any possible explanation?

    (i) a.   The hotel where Gloria stays is being remodelled.
         b.   The day when Jim got fired was a sad day for everyone.
         c.   That is the reason why he resigned.

6. Explain the grammatical differences between the following two. In doing so, draw the tree structures of these two, focusing on the function of *that* in each case:

    (i) a. *The president thought that voted for him.
         b.   The president abandoned the people that voted for him.
         c. *The president abandoned the people that they voted for him.
         d.   The president tried to win the war that everyone thought was already won.

7. Read the following passages and provide the correct verb form for the underlined expressions and their lexical entries.

    (i)   Pied-piping (first identified by John R. Ross) describes the situation where a phrase larger than a single *wh*-word occurs in the fronted position. In the case where the *wh*-word is a determiner such as *which* or *whose*, pied-piping <u>refer</u> to the fact that the *wh*-determiner appears sentence-initially along with its complement. For instance, in the example *Which car does he <u>like</u>?*, the entire phrase *which car* is moved. In the transformational analysis, the *wh*-word *which* moves to the beginning of the sentence, taking *car*, its complement, with it, much as the Pied Piper of Hamelin <u>attract</u> rats and children to follow him, hence the term pied-piping.[7]

    (ii) Certain grammatical structures <u>associate</u> with corresponding functions, as in the interrogative structure *Do you drink tea* the function is questioning. Such a case can <u>describe</u> as a direct speech act. However, when the interrogative structure is used to fulfill a different purpose as in *Can you <u>close</u> the window?* where it clearly is not a question about ability, but a polite request, such a situation is described as an indirect speech act.[8]

---

[7] Adapted from *Wikipedia*, http://en.wikipedia.org/wiki/Wh-movement
[8] Adapted from http://www.tlumaczenia-angielski.info/linguistics/pragmatics.htm

12

Special Constructions

12.1 Introduction

English displays constructions illustrated in (1), respectively known as 'tough movement',[1] 'extraposition', and 'cleft' constructions:

(1)   a.   John is tough to persuade __ . ('Tough' movement)

        b.   It bothers me that John snores. (Subject Extraposition)

        c.   John made it clear that he would finish it on time. (Object Extraposition)

        d.   It is John that I met __ last night in the park. (Cleft)

Though these constructions each involve some kind of nonlocal dependency, they are different from *wh*-question or relative clause constructions in several respects. This chapter looks into the main properties of these new nonlocal dependency constructions.

As we have seen in the previous two chapters, in these *wh*-questions and relative clauses, the gap must match its filler in terms of the syntactic category:

(2)   a.   I wonder [<u>whom</u> [Sandy loves __]]. (*Wh*-question)

        b.   This is the politician [<u>on whom</u> [Sandy relies __]]. (*Wh*-relative clause)

In addition, we can observe that the filler *whom* and *on whom* here are not in the core clause position (subject or object) but are in the adjoined filler position.

Now compare these properties with other examples of the *easy* type:

(3)   a.   <u>He</u> is hard to love __ .

        b.   <u>This car</u> is easy to drive __

The gap in (3a) would correspond to an accusative NP (*him*) whereas the apparent filler in the core position is a nominative subject *he*. The filler and the gap here are thus not exactly identical in terms of their syntactic information, though they are understood as referring to the same individual. Due to the lack of syntactic identity, the dependency between the filler and the gap is considered 'weaker' than the one in *wh*-questions or *wh*-relatives (cf. Pollard and Sag (1994)).

---

[1] The construction is named after adjectives which appear in it, such at *tough, easy, difficult*, etc.

The extraposition and cleft constructions in (1b–d) are also different from *wh*-questions, as well as from *easy* construction examples. In clefts, we have a gap and a corresponding filler, but in extrapositions we have a long-distance relationship between the extraposed clause and the expletive pronoun *it*. In due course, we will see the differences of these constructions in detail.

12.2 'Easy' Constructions

12.2.1 Basic Properties

Adjectives like *easy, tough, difficult*, and so on can appear in three seemlingly-related constructions:

(4)   a.   To please John is easy/tough.

      b.   It is easy/tough to please John.

      c.   John is easy/tough to please.

Superficially, quite similar predicates such as *eager* and *ready* do not allow all these three:

(5)   a.   *To please John is eager/ready.

      b.   *It is eager/ready to please John.

      c.   John is eager/ready to please.

Even though (4c) and (5c) are grammatical and look similar in terms of structure, they are significantly different if we look in detail at their properties. Consider the following contrast:

(6)   a.   Kim is easy to please.

      b.   Kim is eager to please.

One obvious difference between these two examples lies in the semantic roles of *Kim*: in (6a), *Kim* is the object of *please* whereas *Kim* in (6b) is the subject of *please*. More specifically, the verb *please* in (6a) is used as a transitive verb whose object is identified with the subject *Kim*. Meanwhile, the verb *please* in (6b) is used intransitively, not requiring any object. This difference can be shown clearly by the following examples:

(7)   a.   *Kim is easy [to please Tom].

      b.   Kim is eager [to please Tom].

The VP complement of the adjective *easy* cannot have a surface object whereas *eager* has no such restriction. This means that the VP complement of *easy* has to be incomplete in the sense that it is missing an object, and this is so with other *easy* adjectives as well:

(8)   a.   This doll is hard [to see __].

      b.   The child is impossible [to teach __].

      c.   The problem is easy [to solve __].

(9)   a.   *This doll is [hard to see it].

      b.   *The child is impossible [to teach him].

      c.   *The problem is easy [to solve the question].

In all these examples, there must be a gap in the VP complement. Meanwhile, *eager* places no such a restriction on its VP complement which should be internally complete:

(10) a. John is eager [to examine the patient].

 b. John is eager [to find a new home].

(11) a. *John is eager [to examine __].

 b. *John is eager [to find __].

These observations lead us to the following descriptive generalization:

(12) Unlike *eager*-type adjectives, *easy*-type adjectives select an infinitival VP complement which has one missing element semantically linked to their subject.

12.2.2 Transformational Analyses

Let us consider two related examples first:

(13) a. It is easy to please John.

 b. John is easy to please.

Traditional movement analyses have assumed the following deep structure for (13a):

(14) $[_S$ __ is easy $[_{CP}$ $[_S$ PRO to please John]]]

The expletive *it* is introduced at S-structure in the matrix subject position to generate (13a). One might assume direct movement of *John* to the subject position for (13b), but an issue immediately arises with examples like (15):

(15) He$_i$ is easy to please __ $_i$.

The problematic aspect is the status of the subject *He*: how can a direct movement approach move *him* into the subject position and then change the form into *he*?[2] As a solution, Chomsky (1986) proposes an empty operator (Op) movement operation, represented as shown here:

---

[2]In more technical terms, this will violate the 'Case Filter' of Government-Binding Theory, for *he* receives two cases: accusative from the original object position and nominative from the subject position.

(16)

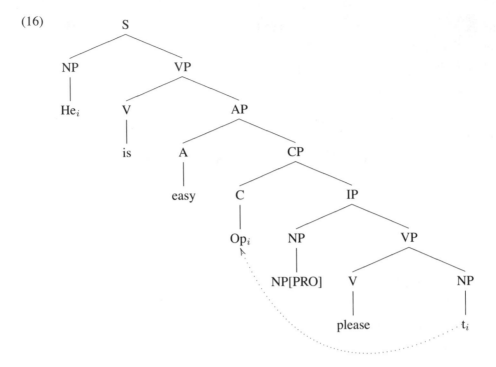

The subject *he* is base-generated in the matrix subject position, while the null operator Op$_i$ moves to the intermediate position from its original object position, leaving the trace (t$_i$). At an interpretive level, this operator is coindexed with the subject, indirectly linking the gap with the filler even though the two have different case markings.

12.2.3   A Lexicalist Analysis

As we have seen earlier, unlike *eager*-type adjectives, *easy*-type adjectives require an incomplete VP complement as a lexical property. This subcategorization restriction appears to be a lexical fact for a family of adjectives and verbs. In addition to adjectives like *easy*, verbs like *take* and *cost* also select an infinitival VP containing an accusative NP gap coindexed with the subject:

(17)   a.   This theorem will take only five minutes to prove __ .

　　　 b.   This theorem will take only five minutes to establish that he proved __ in 1930.

(18)   a.   This scratch will cost Kim $500 to fix __ .

　　　 b.   This $500 bribe will cost the government $500,000 to prove that Senator Jones accepted __ .

Meanwhile, as we have noted in the previous section, *eager*-type adjectives do not have such a subcategorization restriction.

We can represent this lexical difference in terms of lexical information. Let us begin with the *easy*-type which selects a VP complement with one NP missing:

(19)   *easy*-type adjectives

$$
\begin{bmatrix}
\text{HEAD} \mid \text{POS } adj \\[4pt]
\text{VAL} \begin{bmatrix}
\text{SPR } \langle \text{NP}_i \rangle \\[4pt]
\text{COMPS } \left\langle \begin{bmatrix} \text{VFORM } inf \\ \text{GAP } \langle \boxed{1}\text{NP}_i[acc] \rangle \end{bmatrix} \right\rangle
\end{bmatrix} \\[4pt]
\text{TO-BIND} \mid \text{GAP } \langle \boxed{1}\text{NP}_i \rangle
\end{bmatrix}
$$

The lexical entry in (19) specifies that the infinitival complement (VP or CP) of adjectives like *easy* contains a GAP value (NP$_i$) which is coindexed with the subject. This coindexation will ensure the semantic linkage between the matrix subject and the gapped NP. Notice that unlike canonical filler-gap constructions in which the GAP value is discharged when it meets the filler (by the Head-Filler Rule), the feature TO-BIND is introduced to lexically discharge the GAP value in the VP complement. This lexical information will then project the following structure for (6a):

(20)

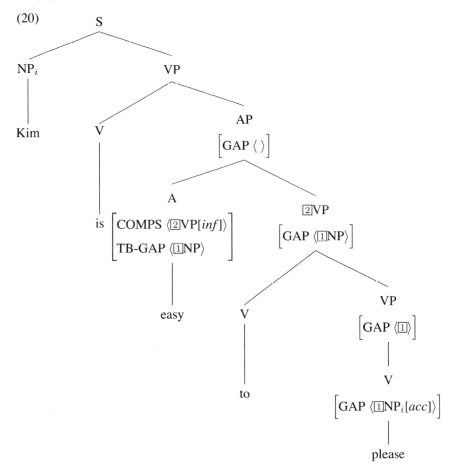

As shown in the tree, the transitive verb *please* introduces its object as the GAP value; hence the mother infinitival VP is incomplete. The adjective *easy* selects this VP and then lexically discharges through the TO-BIND|GAP (TB-GAP) value in accordance with the following revised NIP:

(21)   Nonlocal Feature Inheritance Principle (NIP, final):
         A phrase's nonlocal feature such as GAP and QUE is the union of its daughters' nonlocal feature values minus either the lexically or grammatically bound nonlocal features.

Meanwhile, the lexical information for *eager*-type adjectives is very simple:

(22)   *eager*-type adjectives

$$\begin{bmatrix} \text{HEAD | POS } adj \\ \text{VAL} \begin{bmatrix} \text{SPR } \langle \text{NP} \rangle \\ \text{COMPS } \left\langle \text{VP}[\text{VFORM } inf] \right\rangle \end{bmatrix} \end{bmatrix}$$

These adjectives select a complete infinitival VP with no missing element, eventually generating a simple canonical head-complement structure like the following:

(23)

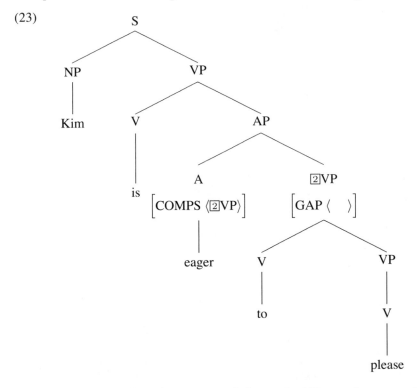

The adjective *eager* thus places no restriction on its VP complement, and so can legitimately combine with the fully saturated VP complement. When its VP complement has a GAP value, it must be later discharged by a filler as seen in the following contrast:

(24) a. *Kim is eager to recommend   .

      b. Who is Kim eager to recommend __ ?

Notice that the present analysis can straightforwardly account for examples in which the VP complement includes more than one GAP element. Compare the following pair of examples:

(25) a. This sonata is easy to play __ on this piano.

      b. Which piano is this sonata easy to play __ on __ ?

The structure of (25a) is similar to that of (20):

(26)

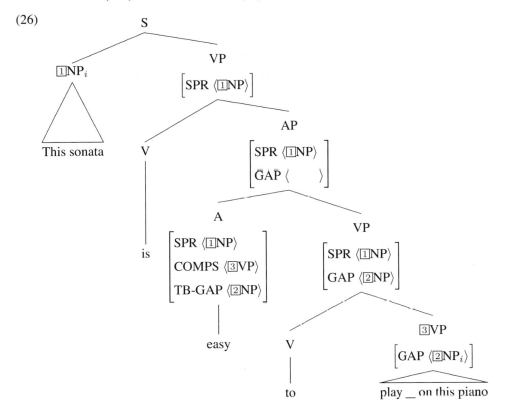

Just like the structure in (20), here the adjective *easy* combines with an incomplete VP whose missing GAP value is lexically discharged and coindexed with the matrix subject. Now consider the structure of (25b) in which the object is linked to the subject *this sonata* whereas the object of *on* is linked to the *wh*-phrase *which piano*:

(27)

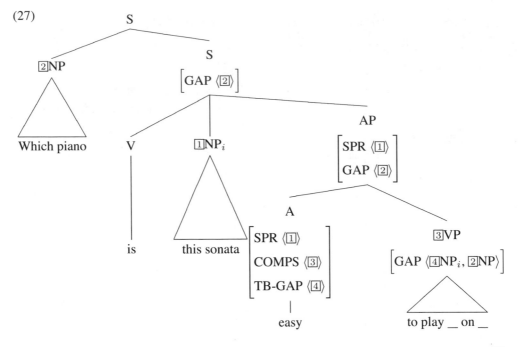

In the structure above, the VP complement of *easy* has two GAP values: one is the object (④NP) and the other is the object (②) of *on*. The first GAP value coindexed with the subject is lexically bound by *easy* through the feature TB-GAP. The remaining GAP value (②NP) is passed up to the second higher S where it is discharged by its filler, *which piano*, through the Head-Filler Rule.

12.3 Extraposition

12.3.1 Basic Properties

English employs an extraposition process that places a heavy constituent such as a *that*-clause, *wh*-clause, or infinitival clause at the end of the sentence:

(28) a. [That dogs bark] annoys people.
      b. It annoys people [that dogs bark].

(29) a. [Why she told him] is unclear.
      b. It is unclear [why she told him].

(30) a. [(For you) to leave so soon] would be inconvenience.
      b. It would be inconvenience [(for you) to leave so soon].

This kind of alternation is quite systematic: given sentences like (31a), English speakers have an intuition that (31b) is possible:

(31) a. That the Dalai Lama claims Tibet independence discomfits the Chinese government.
      b. It discomfits the Chinese government that the Dalai Lama claims Tibet independence.

The extraposition process can also be applicable to a clausal complement:

(32) a. I believe the problem to be obvious.

  b. *I believe [that the problem is not easy] to be obvious.

  c. I believe it to be obvious [that the problem is not easy].

As seen in (32b–c), when a clausal complement is followed by infinitival VP complement, the former is much more preferably extraposed to sentence-final position. In addition to a finite CP, as in (32c), extraposition applies also to an infinitival CP/VP, a simple S, or even a gerundive phrase:

(33) a. I do not think it unreasonable [to ask for the return of my subscription].

  b. He made it clear [he would continue to co-operate with the United Nations].

  c. They're not finding it a stress [being in the same office].

12.3.2 Transformational Analysis

In terms of movement operations, there have been two main ideas to capture the systematic relationships between examples such as the following:

(34) a. [That you came early] surprised me.

  b. It surprised me [that you came early].

One approach assumes that the surface structure of a subject extraposition like (34b) is generated from (34a) as represented in the following (Rosenbaum (1967)):[3]

(35)

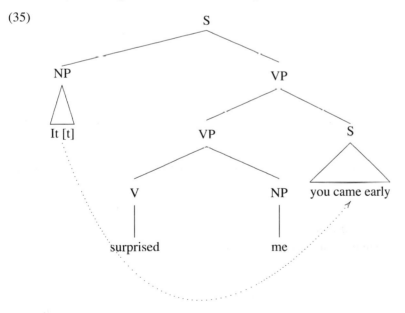

The extraposition rule moves the underlying sentence *you came early* to a sentence-final position. This movement process also introduces the insertion of *that*, generating (34b). To generate

---

[3]The notation [t] means a trace left after a movement.

nonextraposed sentences like (34a) the system posits a process of deleting *it* in (34a) and then adding the complementizer *that*.

A slightly different analysis has also been suggested with the opposite direction of movement (Emonds (1970), Chomsky (1981a), Groat (1995)). That is, instead of extraposing the clause from the subject, the clause is assumed to be already in the extraposed position as in (36a):

(36) a. [[ ] [$_{VP}$ surprised [me] [$_{CP}$ that you came early]]].

  b. [[It] [$_{VP}$ surprised me that you came early]].

The insertion of the expletive *it* in the subject position in (36a) would then account for (36b). When the CP clause is moved to the subject position, the result is the nonextraposed sentence (34a).

Most current movement approaches follow this second line of thought. Though such derivational analyses can capture certain aspects of English subject extraposition, they are not specified in enough detail to predict lexical idiosyncrasies as well as non-local properties of extraposition (see Kim and Sag (2005) for further discussion).

12.3.3 A Lexicalist Analysis

As we have seen, English exhibits a systematic alternation between pairs of non-extraposed and extraposed sentences like the following:

(37) a. [That Chris knew the answer] occurred to Pat.

  b. It occurred to Pat [that Chris knew the answer].

This alternation relation is quite productive. For example, as English acquires new expressions, e.g. *freak out*, *weird out*, or *bite*, it acquires both extraposed and non-extraposed sentence types (cf. Jackendoff (2002)):

(38) a. It really freaks/weirds me out that we invaded Iraq.

  b. That we invaded Iraq really freaks/weirds me out.

(39) a. It really bites that we invaded Iraq.

  b. That we invaded Iraq really bites.

The simple generalization about the process of extraposition is that it applies to a verbal element (CP, VP, and S). Adopting Sag et al. (2003), Kim and Sag (2006), we then can assume that the extraposition process also refers to the *verbal* category whose subtypes include both *comp* and *verb* (see Chapter 5.4.2). In particular, we can adopt the following lexical rule to capture the systematic relationship in extraposition:

(40) Extraposition Lexical Rule (ELR):

$$\left[\text{ARG-ST} \; \langle \, \ldots \, , \boxed{1}\text{XP}[verbal], \, \ldots \, \rangle \right] \Rightarrow \begin{bmatrix} \text{ARG-ST} \; \langle \, \ldots \, , \text{NP}[\text{NFORM } it], \, \ldots \, \rangle \\ \text{EXTRA} \; \langle \boxed{1}\text{XP} \rangle \end{bmatrix}$$

What this rule says is that if a predicative element (actually, adjective or verb) selects a *verbal* argument (either CP or S), this *verbal* element can be realized as the value of the feature EXTRA together with the introduction of *it* as an additional argument.

For example, consider the following data set:

(41)   a.   Fido's barking annoys me.

       b.   That Fido barks annoys me.

       c.   It annoys me that Fido barks.

As shown here, the verb *annoys* can take either a CP or an NP as its subject. When the verb *annoys* selects a *verbal* argument (CP), it can undergo the Extraposition Lexical Rule in (40) as follows:

(42)
$$
\begin{bmatrix} \langle\text{annoys}\rangle \\ \text{ARG-ST } \langle \;\boxed{1}[nominal]\;,\boxed{2}\text{NP}\rangle \end{bmatrix} \Rightarrow \begin{bmatrix} \text{ARG-ST } \langle\text{NP[NFORM } it],\boxed{2}\text{NP}\rangle \\ \text{EXTRA } \langle\; \boxed{1}\text{CP} \;\rangle \end{bmatrix}
$$

Since the verb *annoys* selects a *nominal* (CP or NP since its subtypes are *noun* and *comp*) as one of its arguments, it can undergo the ELR when this argument is realized as a CP (*comp* is a subtype of *verbal*). As shown here, the output *annoy* now selects the expletive *it* as its subject while its original CP now serves as the value of the EXTRA. The two arguments in the output ARG-ST, in accordance with the ARC, will be realized as the SPR and COMPS value, with the EXTRA value intact. This realization will allow us to generate a structure like the following:

(43)

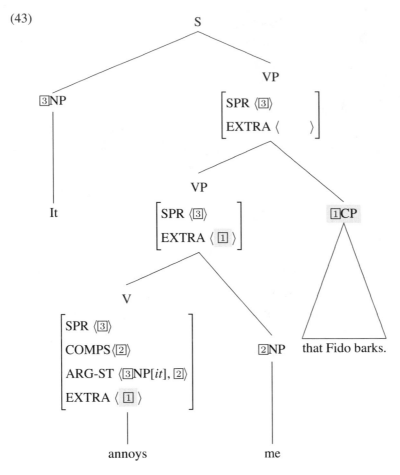

As shown in the tree, the two arguments of the verb *annoys* are realized as SPR and COMPS respectively. When it combines with the NP *me*, it forms a VP with a nonempty EXTRA value. This VP then combines with the extraposed clause CP in accordance with the following Head-Extra Rule:

(44)   Head-Extra Rule:
$$\left[\text{EXTRA } \langle \quad \rangle\right] \rightarrow \mathbf{H}\left[\text{EXTRA } \langle \boxed{1} \rangle\right], \boxed{1}$$

As given here, the rule also discharges the feature EXTRA passed up to the head position. This grammar rule reflects the fact that English independently allows a phrase in which a head element combines with an extraposed element:

(45)

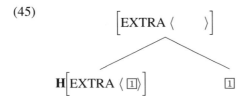

We can observe that English freely employs this kind of well-formed phrase condition even in the extraposition of an adjunct element.

(46) a. [[A man came into the room] [that no one knew]].

  b. [[A man came into the room] [with blond hair]].

  c. I [read a book during the vacation [which was written by Chomsky]].

All of these examples are licensed by the Head-Extra Rule which allows the combination of a head element with an extraposed element.

  Object extraposition is no different – consider the following examples:

(47) a. Ray found the outcome frustrating.

  b. Ray found it frustrating [that his policies made little impact on poverty].

The data indicate that the lexical entry for *find* selects three arguments including a CP and thus can undergo the ELR Rule:

(48) $\begin{bmatrix} \langle \text{find} \rangle \\ \text{ARG-ST } \langle \boxed{1}\text{NP}, \boxed{2}[nominal], \boxed{3}\text{AP} \rangle \end{bmatrix} \Rightarrow \begin{bmatrix} \text{ARG-ST } \langle \boxed{1}\text{NP}, \text{NP}[it], \boxed{3}\text{AP} \rangle \\ \text{EXTRA } \langle \boxed{2}[comp] \rangle \end{bmatrix}$

Since the type *comp* is a subtype of *nominal* and *verbal* at the same time, the verb can undergo the ELR. The output introduces a new element *it* together with the EXTRA value. The three arguments in the output will then be realized as the SPR and COMPS values, projecting a structure like the following:

(49)

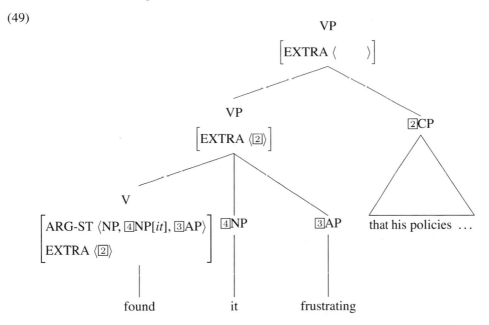

The verb *find* requires an expletive object and an AP as its complement. It also has a clausal element as its EXTRA element. The first VP thus has a nonempty EXTRA value projected from the verb, and this VP forms a well-formed phrase with the extraposed CP clause.

One main difference between subject and object extraposition is that the latter is obligatory:

(50)   a.   *I made [to settle the matter] my objective.

         b.   I made it [my objective] to settle the matter.

         c.   I made [the settlement of the matter] my objective.

(51)   a.   *I owe [that the jury acquitted me] to you.

         b.   I owe it [to you] that the jury acquitted me.

         c.   I owe [my acquittal] to you.

This contrast is due to a general constraint which disprefers any element within VP from occurring after a CP:

(52)   a.   I believe strongly [that the world is round].

         b.   *I believe [that the world is round] strongly.

In the present context this means that there is no predicative expression (verbs and adjectives) whose COMPS list contains an element on the list after a CP complement (see Kim and Sag (2005)).

12.4   Cleft Constructions

12.4.1   Basic Properties

The examples in (53) represent the canonical types of three kinds of cleft construction: *it*-cleft, *wh*-cleft, and inverted *wh*-cleft in English:

(53)   a.   It's their teaching material that we're using. (*it*-cleft)

         b.   What we're using is their teaching material. (*wh*-cleft)

         c.   Their teaching material is what we are using. (inverted *wh*-cleft)

These three types of clefts all denote the same proposition as the following simple declarative sentence:

(54)   We are using their teaching material.

The immediate question that follows is then what is the extra function of the cleft structure instead of the simple sentence (54)? It is commonly accepted that clefts share identical information-structure properties given in (55), for the example in question:

(55)   a.   Presupposition (Background): We are using X.

         b.   Highlighted (Foreground or focus): their teaching material

         c.   Assertion: X is their teaching material.

In terms of the structures, the three types of cleft all consist of a matrix clause headed by a copula and a relative-like cleft clause whose relativized argument is coindexed with the predicative argument of the copula. The only difference is where the highlighted (focused) expression is placed.

12.4.2 Distributional Properties of the Three clefts

It-clefts: As noted before, the *it*-cleft construction consists of the pronoun *it* as the subject of the matrix verb *be*, the highlighted (or focused) phrase XP, and a remaining cleft clause. The pronoun *it* here functions as a place holder, though it is similar in form to the referential pronoun *it*. For example, it is hard to claim that the pronoun *it* in the following dialogue has any referential property:

(56) A: I share your view but I just wonder why you think that's good.

B: Well I suppose <u>it</u>'s the writer that gets you so involved.

As for the type of highlighted XP, we observe that only certain types of phrase can be used:

(57) a. It was [$_{NP}$ the man] that bought the articles from him.

b. It was [$_{AdvP}$ then] that he felt a sharp pain.

c. It was [$_{PP}$ to the student] that the teacher gave the best advice.

d. It was [$_S$ not until I was perhaps twenty-five or thirty] that I read and enjoyed them.

Phrases such as an infinitival VP, AP, or CP cannot function as the XP:

(58) a. *It was [$_{VP}$ to finish the homework] that John tried.

b. *It is [$_{AP}$ fond of Bill] that John seems to be.

c. *It is [$_{CP}$ that Bill is honest] that John believes.

Also notice that in addition to *that*, *wh*-words like *who* and *which* can also introduce a cleft clause:

(59) a. It's the second Monday [that] we get back from Easter holiday.

b. It was the girl [who] kicked the ball.

c. It's mainly his attitude [which] convinced the teacher.

Wh-clefts: Unlike the *it*-cleft, the *wh*-cleft construction places a cleft clause in the subject position followed by the highlighted XP in the postcopular position. This gives a wide range of highlighted phrases. As shown in (60), almost all the phrasal types can serve as the highlighted XP:

(60) a. What you want is [$_{NP}$ a little greenhouse].

b. What's actually happening in London at the moment is [$_{AP}$ immensely exciting].

c. What is to come is [$_{PP}$ in this document].

d. What I've always tended to do is [$_{VP}$ to do my own stretches at home].

e. What I meant was [$_{CP}$ that you have done it really well].

Different from *it*-cleft, the *wh*-cleft allows AP, base VP, and clause (CP, simple S, and *wh*-clause) to serve as the highlighted XP:

(61) a. What you do is [$_{VP}$ wear it like that].

b. What happened is [$_S$ they caught her without a license].

    c.   What the gentleman seemed to be asking is [$_S$ how policy would have differed].

Inverted *wh*-clefts: Though the inverted *wh*-cleft construction is similar to the *wh*-cleft, the possible types of highlighted phrase are in fact different:

(62)   a.   [$_{NP}$ That] is what they're trying to do.

          b.   [$_{AP}$ Insensitive] is how I would describe him.

          c.   [$_{PP}$ In the early morning] is when I do my best research.

(63)   a.   *[$_{VP}$ Wear it like that] is what you do.

          b.   *[$_S$ They caught her without a license] is what happened.

          c.   *[$_{CP}$ That you have done it really well] is what I meant.

In general, all *wh*-words except *which* are possible in inverted *wh*-clefts:

(64)   a.   That's [when] I read.

          b.   That was [why] she looked so nice.

          c.   That's [how] they do it.

          d.   That's [who] I played with over Christmas.

          e.   *That was [which] I decided to buy.

12.4.3   Syntactic Structures of the Three Types of Cleft: Movement Analyses

There have been two main directions in movement analyses to deal with English *it*-cleft constructions: an extraposition analysis and an expletive analysis. The extraposition analysis assumes a direct syntactic or semantic relation between the cleft pronoun *it* and the cleft clause through extraposition (Akmajian (1970), Gundel (1977), Hedberg (1988)).

(65)   a.   [What you heard] was an explosion. (*wh*-cleft)

          b.   It was an explosion, [what you heard]. (right-dislocated)

          c.   It was an explosion [that you heard]. (*it*-cleft)

For example, in Gundel (1977), the *wh*-cleft clause in (65a) is first right dislocated as in (65b) which then can generate the *it*-cleft (65c) with the replacement of *what* into *that*. Analyses of this view basically take the cleft clause to be extraposed to the end of the sentence.

    Meanwhile, the expletive analysis (Chomsky (1977), É. Kiss (1998), Lambrecht (2001)) takes the pronoun *it* to be an expletive expression generated in place, while the cleft clause is semantically linked to the clefted constituent by a 'predication' relation.

(66)   It was [$_{PRED}$ John + who heard an explosion].

An elaborated analysis within this view has been proposed by É. Kiss (1998):

(67)

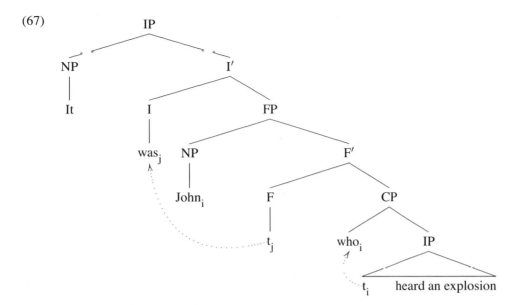

As shown here, the clefted phrase *John*, functioning as focus, is assumed to occupy the specifier of the FP (focus phrase) while the copula is the head of the FP and the cleft clause is the complement of F. The highlighted focus phrase *John* and the cleft clause are thus in a predication relation.

Even though the *wh*-cleft and *it*-cleft are identical in presenting 'salient' discourse information for emphasis, they have different syntactic properties which make it hard to derive one from the other (cf. Pavey (2004)). It is because there are many cases where we can observe clear differences among the three types of clefts. For example, one noticeable difference lies in the fact that only *wh*-clefts allow a base VP as the highlighted XP phrase:

(68)   a.   What you should do is [$_{VP}$ order one first].

       b.   *It is [$_{VP}$ order one first] that you should do first.

       c.   *[$_{VP}$ Order one first] is what you should do.

The three are different as well with respect to the occurrence of an adverbial subordinate clause:

(69)   a.   It was not until I was perhaps twenty-five or thirty that I read them and enjoyed them.

       b.   *When I read them and enjoyed them was not until I was perhaps twenty-five.

       c.   *Not until I was perhaps twenty-five was when I read them and enjoyed them.

As seen here, the *not until* adverbial clause appears only in *it*-clefts.

It is not difficult to find imperfect relationships among the three types of cleft. For example, neither *wh*-clefts nor inverted *wh*-clefts allow the cleft clause part to be headed by *that*:

(70)   a.   It's the writer [that gets you so involved].

       b.   *[That gets you so involved] is the writer.

       c.   *The writer is [that gets you so involved].

In addition, the head of the cleft clause in the *it*-cleft can be a PP, but not in the *wh*-cleft or inverted *wh*-cleft:

(71) a. And it was this matter [[on which] I consulted with the chairman of the Select Committee].

  b. *[[On which] I consulted with the chairman of the Select Committee] was this matter.

  c. *This matter was [[on which] I consulted with the chairman of the Select Committee].

These facts suggest that the different types of cleft cannot be put in direct derivational relationships with each other. Though we cannot provide detailed analyses for them, we sketch out possible directions here.

12.4.4 A Lexicalist Analysis

Wh-clefts: Let us first consider *wh*-clefts:

(72) a. [What I ate] is an apple.

  b. [What we are using] is their teaching material.

Before getting to the specific syntactic structures there are two things to note here: the role of the copula *be* and the cleft clause. The copula in the cleft construction has a 'specificational' use, not a 'predicational' one. In examples like (73a), the copula is predicational, whereas in examples like (73b), the copula is specificational.

(73) a. The student who got A in the class was very happy.

  b. The one who broke the window was Mr. Kim.

One main difference is that in the former the postcopular element denotes a property of the subject whereas in the latter the postcopular element specifies the same individual as the subject. In the *wh*-cleft too, the postcopular expression specifies the same individual as the subject.

As for the properties of the cleft part itself, we can observe that it behaves just like a free relative clause. Not all *wh*-words can occur in free relatives:

(74) a. He got **what** he wanted.

  b. He put the money **where** Lee told him to put it.

  c. The concert started **when** the bell rang.

(75) a. *Lee wants to meet **who** Kim hired.

  b. *Lee bought **which** car Kim wanted to sell to him.

  c. *Lee solved the puzzle **how** Kim solved it.

In the examples in (74), *what, where* and *when* can head a free relative clause in the sense that they are interpreted as 'the thing that, the place where, and the time when'. However, this kind of interpretation is not possible with *who, which* or *how*. As in free relatives, neither *who* nor *which* can appear in *wh*-clefts, for example:

(76) a. *Who achieved the best result was Angela.

  b. *Which book he read the book was that one.

Also note that the syntactic distribution of a free relative clause is as an NP, not as a clause of some kind. For example, the object of *eat* is a diagnostic environment:

(77) a. I ate [what John ate].

    b. I ate [an apple].

Since the verb *ate* requires only an NP as its complement, the only possible structure is as follows:

(78)

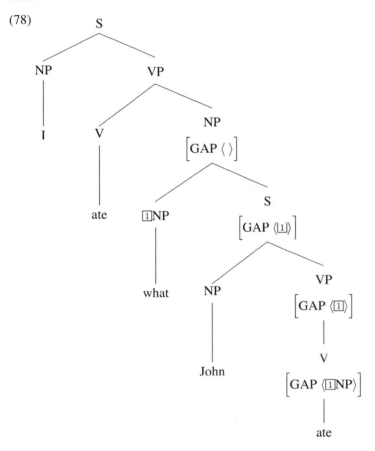

Even though the filler *what* and the head phrase *John ate* form a constituent, the result cannot be an S since *ate* can combine with only an NP. This kind of free relative structure, rather unusual in the sense that the non-head filler *what* is the syntactic head, is formed by the following grammar rule (Pullum (1991)):[4]

(79)   Free-Relative Phrase Rule:

    NP[GAP ⟨ ⟩] → ①NP[FREL *i*], S[GAP ⟨①NP⟩]

---

[4]The feature FREL is assigned to *wh*-words like *what, where,* and *when,* but not to *how* and *why,* to categorize which can head free relatives and which cannot. See Kim (2001b).

This rule ensures that when a free relative pronoun combines with a sentence missing one phrase, the resulting expression is not an S but a complete NP.

On the assumption that the cleft clause in the *wh*-cleft is a free relative, we then can assign the following structure to (72b):

(80)

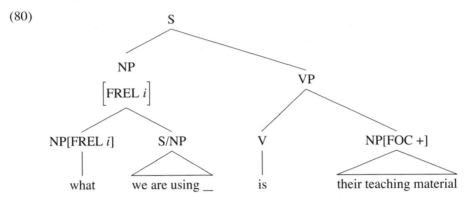

As shown here, the cleft clause is formed by the combination of *what* with an S missing an NP. The index of the free relative is identified with that of the postcopular NP *their teaching material*.

Taking *wh*-clefts as a type of free-relative clause construction headed by an NP, we can understand the ungrammaticality of examples like the following:

(81)   a. *[To whom I gave the cake] is John.

        b. *[That brought the letter] is Bill.

The subjects here are not headed by NPs, and therefore cannot be free relatives.

Inverted Wh-clefts The inverted *wh*-cleft is motivated by a different information structure perspective. In particular, the inverted cleft highlights the phrase in subject position:

(82)

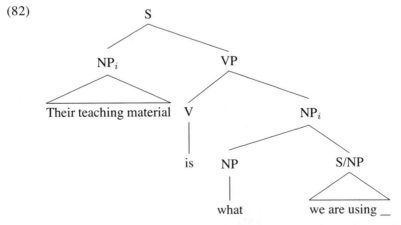

In these structures, the cleft clause has no FREL value to allow almost all *wh*-words to head the relative clause:

(83)　a.　This is how he did it.

　　　b.　This is why he came early.

In other words, while the subject position of a *wh*-cleft is restricted to NPs, the postcopular complement position in the inverted cleft is not restricted – simply due to properties of the copula *be*.

It-clefts: There are two different types of *it*-cleft. Compare the following:[5]

(84)　a.　Type A: It is [$_{PP}$ on Bill] [$_{CP}$ that [John relies [$_{PP}$ ___]]].

　　　b.　Type B: It is [$_{NP}$ Bill] [$_S$ [$_{PP}$ on whom] [John relies [$_{PP}$ ___]]].

In (84a), the cleft clause contains a gap matching the filler PP *on Bill*. If we treat *that* as a relativizer, the PP gap cannot be discharged by *that* because of the category mismatch, for *that* is an NP. However, in (84b) the cleft clause has two parts: one with a missing gap *John relies* and the other with the *wh*-phrase *on whom* functioning as the filler. This second example is similar to ones where the highlighted element is an adverbial:

(85)　a.　It was [then] [when we all went to bed].

　　　b.　It was [only gradually] [that I came to realize how stupid I was].

As noted in the literature, even though a cleft clause is similar in structure to a restrictive relative clause, there are some differences. For example, consider the following:

(86)　a.　It is John that we are looking for.

　　　b. *John that we are looking for showed up.

We can notice here that, unlike a cleft, a canonical restrictive relative clause does not allow a pronoun to function as the antecedent of the relative clause.

　　　Most *wh*-phrases can freely occur in the *it*-cleft, such as *who*, *whose*, or no *wh*-word if *that* is present:

(87)　a.　It's the second Monday [that] we get back from Easter.

　　　b.　It was the peasant girl [who] got it.

　　　c.　It was in 1997 [when] the INS introduced the alien registration receipt card.

　　　d.　It is Uncle John [whose address] I lost.

To capture these two different types and restrictions on the type of *wh*-phrases, we can assume that the copula *be* in the *it*-cleft has its own lexical information:

(88)　　　Copula *be* for Type A *it*-Cleft:

$$
\begin{bmatrix}
\langle \text{be} \rangle \\
\text{SPR} \langle \text{NP}[it] \rangle \\
\text{COMPS} \left\langle \boxed{2}\text{YP}_i[\text{FOCUS} +],\ \text{CP}\!\left[\text{GAP}\ \langle \boxed{2}_i \rangle\right] \right\rangle \\
\text{TO-BIND} \mid \text{GAP} \langle \boxed{2}_i \rangle
\end{bmatrix}
$$

---

[5] See Gazdar et al. (1985) recognizing two different *it*-cleft constructions.

(89)   Copula *be* for Type B *it*-Cleft:

$$\begin{bmatrix} \langle be \rangle \\ \text{SPR } \langle NP[it] \rangle \\ \text{COMPS } \left\langle \boxed{2}\text{YP[FOCUS +], S}\begin{bmatrix} \text{MOD } \langle \boxed{2} \rangle \\ \text{GAP } \langle \quad \rangle \end{bmatrix} \right\rangle \end{bmatrix}$$

In both constructions, the contrastive focus (marked with the feature FOCUS functions as the most salient contextual information. In Type A, the second complement, functioning as the background, is a CP with a GAP value. The lexical head *be* also binds off the GAP inside the CP complement. Notice that the index of the GAP value is identical to that of the focus YP, providing a strict semantic linkage between these two.

In contrast, in Type B, the second COMPS element is a saturated S which modifies the focused element. Let us consider the structure that (88) licenses:

(90)

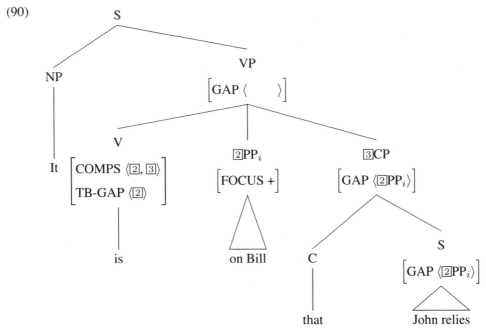

This is a Type A cleft sentence: the copula *be* selects two complements: PP and CP. The cleft clause CP has a PP gap whose GAP value is linked to the focus PP. This GAP value is lexically discharged by the TO-BIND feature. Meanwhile, the lexical information in (89) will license structures like the following:

(91)

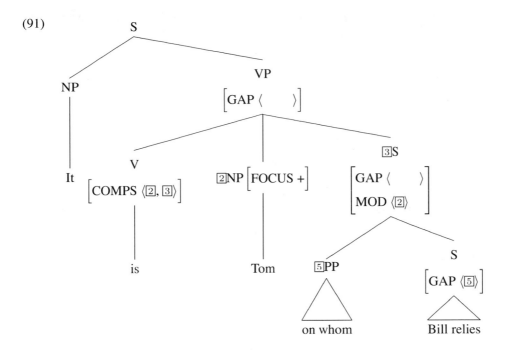

(92)

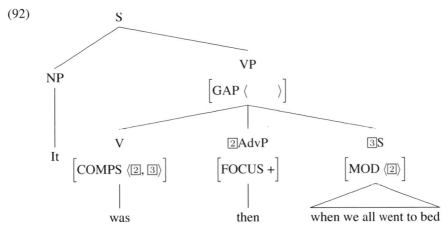

These two structures involve the Type B copula in the sense that the cleft clause contains no GAP element and modifies the highlighted phrase.[6]

Our analysis explains why the following examples are unacceptable:

(93) a. *It is [Kim] [[on whom] [that Sandy relies __]].

    b. *It is [Kim] [[on whom] [Sandy relies on __]].

    c. *It is [Kim] [[whom] [Sandy relies __]].

The example (93a) is ruled out since the combination of *on whom* and *that Sandy relies* is not a well-formed S, even though it could be a CP; (93b) is not allowed because of the mismatch

---

[6]The MOD feature here originates from the subordinator conjunction *when*.

between the gap (NP) and the filler (PP); and (93c) is ruled out similarly. The fragment *Sandy relies* requires a PP but the filler is an NP (*whom*).

Within the present system where the missing element in the cleft clause is taken to be a GAP element, we also expect to see an unbounded dependency relation:

(94) a. It was the director that she wants to meet __ .

   b. It was the director that she said she wants to meet __ .

   c. It was the director that I think she said she wants to meet __ .

In addition, our analysis licenses examples like the following:

(95) a. I wonder who it was __ who saw you.

   b. I wonder who it was __ you saw __ .

   c. I wonder in which pocket it was __ that Kim had hidden the jewels.

Let us look at the structure of (95a), as our system generates it:

(96)

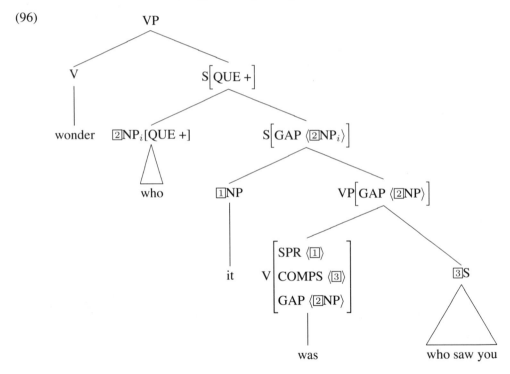

As shown here, the first COMPS value of the cleft copula *be* is realized as a GAP element. This GAP value is passed up to the point where it is discharged by the *wh*-element *who*. This induces an interrogative meaning to the complement clause of the verb *wonder*.

Even though the present system allows the focus phrase (complement of the copula) to be indirectly gapped, a GAP value originating in the cleft clause cannot pass up further:

(97) a. Who do you think it is __ that Mary met __ ?

b. *To whom do you think it is the book that Mary gave __ __ ?

The 'real' gap in (97a) is the one immediately after *be*, which is indirectly connected through the lexical information of *be* to the second one. Notice that in (88) the first GAP value (linked to *the book* originating in the cleft clause is lexically terminated at the level sister to CP, by the copula *be*. Notice that in the lexical entry (89), the cleft clause S does not contain any GAP. Neither realizations of *be* can sanction an example like (97b).

12.5 Exercises

1. Explain the relationship among the following sentences.

    (i) a. It is difficult for me to concentrate on calculus.

    b. For me to concentrate on calculus is difficult.

    c. Calculus is difficult for me to concentrate on.

2. Draw structures for the following sentences and show which grammar rules are involved in generating them.

    (i) a. This problem will be difficult for the students to solve.

    b. Being lovely to look at has its advantages.

    c. This toy isn't easy to try to hand to the baby.

    d. That kind of person is hard to find anyone to look after.

    e. Letters to Grandma are easy to help the children to write.

    (ii) a. It was to Boston that they decided to take the patient.

    b. It was with a great deal of regret that I vetoed your proposal.

    c. It was Tom who spilled beer on this couch.

    d. It is Martha whose work critics will praise.

    e. It was John on whom the sheriff placed the blame.

    f. I wondered who it was you saw.

    g. I was wondering in which pocket it was that Kim had hidden the jewels.

3. Explain why the following examples are ungrammatical, referring to the analysis presented in this chapter.

    (i) a. *It is Kim on whom that Sandy relies.

    b. *It is Kim on whom Sandy relies on.

    c. *It is Kim whom Sandy relies.

    d. *It is on Kim on whom Sandy relies.

    Further, consider the following examples in (ii) and (iii), draw structures for them and show which grammar rules and principles are involved in their generation.

    (ii) a. I wonder who it was who saw you.

    b. I wonder who it was you saw.

    c. I wonder in which pocket it was that Kim had hidden the jewels.

    (iii) a. Was it for this that we suffered and toiled?

    b. Who was it who interviewed you?

4. Analyze the following raising examples and show clearly how the cleft and raising constructions interact.

    (i) a. I believe it to be her father who was primarily responsible.

    b. I believe it to be the switch that is defective.

5. Consider the following set of examples, all of which contain the expression *what Mary offered to him*. Explain whether the phrase functions as an indirect question or an NP and

support your explanations by drawing the syntactic structures:

(i)   a.   Tom ate [what Mary offered to him].

        b.   I wonder [what Mary offered to him].

        c.   [What Mary offered to him] is unclear.

6.   Read the following passage and then provide the correct form of the underlined expressions together with their lexical entries:

(i)   The misfortunes of human beings may <u>divide</u> into two classes: First, those inflicted by the non-human environment and, second, those inflicted by other people. As mankind <u>have</u> progressed in knowledge and technique, the second class has become a continually increasing percentage of the total. In old times, famine, for example, was due to natural causes, and although people did their best to combat it, large numbers of them died of starvation. At the present moment large parts of the world <u>be</u> faced with the threat of famine, but although natural causes have <u>contribute</u> to the situation, the principal causes are human. For six years the civilized nations of the world devoted all their best energies to killing each other, and they <u>find</u> it difficult suddenly to switch over to keeping each other alive. Having destroyed harvests, dismantled agricultural machinery, and disorganized shipping, they find it no easy matter <u>relieve</u> the shortage of crops in one place by means of a superabundance in another, as would easily be done if the economic system were in normal working order. As this illustration shows, it <u>be</u> now man that is man's worst enemy. Nature, it is true, still <u>see</u> to it that we are mortal, but with the progress in medicine it will become more and more common for people to live until they have had their fill of life.[7]

---

[7] From 'Ideas that Have harmed Mankind' by Bertrand Russell.

References

Aarts, Bas. 1997/2001. *English Syntax and Argumentation*. Basingstoke, Hampshire and New York: Palgrave.

Abeillé, Anne and Daniel Godard. 2000. French Word Order and Lexical Weight. In R. Borsley (ed.), *The Nature and Function of Syntactic Categories*, 325–360. New York: Academic Press.

Abney, Steven. 1987. *The English Noun Phrase in Its Sentential Aspect*. Ph.D. dissertation, MIT.

Akmajian, Adrian. 1970. On Deriving Cleft Sentences from Pseudo-cleft Sentences. *Language* 1: 149–168.

Akmajian, Adrian, and Frank Heny. 1975. *Introduction to the Principles of Transformational Syntax*. Cambridge, MA: MIT Press.

Akmajian, Adrian, Susan Steele, and Thomas Wasow. 1979. The Category AUX in Universal Grammar. *Linguistic Inquiry* 10: 1–64.

Akmajian, Adrian, and Thomas Wasow. 1974. The Constituent Structure of VP and AUX and the Position of Verb BE. *Linguistic Analysis* 1: 205–245.

Arnold, Douglas. 2004. Non-restrictive Relative Clauses in Construction-Based HPSG. In Stefan Mueller (ed.), *Proceedings of the HPSG04 Conference*, CSLI Publications.

Bach, Emmon. 1974. *Syntactic Theory*. New York: Holt, Rinehart and Winston.

Bach, Emmon. 1979. Control in Montague Grammar. *Linguistic Inquiry* 10: 515–31.

Baker, C. L. 1970. Double Negatives. *Linguistic Inquiry* 1: 169–186.

Baker, C.L. 1978. *Introduction to Generative-transformational Syntax*. Englewood Cliffs, N.J.: Prentice-Hall.

Baker, C.L. 1979. Syntactic Theory and the Projection Problem. *Linguistic Inquiry* 10: 533–581.

Baker, C.L. 1991. The Syntax of English *not*: The Limits of Core Grammar. *Linguistic Inquiry* 22: 387–429.

Baker, C.L. 1995. *English Syntax*. Mass.: MIT Press.

Baker, Mark. 1997. Thematic Roles and Syntactic Structure. In L. Haegeman (ed.), *Elements of Grammar*, 73–137. Dordrecht: Kluwar.

Baker, Mark. 2001. *The Atoms of Language: The Mind's Hidden Rules of Grammar*. New York: Basic Books.

Bender, Emily, and Dan Flickinger. 1999. Peripheral Constructions and Core Phenomena: Agreement in Tag Questions. In G. Webelhuth, J.-P. Koening, and A. Kathol (Eds.), *Lexical and Constructional Aspects of Linguistic Explanation*, 199–214. Stanford, CA: CSLI.

Blake, Barry J. 1990. *Relational Grammar*. London: Routledge.

Bloomfield, Leonard. 1933. *Language*. New York: H. Holt and Company.

Borsley, Bob. 1989a. Phrase Structure Grammar and the Barriers Conception of Clause Structure. *Linguistics* 27: 843 863.

Borsley, Bob. 1989b. An HPSG Approach to Welsh. *Journal of Linguistics* 25: 333 354.

Borsley, Bob. 1991. *Syntactic Theory: A Unified Approach*. Cambridge: Arnold.

Borsley, Bob. 1996. *Modern Phrase Structure Grammar*. Cambridge: Blackwell.

Bouma, Gosse, Rob Malouf, and Ivan A. Sag. 2001 Satisfying Constraints on Extraction and Adjunction. *Natural Language and Linguistic Theory* 19: 1–65.

Brame, Michael K. 1979. *Essays Toward Realistic Syntax*. Seattle: Noit Amrofer.

Bresnan, Joan. 1978. A Realistic Transformational Grammar. In M. Halle, J. Bresnan, and G. A. Miller (Eds.), *Linguistic Theory and Psychological Reality*. Cambridge, MA: MIT Press.

Bresnan, Joan. 1982a. Control and Complementation. In *The Mental Representation of Grammatical Relations* (Bresnan 1982c).

Bresnan, Joan. 1982b. The Passive in Lexical Theory. In *The Mental Representation of Grammatical Relations* (Bresnan 1982c).

Bresnan, Joan. (Ed). 1982c. *The Mental Representation of Grammatical Relations*. Cambridge, MA: MIT Press.

Bresnan, Joan. 1994. Locative Inversion and the Architecture of Universal Grammar. *Language* 70: 1–52.

Bresnan, Joan. 2001. *Lexical-Functional Syntax*. Oxford and Cambridge, MA: Blackwell.

Briscoe, Edward, and Ann Copestake. 1999. Lexical Rules in Constraint-based Grammar. *Computational Linguistics* 25(4):487–526.

Briscoe, Edward, Ann Copestake, and Valeria de Paiva (Eds.). 1993. *Inheritance, Defaults, and the Lexicon*. Cambridge: Cambridge University Press.

Brody, Michael. 1995. *Lexico-Logical Form: A Radically Minimalist Theory*. Cambridge, MA: MIT Press.

Burton-Roberts, N. 1997. *Analysing Sentences: An Introduction to English Syntax*. 2nd Edition. Longman.

Carnie, Andrew. 2002. *Syntax: A Generative Introduction*. Oxford: Blackwell.

Carpenter, Bob. 1992. *The Logic of Typed Feature Structures: with Applications to Unification Grammars, Logic Programs, and Constraint Resolution*. Cambridge: Cambridge University Press.

Chaves, Rui. 2007. *Coordinate Structures – Constraint-based Syntax and Semantics Processing*. Ph.D. Dissertation. University of Lisbon.

Chierchia, Gennaro, and Sally McConnell-Ginet. 1990. *Meaning and Grammar: An Introduction to Semantics*. Cambridge, MA: MIT Press.

Chomsky, Noam. 1957. *Syntactic Structures*. The Hague: Mouton.

Chomsky, Noam. 1963. Formal Properties of Grammars. In R. D. Luce, R. Bush, and E. Galanter (Eds.), *Handbook of Mathematical Psychology,* Volume II. New York: Wiley.

Chomsky, Noam. 1965. *Aspects of the Theory of Syntax*. Cambridge, MA: MIT Press

Chomsky, Noam. 1969. Remarks on Nominalization. In R. Jacobs and P.S. Rosenbaum(eds), *Readings in English Transformational Grammar*, 184–221. Waltham, MA: Ginn.

Chomsky, Noam. 1973. *Conditions on Transformations*. In S. Anderson and P. Kiparsky (eds.), A Festschrift for Morris Halle. New York: Holt, Rinehart and Winston.

Chomsky, Noam. 1975. *The Logical Structure of Linguistic Theory*. Chicago: University of Chicago Press.

Chomsky, Noam. 1977. On Wh-movement. P. Culicover, A. Akmajian, and T. Wasow (eds.), *Formal Syntax*, 71–132. New York: Academic Press.

Chomsky, Noam. 1980. *Rules and Representations*. New York: Columbia University Press.

Chomsky, Noam. 1981a. *Lectures on Government and Binding*. Dordrecht: Foris.

Chomsky, Noam. 1981b. *Principles and Parameters in Syntactic Theory*. In Hornstein and Lightfoot 1981, 32–75.

Chomsky, Noam. 1982. *Some Concepts and Consequences of the Theory of Government and Binding*. Cambridge, MA: MIT Press.

Chomsky, Noam. 1986. *Barriers*. Cambridge, MA: MIT Press.

Chomsky, Noam. 1995. *The Minimalist Program*. Cambridge, MA: MIT Press.

Chomsky, Noam, and Howard Lasnik. 1977. Filters and control. *Linguistic Inquiry* 8: 425–504.

Copestake, Ann. 2002. *Implementing Typed Feature Structures Grammars*. Stanford: CSLI Publications.

Copestake, Ann, Dan Flickinger, Carl Pollard, and Ivan A. Sag. 2006. Minimal Recursion Semantics: an Introduction. *Research on Language and Computation* 3.4: 281–332.

Cowper, Elizabeth A. 1992. *A Concise Introduction to Syntactic Theory: The Government-Binding Approach*. University of Chicago Press.

Crystal, David. 1985. *A Dictionary of Linguistics and Phonetics*. London: Blackwell.

Culicover, Peter, Adrain Akmajian, and Thomas Wasow (eds.). 1977. *Formal Syntax*. New York: Academic Press.

Culicover, Peter. 1993. Evidence against ECP Aaccounts of the that-t Effect. *Linguistic Inquiry* 24: 557–561.

Culicover, Peter, and Jay Jackendoff. 2005. *Simpler Syntax*. Oxford University Press.

Dalrymple, Mary. 2001. *Lexical Functional Grammar*. (Syntax and Semantics, Volume 34). New York: Academic Press.

Dalrymple, Mary, Annie Zaenen, John Maxwell III, and Ronald M. Kaplan (eds.) 1995. *Formal Issues in Lexical-Functional Grammar*. Stanford: CSLI Publications.

Davidson, Donald. 1980. *Essays on Actions and Events*. Oxford: Clarendon Press; New York: Oxford University Press.

Davis, Anthony. 2001. *Linking by Types in the Hierarchical Lexicon*. Stanford: CSLI Publications.

Dowty, David, Robert Wall, and Stanley Peters. 1981. *Introduction to Montague Semantics*. Dordrecht: Reidel.

Dowty, David. 1982. Grammatical Relations and Montague Grammar. In P. Jacobson and G. Pullum (eds.), *The Nature of Syntactic Representation*, 79–130. Dordrecht: Reidel.

Dowty, David. 1989. On the Semantic Content of the Notion of Thematic Role. In G. Chierchia, B. Partee, and R. Turner (eds.), *Properties, Types, and Meanings*, Volume 2, 69–129. Dordrecht: Kluwer Academic Publishers.

Dubinksy, Stanley and William Davies. 2004. *The Grammar of Raising and Control: A Course in Syntactic Argumentation*. Oxford: Blackwell.

É. Kiss, Katalin. 1998. Identificational Focus Versus Information Focus. *Language* 74: 245–273.

Emonds, Joseph. 1970. *Root and Structure-preserving Transformations*. Ph.d. Dissertation, MIT.

Emonds, Joseph. 1975. *A Transformational Approach to Syntax*. New York: Academic Press.

Fabb, Niegel. 1990. The Difference Between English Relative and Non-Restrictive Relative Clauses. *Journal of Linguistics* 26, 57–78.

Fillmore, Charles. 1963. The Position of Embedding Transformations in a Grammar. *Word* 19: 208–231.

Fillmore, Charles. 1999. Inversion and Constructional Inheritance. In G. Webelhuth, J.P Koenig, and A. Kathol (eds.), *Lexical and Constructional Aspects of Linguistics Explanation*, 113–128. Stanford: CSLI Publications.

Fillmore, Charles J., Paul Kay, and Mary O'Connor. 1988. Regularity and Idiomaticity in Grammatical Constructions: The Case of *Let Alone*. *Language* 64(3): 501–538.

Flickinger, Daniel. 1983. Lexical Heads and Phrasal Gaps. In Michael Barlow, Daniel Flickinger, and Michael T. Wescoat (eds.), *Proceedings of the 2nd West Coast Conference on Formal Linguistics*, 89-101. Stanford, CA: Stanford Linguistics Association.

Flickinger, Daniel, Carl Pollard, and Thomas Wasow. 1985. Structures sharing in lexical representation. In *Proceedings of the 23rd Annual Meeting of the Association for ComputationalLinguistics*, Morristown, N. J. Association for Computational Linguistics.

Fodor, Jerry A. 1983. *The Modularity of Mind*. Cambridge, MA: MIT Press

Fodor, Jerry A., and Jerrold J. Katz, (eds). 1964. *The Structure of Language*. Englewood Cliffs, NJ: Prentice-Hall.

Fraser, Bruce. 1970. Idioms within a Transformational Grammar. *Foundations of Language* 6: 22–42.

Gazdar, Gerald. 1981. Unbounded Dependencies and Coordinate Structure. *Linguistic inquiry* 12: 155–184.

Gazdar, Gerald. 1982. Phrase Structure Grammar. In P. Jacobson and G. K. Pullum (eds.), *The Nature of Syntactic Representation*. Dordrecht: Reidel.

Gazdar, Gerald, Ewan Klein, Geoffrey K. Pullum, and Ivan A. Sag. 1985. *Generalized Phrase Structure Grammar*. Cambridge, MA; Havard University Press and Oxford; Basil Blackwell.

Gazdar, Gerald, and Geoffrey K. Pullum. 1981. Subcategorization, Constituent Order, and the Notion 'head'. In M. Moortgat, H. van der Hulst, and T. Hoekstra (eds.), *The Scope of Lexical Rules*. Dordrecht: Foris.

Gazdar, Gerald, Geoffrey K. Pullum, and Ivan A. Sag. 1982. Auxiliaries and Related Phenomena in a Restrictive Theory of Grammar. *Language* 58: 591–638.

Ginzburg, Jonathan, and Ivan A. Sag. 2000. *Interrogative Investigations: The Form, Meaning and Use of English Interrogatives*. Stanford: CSLI Publications.

Goldberg, Adele E. 1995. *A Construction Grammar Approach to Argument Structure*. Chicago: University of Chicago Press. Green,

Goldberg, Adele. 2006. *Constructions at Work*. Oxford University Press.

Grimshaw, Jane. 1997. Projection, Heads, and Optimality. *Linguistic Inquiry*, 28: 373—422.

Green, Georgia M. 1976. Main Clause Phenomena in Subordinate Clause. *Language* 52: 382–397.

Green, Georgia M. 1981. Pragmatics and Syntactic Description. *Studies in the Linguistic Sciences* 11.1: 27–37.

Greenbaum, Sidney. 1996. *The Oxford English Grammar*. Oxford: Oxford University Press.

Groat, Erich M. 1995. English Expletives: A Minimalist Approach. *Linguistic Inquiry* 26.2: 354–365.

Grosu, Alexander. 1972. *The Strategic Content of Island Constraints*. Ohio State University Working Papers in Linguistics 13: 1–225.

Grosu, Alexander. 1974. On the Nature of the Left Branch Constraint. *Linguistic Inquiry* 5: 308–319.

Grice, H. Paul. 1989. *Studies in the Way of Words*. Cambridge, MA: Harvard University Press.

Gundel, J. K. 1977. Where do cleft-sentences come from? *Language* 53. 543-59.

Haegeman, Liliance. 1994. *Introduction to Government and Binding Theory*. Oxford and Cambridge, MA: Basil Blackwell.

Harman, Gilbert. 1963. Generative Grammar Without Transformation Rules: A Defense of Phrase Structure. *Language* 39: 597–616.

Harris, Randy Allen. 1993. *The Linguistic Wars*. Oxford: Oxford University Press.

Harris, Zellig S. 1970. *Papers in Structural and Transformational Linguistics*. Dordrecht: Reidel.

Hedberg, Nancy. 2000. The Referential Status of Clefts. *Language*, 76: 891–920.

Hooper, Joan, and Sandra Thompson. 1973. On the Applicability of Root Transformations. *Linguistic Inquiry* 4: 465–497.

Hornstein, Norbert, and Daivd Lightfoot, (eds.) 1981. *Explanation in linguistics: The logical problem of language acquisition*. London: Longman.

Huddleston, Rodney, and Geoffrey K. Pullum. 2002. *The Cambridge Grammar of the English Language*. Cambridge University Press.

Hudson, Richard. 1984. *Word Grammar*. Oxford: Blackwell.

Hudson, Richard. 1990. *English Word Grammar*. Oxford: Blackwell.

Hudson, Richard. 1998. Word Grammar. In V. Agel, et al (eds.), *Dependency and Valency: An International Handbook of Contemporary Research*. Berlin: Walter de Gruyter.

Huang, James. 1982. *Logical Relations in Chinese and the Theory of Grammar*. Ph.D. Dissertation, MIT.

Jackendoff, Ray. 1972. *Semantic Interpretation in Generative Grammar*. Cambridge, MA: MIT Press.

Jackendoff, Ray. 1975. Morphological and semantic regularities in the lexicon. *Language* 51: 639–671.

Jackendoff, Ray. 1977. *X'-syntax*. Cambridge, MA: MIT Press.

Jackendoff, Ray. 1994. *Patterns in the Mind*. New York: Basic Books.

Jackendoff, Ray. 1990. *Semantic Structures*. MIT Press.

Jackendoff, Ray. 2002. *Foundation of Language: Brian, Meaning, Grammar, Evolution*. Oxford: Oxford University Press.

Jacobs, Roderick. 1995. *English Syntax: A Grammar for English Language Professionals*. Oxford University Press.

Johnson, David, and Paul Postal. 1980. *Arc-Pair Grammar*. Princeton: Princeton University Press.

Johnson, David, and Shalom Lapin. 1999. *Local Constrains vs. Economy*. Stanford: CSLI Publication.

Kager, Rene. 1999. *Optimality Theory*. Cambridge: Cambridge University Press.

Kaplan. Ronald M., and Annie Zaenen. 1989. Long-distance Dependencies, Constituent Structure and Functional Uncertainty. In M. R. Baltin and A. S. Kroch (eds.), *Alternative Conceptions of Phrase Structure*, 17–42. University of Chicago Press.

Katz, Jerrold J., and Paul M. Postal. 1964. *An Integrated Theory of Linguistic Descriptions*. Cambridge, MA: MIT Press.

Katz, Jerrold J., and Paul M. Postal. 1991. Realism versus Conceptualism in Linguistics. *Linguistics and Philosophy* 14: 515–554.

Kay, Paul. 1995. Construction grammar. In J. Verschueren, J.-O. Ostman, and J. Blommaert (Eds.), *Handbook of Pragmatics*. Amsterdam and Philadelphia: John Benjamins.

Kay, Paul, and Charles J. Fillmore. 1999. Grammatical Constructions and Linguistic Generalizations: The What's x Doing y Construction. *Language* 75.1: 1–33.

Kayne, Richard, and Jean-Yves Pollock. 1978. Stylistic Inversion, Successive Cyclicity, and Move NP in French. *Linguistic Inquiry* 9: 595–621.

Keenan, Deward. 1975. Some Universals of Passive in Relational Grammar. In Robin E. Grossman, L. James San, and Timothy J. Vance (eds.), *Papers from the 11th Regional Meeting, Chicago Linguistic Society*, 340–352. Chicago: Chicago Linguistic Society.

Keenan, Edward, and Bernard Comrie. 1977. Noun phrase accessibility and universal grammar. *Linguistic Inquiry* 8: 63–99.

Kim, Jong-Bok. 2001a. On the Types of Prepositions and Their Projections in Syntax. *Studies in Modern Grammar*. 26. 1–22.

Kim, Jong-Bok. 2001b. Constructional Constraints in English Free Relative Constructions: *Language and Information* 5.1: 35–53.

Kim, Jong-Bok. 2002a. On the Structure of English Partitive NPs and Agreement. *Studies in Generative Grammar* 12.2: 309–338.

Kim, Jong-Bok. 2002b. English Auxiliary Constructions and Related Phenomena: From a Constraint-based Perspective. *Language Research*, 38.4 1037–1076

Kim, Jong-Bok. 2002c. *The Grammar of Negation: A Constraint-Based Approach*. Stanford: CSLI Publications.

Kim, Jong-Bok. 2003. Similarities and Differences between English VP Ellipsis and VP Fronting: An HPSG Analysis. *Studies in Generative Grammar*. 13.3: 429–459.

Kim, Jong-Bok. 2004a. Hybrid English Agreement. *Linguistics* 42.6: 1105–1128.

Kim, Jong-Bok. 2004b. *Korean Phrase Structure Grammar* (In Korean). Seoul: Hankwuk Publishing.

Kim, Jong-Bok, and Ivan Sag. 1995. The Parametric Variation of French and English Negation. In Jose Camacho, Lina Choueiri, and Maki Watanabe (eds), *Proceedings of the Fourteenth West Coast Conference on Formal Linguistics(WCCFL)*, 303–317. Stanford: SLA CSLI Publications.

Kim, Jong-Bok and Ivan A. Sag. 2002. Negation Without Movement. *Natural Language and Linguistic Theory,* 20.2: 339–412.

Kim, Jong-Bok, and Ivan A. Sag. 2005. English Object Extraposition: A Constraint-Based Approach. In Stefan Mueller (ed.), *Proceedings of the HPSG05 Conference*, 192–212. CSLI Publications.

King, Paul J. 1989. *A Logical Formalism for Head-Driven Phrase Structure Grammar*. PhD thesis, University of Manchester.

Koenig, Jean-Pierre. 1999. *Lexical Relations*. Stanford: CSLI Publications.

Kornai, Andras, and Geoffrey K. Pullum. 1990. *The X-bar Theory of Phrase Structure*. Language 66: 24–50.

Koster. Jan. 1987. *Domains and Dynasties, the Radical Autonomy of Syntax*. Dorarecht: Foris.

Langacker, Ronald. 1987. *Foundations of Cognitive Grammar*. Stanford, CA: Stanford University Press.

Lambrecht, Knud. 2001. A Framework for the Analysis of Cleft Constructions. *Linguistics*, 39.3: 463–516.

Lappin, Shalom, Robert Levine, and David Johnson. 2000. The structure of unscientific revolutions. *Natural Language and Linguistic Theory* 18: 665–671.

Larson, Richard. 1988. On the Double Object Constructions. *Linguistic Inquiry*, 19: 335-392.

Lasnik, Howard, Marcela Depiante, and Arthur Setpanov. 2000. *Syntactic Structures Revisited: Contemporary Lectures on Classic Transformational Theory*. Cambridge, MA: MIT Press.

Levin, Beth. 1993. *English verb Classes and Alternations: A Preliminary Investigation*. Chicago: University of Chicago Press.

Levin, Beth. and M. Rappaport Hovav. 2005. *Argument Realization, Research Surveys in Linguistics Series*. Cambridge: Cambridge University Press.

Lees, Robert B. and Edward S. Klima. 1963. Rules for English Pronominalization. *Language* 39: 17–28.

Li, Charles, and Sandra A. Thompson. 1976. Subject and Topic: A New Typology of Languages. In Li, Charles N. (ed.) *Subject and Topic*, New York/San Francisco/London: Academic Press, 457–490.

Lambrecht, Knud. 1994. *Information Structure and Sentence Form*. Cambridge: Cambridge University Press.

Malouf, Rob. 2000. *Mixed Categories in the Hierarchical Lexicon*. Stanford: CSLI Publications.

McCawley, James D. 1968. Concerning the Base Component of a Transformational Grammar. *Foundations of Language* 4: 243–269.

McCloskey, James. 1988. Syntactic theory. In Frederick J. Newmeyer (ed.), *Linguistics: The Cambridge Survey* 18–59. Cambridge: Cambridge University Press.

McCawley, James D. 1988. *The Syntactic Phenomena of English*. Chicago: University of Chicago Press.

Michaelis, Laura, and Knud Lambecht. 1996. Toward a construction-based theory of language function: The case of nominal extraposition. *Language* 72: 215–248.

Montague, Richard. 1973. The Proper Theory of Quantification. *Approaches to Natural Language*, ed. by J. Hintikka, J. Moravcsik, and P. Suppes. Dordrecht: Reidel.

Moortgat, Michael. 1988. *Categorial Investigations*. Dordrecht: Foris.

Nunberg, Geoffrey, Ivan A. Sag, and Thomas Wasow. 1994. Idioms. *Language* 70: 491–538.

Nunberg, Geoffrey. 1995. Transfer of Meaning. *Journal of Semantics*, 12.2: 109–132.

Pavey, Emma. 2004. *The English it-cleft construction: A Role and Reference Grammar Analysis*. Ph.D. dissertation, SUNY.

Perlmutter, David M., (ed.) 1983. *Studies in Relational Grammar 1*. Chicago: University of Chicago Press.

Perlmutter, David M., and Carol Rosen. 1984. *Studies in Relational Grammar 2*. Chicago: University of Chicago Press.

Perlumutter, David, and Paul Postal. 1977. Toward a Universal Characterization of Passivization. In *Proceedings of the 3rd Annual Meeting of the Berkeley Linguistics Society*, Berkeley. University of California, Berkeley. Reprinted in Perlmutter (1983).

Perlmutter, David, Scott Soames. 1979. *Syntactic Argumentation and the Structure of English*. Berkeley: University of California Press.

Pinker, Steven. 1994. *The Language Instinct*. New York: Morrow.

Pollard, Carl, and Ivan A. Sag. 1987. *Information-Based Syntax and Semantics, Volume 1: Fundamentals*. Stanford: CSLI Publication.

Pollard, Carl, and Ivan A. Sag. 1992. Anaphors in English and the scope of binding theory. *Linguistic Inquiry* 23:261–303.

Pollard, Carl, and Ivan A. Sag. 1994. *Head-Driven Phrase Structure Grammar*. Chicago: University of Chicago Press.

Pollock, Jean-Yves. 1989. Verb Movement, Universal Grammar, and the structure of IP. *Linguistic Inquiry* 20: 365–422.

Postal, Paul M. 1971. *Crossover Phenomena*. New York: Holt, Rinehart, and Winston.

Postal, Paul. 1974. *On Raising*. Cambridge, MA: MIT Press.

Postal, Paul. 1986. *Studies of Passive Clause*. Albany: SUNY Press.

Postal, Paul, and Brian Joseph (eds.). 1990. *Studies in Relational Grammar 3*. Chicago: University of Chicago Press.

Postal, Paul, and Geoffrey K. Pullum. 1998. Expletive Noun Phrases in Subcategorized Positions. *Linguistic Inquiry* 19: 635–670.

Pullum, Geoffrey K., Gerald Gazdar. 1982. Natural languages and context-free languages. *Linguistics and Philosophy* 4: 471–504.

Pullum, Geoffrey. 1979. *Rule Interaction and the Organization of a Grammar*. New York: Garland.

Pullum, Geoffrey. 1991. English Nominal Gerund Phrases as Noun Phrases with Verb-Phrase Heads. *Linguistics* 29: 763–799.

Pullum, Geoffrey K. and Barbara C. Scholz. 2002. Empirical Assessment of Stimulus Poverty Arguments. *The Linguistic Review 19*, 9–50.

Pullum, Geoffrey K. and Babara Scholz. 2002. Empirical Assessment of Stimulus Poverty Arguments. *The Linguistic Review* 19, 9–50.

Prince, Alan, and Paul Smolensky. 1993. Optimality Theory: Constraint Interaction in Generative Grammar. Tech Report RuCC-TR-2. ROA-537: Rutgers University Center for Cognitive Science.

Quirk, Randoph, Sidney Greenbaum, Geoffrey Leech, and Jan Svartvik. 1972. *A Grammar of Contemporary English*. London and New York: Longman.

Quirk, Randoph, Sidney Greenbaum, Geoffrey Leech, and Jan Svartvik. 1985. *A Comprehensive Grammar of the English Language*. London and New York: Longman.

Radford, Andrew. 1981. *Transformational Syntax: A Student's Guide to Chomsky's Extended Standard Theory*. Cambridge: Cambridge University Press.

Radford, Andrew. 1988. *Transformation Grammar*. Cambridge: Cambridge University Press.

Radford, Andrew. 1997. *Syntactic Theory and the Structure of English*. New York and Cambridge: Cambridge University Press. Richter.

Radford, Andrew. 2004. *English Syntax: An Introduction*. Cambridge: Cambridge University Press.

Riemsdijk, Henk van, and Edwin Williams. 1986. *Introduction to the Theory of Grammar*. Cambridge, Mass.: MIT Press.

Rosenbaum, Peter S. 1967. *The Grammar of English Predicate Complement Constructions*. Cambridge, Mass.: MIT Press.

Ross, John R. 1967. *Constraints on Variables in Syntax*. PhD thesis, MIT. Published as Infinitive Syntax. Norwood, NJ: Ablex, 1986.

Ross. John R. 1972. Doubl-ing. *Linguistic Inquiry* 3: 61–86.

Ross. John. R. 1969. Auxiliaries as Main Verbs, In W. Todd(Ed.), *Studies in Philosophical Linguistics 1*. Evanston, Ill.: Great Expectations Press.

Sag, Ivan A. 1997. English Relative Clause Constructions. *Journal of Linguistics* 33(2): 431-484.

Sag, Ivan A. 2000. Another Argument Against Wh-Trace. Jorge Hankamer Webfest.

Sag, Ivan A. 2006. Remarks on Locality. In Stefan Mueller ed., *Proceedings of the HPSG07 Conference*, Stanford University, CSLI Publications.

Sag, Ivan A. 2007. Sign-Based Construction Grammar: An informal synopsis. Manuscript, Stanford University.

Sag, Ivan A. 2007. English Filler-Gap constructions. Manuscript, Stanford University.

Sag, Ivan A. 2008. Feature Geometry and Predictions of Locality. In Greville Corbett and Anna Kibort (eds.), *Proceedings of the Workshop on Features*. Oxford: Oxford University Press.

Sag, Ivan A. to appear. Rules and Exceptions in the English Auxiliary System. *Journal of Linguistics*.

Sag, Ivan A., and Janet D. Fodor. 1994. Extraction without Traces. In *Proceedings of the Thirteenth annual Meeting of the West Coast Conference on Formal Linguistics*, Stanford. CSLI Publication.

Sag, Ivan A., Philip Hofmeister, and Neal Snider. to appear. Processing Complexity in Subjacency Violations: The Complex Noun Phrase Constraint. Proceedings of the 43rd Annual Meeting of the Chicago Linguistic Society. Chicago: CLS.

Sag, Ivan A., and Carl Pollard. 1991. An Integrated Theory of Complement Control. *Language* 67: 63-113.

Sag, Ivan A., Thomas Wasow, and Emily M. Bender. 2003. *Syntactic Theory: A Formal Introduction*. Stanford: CSLI Publications.

Saussure, Ferdinand de. 1916. *Course of General Linguistics*. Illinois: Open Court.

Savitch, Walter J., Emmon bach, William Marsh, and Gila Safran-Naveh. 1987. *The Formal Complexity of Natural Language*. Dordrecht: D. Reidel.

Schutze, Carson T. 1996. *The Empirical Base of Linguistics*. Chicago: University of Chicago Press.

Sells, Peter. 1985. *Lectures on Contemporary Syntactic Theories*. Stanford: CSLI Publications.

Sells, Peter (ed.). 2001. *Formal and Empirical Issues in Optimality Theoretic Syntax*. Stanford: CSLI Publications.

Shieber, Stuart. 1986. *An Introduction to Unification-based Approaches to Grammar*. Stanford: CSLI publications.

Skinner, B. F. 1957. *Verbal Behavior*. New York: Appleton-Century-Crofts.

Smith, Jeffrey D. 1999. English Number Names in HPSG. In G. Webelhuth, J.-P. Koenig, and A. Kathol (eds.), *Lexical and Constructional Aspects of Linguistic Explanation*, 145–160. Stanford: CSLI Publications.

Steedman, Mark. 1996. *Surface Structure and Interpretation*. Cambridge, MA: MIT Press.

Steedman, Mark. 2000. *The Syntactic Process*. Cambridge, MA: MIT Press/Bradford Books.

Steele, Susan.1981. *An Encyclopedia of AUX*. Cambridge, MA: MIT Press.

Stockwell, Robert P., Paul Schachter, and Barbara H. Partee. 1973. *The major Syntactic Structures of English*. New York: Holt, Rinehart and Winston.

Trask, Robert Lawrence. 1993. *A Dictionary of Grammatical Terms in Linguistics*. London and New York: Routledge.

Ward, Gregory. 1985. *The Semantics and Pragmatics of Preposing*. Ph.D. Dissertation., University of Pennsylvania.

Warner, Anthony. 2000. English Auxiliaries Without Lexical Rules. In R. Borsley (ed.), *The Nature and Function of Syntactic Categories*, 167–218. New York: Academic Press.

Wasow, Thomas. 1977. Transformations and the lexicon. In *Formal Syntax* (Culicover et al. 1977).

Wasow, Thomas. 1989. Grammatical Theory. In *Foundations of Cognitive Science*.

Webelhuth, Gert (ed.). 1995. *Government and Binding Theory and the Minimalist Program*. Oxford: Basil Blackwell.

Zwicky, Arnold, and Geoffrey K. Pullum. 1983. Cliticiziation vs. Inflection: English n't. *Language* 59: 502–13.

Index